365 Animal Bedtime Stories

YoYo

BOOKS

January

Bonfire Day

1 JANUARY

Bouncer Brachio is excited! For the first time, his mummy and daddy are letting him help build their village's New Year's bonfire. 'This is the way we start every new year on Firefly Island, Bouncer', says Mummy as they put on jackets, mittens and scarves.

They head up the path through the woods towards Firefly Meadow. Before long, they see friends and neighbours, pushing piles of branches and logs on carts.

'Tonight's the night!' calls Bouncer's daddy happily to them. He runs the camping ground on Firefly Island, where they live. The huge mountain of wood is getting bigger and bigger.

Bouncer jumps and yells, 'Whoopee! I can't wait! The sun has set! We can start!'

Bouncer's daddy lights a big torch and sets fire to the pile. The villagers gather around the huge blaze, watching it crackle and shoot sparks into the dark sky.

'Hooray! Happy New Year!' they cry, clapping and laughing and hugging each other. Shadows dance. The smoke smells wonderful.

'I wish New Year's bonfire came every day!' shouts Bouncer to his friends. Together, Nolo Giraffe, Slye Snake, Baabra Sheep and Bouncer make a circle. They spin faster and faster, shouting and laughing until they all fall down. What a wonderful start to the new year!

Warm Memories

2 JANUARY

'What a fantastic night!' Bouncer says to himself this morning. He wakes up slowly, remembering the fun. Everyone sipped hot chocolate.

'Let's sing something', someone said, and everybody joined in, standing around the bonfire. 'How about the Firefly Island song?' asked Bouncer and everybody sang together.

We love Firefly Island,
Its woods and meadows and shores.
Our village is a friendly home
That welcomes everyone.

Bouncer can't wait to see what this new year will bring.

January

Baabra Sheep

3 JANUARY

'Welcome to my tea party! Please sit here Teddy', says Baabra Sheep, and she puts him on his chair.

'Would you like some tea?' Baabra asks Teddy politely. Baabra loves taking care of him.

Baabra pours water into Teddy's tiny cup and her own. She sips. 'Yummy'.

Teddy Bear isn't sipping. Baabra asks, 'Teddy, can I help you?' Teddy seems to nod yes.

'Here you are. Sssippp!' she whispers.

She drinks the rest of her tea. 'It's very good!' she says. 'I think I'll have some more'.

She starts to pour a second cup, but the lid of the teapot falls off and water spills everywhere.

'Oh no!' she cries. She sees her new party dress, grabs it and starts to mop up the water. But just then Mummy Sheep comes in.

'Oh Baabra! what happened?' Mummy cries, putting her hands to her mouth.

'I spilled the water!' Baabra sobs, mopping faster.

'I'm not worried about the water, dear. But your dress... !'

Mummy looks it over and gives Baabra a hug. 'It's fine Baabra. Just be careful. And please don't use your dress to mop things up if you spill water next time!'

'I won't Mummy', sighs Baabra. Teddy looks relieved.

Nolo Giraffe

4 JANUARY

'Nolo, could you please pick up our post this morning?' Nolo Giraffe's daddy asks. Nolo loves doing important jobs and being a leader.

He hurries to the Firefly Island post office. Mrs. Trico, the postmistress, smiles as he comes in. 'Good morning, Nolo! Is the new year off to a good start for you?' she asks.

'Yes, thank you!' Nolo nods, feeling grown up. He finds his family's post office box and turns the pointer on the lock so that it points to two, then six, then eight. His favourite numbers! He turns a shiny knob and the little door pops open.

'Good! There's a letter in there!' he exclaims.

Nolo can't read yet, but Mummy or Daddy will tell him what it's all about.

'Bye, Mrs. Trico', he calls, and he heads off.

At home, Daddy opens the letter. 'Guess what, Nolo?' he exclaims, 'Our island is getting a new ferry!'

'Really?' answers Nolo, who loves ferry boats. 'I love the old one. But I can't wait to see the new one'.

'*Tooot!*' he yells, pretending he's the new ferry captain, blowing its horn. He steams around the kitchen. Perhaps he'll get a chance to go on the new ferry really soon!

Slye Snake

Slye Snake is very clever. She can already read and write a little and she always says exactly what she thinks. Sometimes that can get her into trouble!

'Hello Mr. Horse', she says when she sees the Mayor of Firefly Island this afternoon.

'Hello Slye. How are you?' he asks kindly.

'Fine, thank you', replies Slye. 'But I wanted to ask you something'.

'Of course! What is it?' Mr. Horse answers.

'Why do you stand on that box when you make a speech? For instance, the one you gave at the New Year's bonfire party?' she asks.

'Oh, that's simple', chuckles Mr. Horse. 'I stand on my soapbox – that's what that box is called – so that everybody can see and hear me', he smiles proudly.

'I understand', Slye nods. 'But you don't really say much, do you? I mean, you talk and talk, but you don't really tell us much. So it doesn't matter if we hear you or not, does it?' Slye fixes her little eyes on the mayor.

Mr. Horse twitches and pulls himself up a little taller.

'So you don't think I make very good speeches?' he asks. He clears his throat and looks a little cross. Or perhaps his feelings are hurt.

'Well…', Slye continues bravely, 'I can see that nobody really wants to listen. Perhaps if you made your speeches shorter, or funnier or something, we would', she adds helpfully.

'Humph! You think so?' Mr. Horse asks slowly. Then he laughs. 'I suppose I'll give it a try! Thank you Slye'. And he hurries away.

'His speeches really are bad', Slye thinks. 'I hope he can be funnier next time!'

3

January

6 JANUARY
Hoopla Hippo's Surprise Party

Hoopla Hippo was unwell and had to stay at home, so he missed the New Year's bonfire. His friends are planning a surprise New Year's party for him, a few days late.

Baabra Sheep asked her mummy to help her make a New Year's cake. 'It came out a little funny looking', Baabra thinks, 'but I know it's delicious, because I tasted the mix as we made it!'

'I have missed Hoopla's big laughs and jokes', Baabra tells her mummy. 'And I know how he loves to eat! So he should enjoy this cake!'

Bouncer Brachio and Nolo Giraffe are in charge of the party decorations and a little present.

'Let's hang balloons, streamers and a big Happy New Year banner in my room', says Nolo.

With a little money from each of the friends, Bouncer and Nolo buy Hoopla a really lovely book that has pages to colour, stickers and shiny tags that you can peel off and put on your things.

Now it's party time! Everybody is hiding in Nolo's room. Baabra brings Hoopla into the room.

'Happy New Year!' they all yell as Hoopla walks in. He is amazed to see everything his friends have done, and he starts laughing as only he can.

'HOOO, HO-HO-HO-HO!'

'HOOO, HO-HO-HO-HO!'

Hoopla's laugh is so funny that his friends just explode, laughing until their tummies ache.

They crowd around Hoopla as he opens his present, and then ooh and aah over it. Then it's time for the cake. It's a perfect surprise New Year's party!

7 JANUARY
Firefly Island

It's bedtime at the Sheep family's house. Baabra Sheep and her little brother Lammie are cosily snuggled beside their mummy.

'Tell us a story, please', says Baabra.

'I'd love to', Mummy answers. 'Have I ever told you how our island got its name?'

'No', Baabra replies. Actually, Mummy has, many times, but it's always fun to hear it again.

'Long ago, nobody lived on our island. But one

day a little boat filled with visitors stopped in the harbour. They thought it was such a nice place that they decided to build houses and live here. Bit by bit, boats brought more people, and they also decided to live here, helping each other and enjoying our island life'. Mummy starts.

'A little village grew up and when you look around, you see all sorts of creatures living here happily together. It's part of the fun of our life on the island. We welcome others'. Mummy smiles.

'The villagers named our island Firefly Island, because they loved to see the fireflies' twinkling lights up at Firefly Meadow on warm summer evenings'.

Baabra and Lammie haven't heard the last part of the story. They have been snuggling next to Mummy and have dropped off to sleep. Perhaps next time they'll manage to hear the end!

New Friends

8 JANUARY

The village is excited today. Nolo Giraffe and Slye Snake spot a crowd of villagers at the dock.

'A new family is moving to our island', cries Mr. Horse, the mayor, standing on his soapbox. 'Let's all give them a warm welcome and help them to get settled in!'

He gives Slye a little wink after his extra-short speech.

Slye laughs and gives the Mayor a nod.

Nolo tells Slye, 'I hope we can make new friends if there are children in this family'.

'But what if they are horrible?' asks Slye. She's always ready to speak her mind.

'Oh, I'm sure they'll be nice', smiles Nolo. 'We can show them things, like our toys, the Hideout, and...'

Tooooooooot! The ferry is arriving, with the new family peering over its rails. Villagers wave their hats and scarves and the new family waves back.

'I can see two children!' calls Nolo. 'Come on, let's go and say hello to them!'

A zebra family steps off the ferry. Nolo walks gracefully over to the two youngsters and gives them a big smile.

'Welcome to our island!' he says in an official-sounding voice. He likes being a leader.

The two youngsters look a little shy, but they smile back and nod happily. One of them digs into a pocket and pulls out a chocolate bar, breaks off two pieces and hands them to Nolo and Slye.

The year is already off to a good start!

January

Zig and Zag

9 JANUARY

'Let's go and meet the newcomers', says Baabra Sheep to the friends when they are playing today. She's very friendly!

'What a good idea', nods Slye Snake, 'but did you notice? They look exactly like each other!'

'No. Really?' blinks Bouncer Brachio.

The friends knock at the Zebra family's door. Mrs. Zebra opens it and smiles at them.

Nolo Giraffe takes the lead. 'Hello. My name is Nolo, and these are my friends, Baabra, Bouncer, Hoopla and Slye. Would your children like to play with us?'

'Oh, how nice of you all to ask', Mrs. Zebra answers. She calls out, 'Zig and Zag, come and meet some new friends!'

Two little zebras peek out from behind their mummy. It's true, they look exactly the same!

'I'm Zig', says one. The other shyly adds, 'And I'm Zag'.

'Would you like to play with us?' Nolo asks politely.

'Yes!' they exclaim together, and they all trot out into the wintry sunshine.

'So, are you really twins?' asks Slye, always coming straight to the point.

'Yes. We were born at the same time', Zig explains.

'Well, you were born two minutes before me, so I'm the baby', laughs Zag.

'Real twins!' Bouncer says, hardly believing it. He's never seen twins before.

'Oh, this is difficult', thinks Baabra. 'I've already lost track of who is who!'

Lammie's First Snow

10 JANUARY

It snowed last night! The island sparkles, white and silent in the morning sunlight.

Lammie Sheep is Baabra's little brother. He was born last spring, so he's never seen snow before.

Baabra asks, 'Mummy, can we go outside?'

'Of course!' smiles her mummy.

Soon they are out in the snow, dancing around.

'Cold!' says Lammie, scooping up a handful of snow. He takes a bite, thinking it would taste like ice cream, but it tastes more like water.

He scoops up some more, then throws it into the air and it flutters down.

'Pretty!' he cries.

'Watch, Lammie, we can make snow angels!' Baabra calls. She flops down on her back. 'You just move your arms and legs sideways like this', she says, sliding through the flakes.

'Look', she says, getting up and pointing to the

6

shape she's made. It has a head, two wings, and a long robe. 'See, Lammie? It looks like an angel', Baabra cries.

'Me too!' cries Lammie, and he flops down and squirms around on the snow. Then he stands up. His creature looks more like a snow worm, but he's proud. 'Angel!' he whispers, pointing.

'Not quite, Lammie, but a good try! Let's have a snow shower. Come over here!' Baabra orders.

They stand under the snow-covered apple tree. Baabra shakes a low branch. The whole tree shivers and drops snow all over them! Lammie whoops and dances around in the snow shower.

'Ooooh! It's cold!' yells Baabra. A wonderful day!

Frozen Summer

11 JANUARY Bouncer Brachio is going to visit his grandad and grandmother. They live on a small farm on the edge of the village.

'Hello Grandad! Hello Grandmother!' Bouncer calls out. 'Isn't the snow wonderful?'

'It certainly is. Look, the garden is sleeping now', his grandad chuckles, pointing to it. 'All you can see is snow. Bouncer, would you like to have your very own garden this year?'

'Oh yes! What do I need to do?' Bouncer asks.

'Let's look at the seed catalogues so you can choose what you want to grow', Grandad says, and they go inside.

Grandad brings out a pile of books filled with colourful little pictures of flowers and vegetables. 'What do you think?' he asks. Flowers?'

'Vegetables!' Bouncer says.

'A good choice!' laughs Grandmother. 'That yummy soup I make is full of vegetables Grandad grew last summer. I store them in our freezer. I call that machine my frozen summer!'

Bouncer looks at each picture. 'I like carrots', he announces. Grandad grins. 'Not tomatoes?'

'No. I hate tomatoes', Bouncer declares.

'But you love my spaghetti sauce', laughs Grandmother. 'You can't make that without tomatoes!'

'Hmmm… all right then. Tomatoes as well'.

Everybody laughs. 'We'll see what we can do, Bouncer', Grandad says.

January

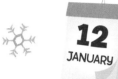

Stormy Night

12 JANUARY

The wind is howling tonight. Snow flies sideways in the gusts. The villagers all snuggle deeper into their beds, glad they are not outside.

'Gosh, that wind is howling like mad', whispers Slye Snake to herself, pulling her covers up. 'The trees must feel awful out there in the cold'.

Suddenly there's a loud cracking sound and Slye's house shivers and shakes. Her eyes open wide!

'What was that?' Slye asks herself, jumping in fright. She slips out of bed and quickly runs to her parents' bedroom.

'Mummy, Daddy, I'm frightened!' she cries. Slye jumps into bed with them. Mummy cuddles her and whispers, 'Don't worry, we're here'.

Daddy gets up, though, and peeks out of the window. It's dark, but he can see a little.

'Oh! The wind has blown down our tree. It's landed on the corner of our roof!' he says, looking into the snowy garden.

'It looks as though it will be fine for tonight', he says after looking at it a little longer. 'We'll see what we need to do tomorrow when the sun is up'.

'Would you like to stay in our bed tonight?' Mummy asks Slye.

'Oh yes please', answers Slye, snuggling in, and in a few minutes she's back asleep.

Village Meeting

13 JANUARY

It is morning. The snow storm has stopped, but branches have broken off trees, dustbins have blown over and deep snow drifts cover the village. A bell rings from the top of the village hall. That tells the villagers to come to a meeting there.

'I'll go and see what the news is', says Slye Snake's daddy. 'I'll be back soon!'

He hurries through the snow to the village hall. Mr. Horse, the mayor, starts the meeting.

'I've walked around the village. It was a bad storm'. reports the Mayor. 'Luckily, nobody was hurt. Let's

make a list of things to repair and clean up'.

'The clock on the village hall tower is broken', says Mrs. Brachio, the gift shop's owner.

'My little rowing boat has blown over in the harbour', says Ivan Monkey. He's a mad scientist.

'A tree is leaning on our roof', says Mr. Slye. 'Our roof is fine, but we need to cut the tree down'.

'Right', says Mr. Horse. 'Your tree', he nods to Mr. Slye, 'needs to be cut down first thing tomorrow. It's not safe, leaning on your house'.

'Who is going to repair the clock? Who will pay for it?' asks Mrs. Brachio, worried. 'We need to know what time it is!'

'We must come up with a plan', says Mr. Horse, wisely. Everyone agrees. Then the villagers walk back to their warm, cosy homes.

Tim-berrr!

14 JANUARY

Slye Snake wakes up early. Their tree is going to be cut down today!

'Hello Mr. Horse', she says when the mayor arrives.

'Good morning, Slye! How was my speech, when the Zebra family arrived?' he asks, a little worried.

'Much better', Slye smiles. 'Short and to the point'.

Then she says smiling 'Look! Here come our friends!'

The villagers arrive with ladders, saws, clippers and ropes. This will be a big job!

'First let's cut off the branches', directs Mr. Horse. Soon only the main trunk is leaning against the house.

'Now let's tie ropes to the trunk', says Mr. Horse.

'Time to cut the trunk – careful!' says Mr. Horse. A big chainsaw buzzes and snarls.

When that's done, he says, 'Right! When I yell 'Pull!' everybody has to pull. Agreed?'

The villagers hold their ropes tightly and get ready to tug.

'One, two, three, PULL!' yells Mr. Horse.

They pull and pull. Slowly the tree falls away from the house and lands on the ground.

'Hurray!' everybody cheers. It was a big, big tree! Slye's mummy serves coffee and hot chocolate.

'Thank you all for your hard work', Slye's daddy says, lifting his coffee cup to salute the villagers.

'That's what neighbours are for', replies Mr. Horse, and everybody smiles. 'Now we just have to cut the trunk into logs and stack them in a neat pile. Next winter Slye's family will have lots of firewood. They will really enjoy their fireplace!'

January

Good Friends

15 JANUARY

Not everyone was as lucky as Slye Snake's family in the snow storm.

At Bouncer Brachio's house, a tree branch broke a window in his playroom.

Yesterday Bouncer walked into the playroom, and wailed, 'My toys! My toys! They're broken!'

Almost all of Bouncer's toys were damaged by the wind and the melting snow.

Bouncer helps his mummy and daddy clean up the mess. He picks up a toy truck that used to push around, but it won't move any more.

'I loved playing with that truck', he says sadly, putting it into a big rubbish bag.

He spots a colouring book that is soaking wet and smelly. 'You go into the rubbish too', he sighs.

Bouncer kicks angrily at the bag, yelling, 'Arghhh! Mummy! I don't want my toys to be broken!'

'Poor Bouncer', his mummy says. 'You are such a good sport every day. We will get you some new ones'.

'But I don't want new ones', Bouncer sobs.

They fill the bag and take it to the dustbin.

Bouncer is sitting in the empty playroom when Nolo Giraffe comes to visit.

'Oh dear Bouncer. What happened?' he asks.

'The storm wrecked my toys!' Bouncer moans.

Nolo has an idea. 'Bouncer, I'm really sorry about your toys. I'll make things better tomorrow!'

What is Nolo up to now?

Help Arrives

16 JANUARY

This morning Nolo Giraffe, Baabra Sheep, Hoopla Hippo, Slye Snake, and Zig and Zag Zebra walk up the path to Bouncer Brachio's house, carrying packages.

'We thought we would give you some of our toys, so that you won't feel so sad', Baabra says.

Bouncer smiles for the first time today. 'Really? But you mean I can borrow them, yes?'

'Here's a truck that runs on batteries', Nolo says, handing it to Bouncer. 'It's yours'.

'You can have my sticker book, too. I don't like it anymore', says Baabra, smiling and telling a little white lie.

'I've already read this story book, so you can keep it', says Slye, handing it to Bouncer.

'And we want you to have these cartoon videos', Zig giggles and Zag nods.

'This is my favourite board game', says Hoopla.

'So I want it back!' And he starts laughing.

'HOOO, HO-HO-HO-HO!'

'HOOO, HO-HO-HO-HO!'

Everybody laughs with him. Especially Bouncer. The friends put their toys on Bouncer's shelves.

'What should we play first?' Nolo asks. 'It's very cold outside, so how about watching some of the cartoons?'

'Yes!' they yell. Bouncer starts one. Later, his mummy comes in with cups of hot chocolate.

'Hooray!' they cheer. Bouncer is happy again.

Hide and Seek

17 JANUARY

The friends are playing outside.

'Let's play hide and seek!' Bouncer says with a grin.

'We don't know that game. Can you tell us how to play it?' Zag smiles.

'Of course! I'll be IT for the first time. I stand on this stone, which is called the home base. I close my eyes and slowly count up to ten out loud. Everybody runs and hides. When I get to ten, I open my eyes and come looking for all of you.

'If I see you, I say, "I see Zig, behind the rose bush", or wherever you are. Then you are caught'.

'If you can run to the home base without me tagging you, you are free. The last one to be found wins. Understand?' Zig and Zag nod.

Bouncer starts counting, 'One! Two! Three! Four!...' Zig and Zag decide to hide together.

Bouncer gets to ten and starts finding his friends, one by one, but he can't spot Zig and Zag! He's found everyone except them now.

Finally Bouncer gives up on finding Zig and Zag and calls, 'All home free!' The twins have won!

Suddenly the friends see Zig and Zag move away from in front of a fence. They were completely invisible before. Their stripes hid them perfectly!

'We used to do that at our old home', Zig explains. Everybody laughs as they show how they can match the background and almost disappear.

January

A Mysterious Project

Grandad Brachio hears about Bouncer's wrecked toys. He visits him, to help cheer him up.

'Let's make something together', he says. Bouncer's face lights up.

'We need newspaper, flour, water, a bowl, a spoon, cooking oil, an apple, glue, a knife and red paint'.

'What can you make from all that?' Bouncer asks, curious.

Grandad won't say, so Bouncer just finds them.

'First, tear up the newspaper into thin strips', says Grandad, showing Bouncer how. 'I'll mix the flour and water while you do that', he adds, stirring them to make some paste.

'Now let's soak the newspaper strips in our paste. The paper needs to get really wet', Grandad says.

It feels and smells odd, but Bouncer has fun mixing the paper into the paste with his hands.

'Now rub the oil all over that apple', Grandad says, pointing to the oil.

Bouncer is puzzled. 'It feels strange!' he laughs.

'Next, wrap the newspaper strips around your apple, one by one. Smooth them tightly all over your apple until it's completely covered'.

'Are you sure you know what you're doing?' asks Bouncer. Grandad grins and nods.

'Put your apple on the radiator until the newspaper is dry', he answers. 'I'll come back then'.

'I can't guess what happens next!' Bouncer laughs.

The Mystery is Solved

Grandad says, 'it looks as though your newspaper apple is completely dry now Bouncer. We need two halves'. Grandad cuts it in two and the oily apple slides out.

'I found this little stick to make your new apple's stem. And here's some green paper to make leaves', says Grandad, handing Bouncer the paper and a pair of scissors.

'This is fun!' Bouncer says, cutting two leaves.

'Now use this glue to stick the two parts of your newspaper apple back together, Bouncer. We'll glue the stem and leaves on the top', says Grandad. Soon, the glue is dry. 'See, Bouncer? You've made a perfect newspaper apple!' laughs Grandad. 'What am I going to do with a newspaper apple?' Bouncer asks, still puzzled.

'A good question! Let's cut a slot near the top of

your apple', says Grandad. 'And now you can paint it all over with that beautiful red paint', he smiles. 'Make sure to paint into that slot, too'. Before long, the red paint is dry.

'Now I understand!' exclaims Bouncer. 'It's a bank'.

'You know, if you start saving your money, soon you can buy a new toy! I'll start you off', says Grandad. He fishes around in his pockets until he finds a large, shiny coin and gives it to Bouncer.

'Thank you! That was fun! I never thought I could make an apple! Or a bank!' chuckles Bouncer.

Spying

20 JANUARY

'What shall we do for fun?' Nolo Giraffe asks.

'Let's spy on somebody!' Hoopla Hippo whispers. He loves making mischief.

'Who?' asks Slye Snake, squinting.

'How about Roota Rooster?' suggests Hoopla. 'He's always up to something'.

'You're right', says Nolo, and everybody nods.

They head over to the chicken coop, where Roota is the chief rooster. He's a little silly and thinks he's more important than he really is. But he's funny. Before they get too close, they crouch down and sneak along a hedge, looking for Roota.

'There he is! He's busy scratching in the earth. It looks as though he's digging for buried treasure', Hoopla whispers.

'Shhh! He's found something!' hisses Slye.

The friends hold their breath and watch.

'I'll get you yet!' Roota mutters to himself.

He scratches deeper and deeper in the earth, tilting his head every now and then. Suddenly he stabs something with his beak.

'What is it?' whispers Nolo.

The friends lean closer, dying to see it.

In a flash, Roota pulls a fat worm out of the ground, flips it into the air, and swallows it in one gulp.

'Oh, yuck!' cries Slye, making a face.

'That's not much of a treasure, if you ask me!' snorts Nolo. Still, it was fun being a spy!

21 JANUARY — Firefly Island Map

The friends meet at the village's news board today.

Nolo Giraffe explains to Zig and Zag Zebra, 'Whenever there is some news, our villagers put up a notice on the news board'. The twins nod.

'Hello, everybody', old Mr. Ptera smiles. His general store sells food, clothes, toys, paint – nearly everything in fact. He is about to paint something on the back of the news board. 'I'm making a map of Firefly Island. Do you want to help?'

Everyone cries, 'Yes please!'

'This is the shape of our island', says Mr. Ptera. He paints a big, lumpy shape on the board. 'I think it looks like that. Now for all the places'.

'How about the beach and the dock where the ferry boat stops?' asks Nolo. Mr. Ptera paints them in. 'The café!' 'The general store!' 'The fire station!' 'The post office!' 'The clinic!' 'The village hall!' 'The gift shop!' 'The school and playground!' As the friends call the places out, Mr. Ptera adds them to the map.

'Phew! There are more places here than I thought', says Baabra. 'But it certainly looks nice!'

'And there's still more to add', says Nolo. 'We haven't done any of the rest of the island!'

Claaang! 'Oops, dinner bell! See you tomorrow!' calls Slye. They are all starving, so they hurry off to their homes!

22 JANUARY — The Map Is Done

The friends and Mr. Ptera are ready to finish the map of Firefly Island.

'You know what we forgot yesterday? Our Hideout!' says Slye Snake. Everybody laughs.

'What's the Hideout?' asks Zig Zebra, her eyes big with wonder.

'The Hideout is a little hut in the woods. We play there sometimes. If you pass a test, we'll let you play there too', Slye explains.

'I'll do that. It should be easy!' Zig replies.

'What else should we add to the map?' asks Bouncer Brachio.

'Well, there are our houses, and Firefly Meadow, and the lake…' starts Nolo Giraffe.

'And the camping ground – oh, and the watch tower!' exclaims Baabra Sheep.

'What's a watch tower?' asks Zag.

'It's a really tall tower you can climb up. And then you can see forever!' explains Baabra excitedly. 'When it gets warm again we can go there and climb to the top'.

'Can you please put on the names of all the places?' asks Hoopla. Mr. Ptera nods and gets busy.

'Thank you for all your help', smiles Mr. Ptera. 'I really couldn't have done it without you!' The friends all clap and cheer.

January

Ferry Ride

23 JANUARY

'Hurry, Zig and Zag, we don't want to miss the boat!' calls Mummy Zebra this morning. They are going for a ferry ride today.

Near Firefly Island lies another island, Big Island. A ferry boat goes back and forth between them.

'Watch your step', says Mummy as they get on the ferry. Captain Cow clangs her bell and toots her horn. The ferry pulls away from the dock.

'Our village is so pretty!' cries Zig.

'Let's wave!' calls out Zag, and they wave madly.

The villagers on the dock and along the beach wave back and shout, 'Have fun!'

Firefly Island grows smaller and smaller.

Zig looks down into the clear water below them.

'Look! A huge fish!' she cries.

They all lean over and spot an enormous, beautiful golden fish, swimming beside the ferry. It looks up at them.

'Oooh, it's swimming really fast!' cries Zag.

'Maybe it's going shopping on Big Island', jokes Daddy, 'but it missed the boat'. They all laugh.

The Zebra family gets off. They sip hot chocolate at a little stall on the harbour. Then they get back on board and head off home to Firefly Island.

'Maybe our fish will swim back with us', thinks Zig. But it doesn't appear. Still, it's exciting to feel the wind in your face and be chugging home to Firefly Island.

A Competition

24 JANUARY

A large group of villagers stands by the news board, talking excitedly.

Since he has such a long neck, Nolo Giraffe can see over the villagers' heads.

He spots a yellow sheet on the board. It has a picture of a shiny ferry boat and some words.

'What is happening?' Nolo asks Mr. Horse, the mayor.

'You've heard we are getting a brand new ferry?' asks Mr. Horse. Nolo nods. 'We're having a competition to pick the best name for it'.

Nolo loves the old ferry. But a new one is exciting too. 'Can I enter the competition?' he asks.

'Of course you can', says Mr. Horse. 'Each villager can put in one name. The winner will get a free

16

ferry ride around the island!'

'How can I come up with a good name?' he asks himself.

He thinks hard. 'What about *Water Queen*? Or *Splasher*? Gosh, this isn't easy'.

Finally he comes up with a name.

'Aha! It should be the *Tinker Bell*. She was a fairy in my Peter Pan book. And Captain Cow rings a bell when she starts the ferry's engine'.

He goes to the post office. 'Mrs. Trico, could you please write something for me?' he asks the postmistress.

'Of course, Nolo', she replies. Nolo explains. She writes *Tinker Bell* and *Nolo Giraffe* on the paper, chuckling as she writes. Then she hands the slip back to Nolo.

'Good luck! I think your name is wonderful', she says with a smile.

Nolo puts his slip into the competition box.

'I hope I win!' he thinks, as he walks home.

Ordering Seeds

Bouncer Brachio is at his grandmother and grandad's farm.

'It's time to order the seeds for your garden', Grandad says.

'What do we do?' Bouncer asks.

'Let's use my computer. Hop up!' Grandad says. Bouncer jumps onto his lap and looks at the screen.

'Gosh! Look at all the flowers and vegetables!'

'Can you remember what you chose?' Grandad laughs.

'I still want carrots and tomatoes', Bouncer says firmly. He adds a few other things too.

'OK, now click here, Bouncer. That sends your order to the seed company', Grandad explains. Bouncer grins and clicks. *Bing-bong*! 'They've got it!' Grandad says. 'In a few days, your seeds will be in your postbox'.

Grandad's eyes twinkle as he turns the computer off. The screen goes black.

'I also ordered some secret seeds, Bouncer. You'll just have to plant them and see what comes up. I know you'll love them both!'

'Can't you tell me?' Bouncer is dying to know.

'No! Wait until the summer!' Grandad chuckles.

'Oh, this is going to feel wonderful', she says to herself, smiling. 'I do love a lovely, long bath in the winter'.

Then she steps into the bath. But something's wrong. There's no water! The water is running – not too hot, and not too cold – but it's running straight down the drain!

'Oh my goodness!' she cries. 'I forgot to put the plug in!' Quickly she puts it in and the bath starts to fill. She laughs, shakes her head, and says to herself, 'Silly me! What will I forget next time?'

26 JANUARY — Grandmother Brachio's Bath

Grandmother Brachio is very sweet and kind, but she is always forgetting things.

'I'd like to have a bath', she says to herself.

She gets clean clothes and puts them by the bath.

'I love this soap, because it smells like apples', she says, putting it on the edge of the bath.

'I'll use my favourite towel', she murmurs. She hangs a big fluffy pink towel on a hook. Then she turns the water on, and puts a finger into it.

'Not too hot, not too cold', she says, happily.

'I mustn't forget to close the door', she thinks, 'to keep the warm air inside'.

She takes off her long blue dressing gown and hangs it up on another hook. Then she puts her blue slippers on the floor, right under her dressing gown.

27 JANUARY — Sardines

All the youngsters are at a sleepover at the village hall tonight. They are allowed to stay up late and play games.

Some parents will sleep there too, just to be safe.

'What shall we play?' asks Hoopla Hippo.

'How about sardines?' suggests Zig Zebra. The rest have never heard of sardines, so she explains.

'It's like hide and seek. But in sardines, the person who's IT hides. Then we all try to find them.

'When you find them, you quietly join them in the hiding place. Soon everyone is crammed together like sardines in a tin. The last person to find the place is IT next time'.

'Right! I'm IT!' Hoopla cries. 'So all close your eyes and count to ten'. He scurries out of sight as the rest begin: 'One! Two! Three!...'

Hoopla wriggles behind the piano in the dark hall. The friends start looking.

Zig spots him. 'There you are!' she whispers. And she squeezes in.

Nolo Giraffe hears 'Tee-hee!' coming from behind the piano, and he squashes in next to Zig.

Slye Snake spots Nolo's tail sticking out and wriggles in. Soon there's a crowd behind the piano, trying not to laugh. Still, muffled sounds come out: 'Hoo-hoo! Hee-hee! Giggle-giggle!' It's impossible to keep quiet.

Finally Baabra hears everyone.

She comes over and sees the pile of friends. She laughs and says, 'Found you! I'm last, so I'm IT now!'

'Sardines is such fun!' gasps Hoopla.

Tops and Bottoms

28 JANUARY

It's bedtime for Lammie Sheep.

'Pyjamas, pyjamas, me put on', he yawns.

Mummy gets them out of the drawer and says, 'Come and give me a goodnight kiss when you're ready'.

She goes to help Baabra brush her teeth. Soon a terrible noise comes from Lammie's room.

Bang! Thud! Ow! It sounds like a wild animal is trapped in there! A lamp crashes to the floor. The room goes dark, but the struggling sounds carry on and on.

'What in the world is happening?' cries Mummy. She and Baabra rush to go and see what is going on in Lammie's room.

Mummy turns on the ceiling light.

She sees the broken lamp. A strange, headless creature is stumbling around the room, roaring!

'Mummy! Mummy! Can't get out!' cries the headless creature, waving its arms in the air.

'It's alright, Lammie, it's alright', she says hugging him, but she's laughing a little too. She pulls Lammie's pyjama bottoms off his arms and head. He blinks and wipes his tears away.

Baabra laughs and hugs him too.

'Poor Lammie!' Mummy says. 'You were trying to put on your pyjama bottoms, not your pyjama top, so there was no hole for your head! I can well believe you were scared!'

January

29 JANUARY Decorating the Toy Chest

Hoopla Hippo is having fun today with the wonderful book his friends gave him at his surprise New Year's party. It's a colouring book, but in the back it's got lots of sparkly, colourful stickers.

'I'll use the stickers to decorate my toy chest. It's nice, but a bit plain looking', he thinks.

He peels off a red rocket ship and sticks it on the top of the toy chest, in the corner.

'That looks really good!' he says to himself. 'How about a moon for the rocket ship to land on?' he mutters, putting a moon sticker above the rocket.

He keeps on adding stickers. Soon he has planets, stars, space creatures and lots of other rockets and space stations on his toy chest.

'Now, that is really beautiful', he thinks happily, carrying on.

'I suppose that's it', he says, sitting back to admire his chest. 'I've used them all up!'

Suddenly, Mummy comes into his room. She stops when she sees his toy chest.

'What in the world? Or rather, what in outer space?' she exclaims, surprised.

'I wanted to make my toy chest look prettier, Mummy', Hoopla explains.

Mummy smiles and gives him a hug. 'It looks wonderful, Hoopla', she says. 'Good idea!'

30 JANUARY Story Time

'It's story day at the gift shop – yippee!' cries Zig Zebra.

'I can't wait', answers her twin sister Zag. 'Let's go early so we can sit in the first row!'

'Why hello, Zig and Zag!' says Bouncer Brachio's mummy. She runs the gift shop. 'Can you please help me scatter these cushions on the floor?'

'I'll put our mittens on these cushions, to save them for us', says Zag, picking two in the front row. The shop soon fills up.

Bouncer's mummy smiles and says, 'Welcome! Please sit down. I have picked a special book today'. She shows them the cover. 'It's called *We Are Wolves*, by Melinda Julietta. It's about baby wolves, learning how to be good grown-up wolves'. She starts reading

'I wish I was a wolf', Zag thinks, forgetting where she is, and falling into the world of wolves.

But suddenly Zag has a problem. 'Oh dear! I have to go to the bathroom!' And she's in the front row! She crouches and rushes to the bathroom – just in time. Zag comes back quickly and sits on her cushion again, curious about the wolves.

'The end!' she hears Mrs. Brachio say.

'Oh no. I missed the rest of the book!' she thinks crossly. 'Story time is over'.

Mrs. Brachio comes over to her and says, 'Poor Zag, I know you didn't hear the whole story. Would you like to borrow this book for a few days?'

'Oh yes! Can I?' Zag asks.

Mrs. Brachio nods. 'Yes! Just bring it back soon'. 'Of course!' Zag says. Things turned out perfectly after all.

The Winner

31 JANUARY

All the villagers are really excited today. Mr. Horse, the mayor, will announce the winning name for the new ferry boat. Every villager has entered the competition.

Nolo Giraffe can't wait. 'Wouldn't it be wonderful if I thought up the winning name?' he thinks. But he also thinks about the prize. 'If I win, I'll get a free ride around the island on the new ferry. And I love going on any ferry, new or old!'

Mr. Horse is standing on his soapbox so that everybody can see him.

'Ahem. Ahem!' He clears his throat loudly to get everyone to be quiet. Then he begins to speak in his speech-making voice.

'Dear villagers, thank you for coming today. As you know, we have held a competition to find the best name for our new ferry boat. There is a prize for the villager who put in the winning name. I am happy to tell you that our ferry will be launched in three days, and that the winning name is… *Tinker Bell!*' He turns and points to Nolo.

'Nolo Giraffe, congratulations! You won!'

Everybody laughs and claps and turns to look at Nolo, whose eyes are wide with surprise.

'I can't believe my ears!' he exclaims.

He's so excited that he does a little dance, kicking up his heels in happiness.

'Let me also tell Nolo more about his prize', Mr. Horse continues after Nolo has finished his dance. 'As the winner, next summer you can invite all your friends to go on a ferry ride with you, all around Firefly Island. We will make a picnic for you at the picnic shelter and you can sleep in tents that night at the camping ground! So many congratulations, Nolo!'

Nolo's friends run to him, cheering, and pat his back. They are thrilled to hear about his prize. They can't wait for their ferry ride. And now the new ferry has a wonderful name.

February

Ice Skating

'Let's go skating!' calls Nolo Giraffe.

It has been very cold, so the lake on Firefly Island is covered with thick ice and perfect for skating. The friends hike up the snowy path to the picnic shelter by the lake. They are throwing snowballs and laughing.

'Come in and warm up!' calls Mr. Trico, the park ranger. He swings open the picnic shelter's door. Hot air from the fireplace hits them.

In no time they have their skates laced up.

'Is everybody ready?' calls Nolo.

'Yes!' they all shout. They walk out to the lake. Baabra Sheep has been skating for years.

'Yippee!' she yells, whizzing by on the grey ice. Her hair ribbons flutter and flap.

Zig and Zag Zebra have never skated before. They totter, fall, get up, fall, then skate a little more.

'Look! We can skate!' crows Zig, as she and Zag wobble by. It's not easy, but they're getting better.

'Let's play tag!' shouts Hoopla Hippo. 'I'm IT!' He tries to tag Zig. She falls, so he misses. He catches Slye Snake instead. 'Now you're IT!' he laughs. Slye tags Zag, Zag tags Baabra, Baabra tags Nolo and Nolo tags Bouncer Brachio.

'Phew! I'm thirsty', says Hoopla. 'Let's go and have some hot chocolate in the shelter'.

They head inside, rubbing their bottoms and laughing. Mr. Trico has mugs waiting.

'Mmm, delicious!' they murmur.

The New Ferry Arrives

Nolo Giraffe wakes up early today. 'I can't wait to see the *Tinker Bell*', he whispers. Ever since he won the ferry naming competition, villagers have been asking him when 'his' boat is coming. Today is the day! He hurries to the dock. 'Gosh! The village band is already here!' he says, impressed. Mr. Horse, the mayor, is already standing on his soap box, ready to make a speech.

'A perfect name for our ferry, Nolo!' One villager after another claps him on the back.

'There she is!' somebody cries, pointing to a plume of smoke in the distance, and soon the ferry cruises into the harbour.

Tooooot! Captain Cow blows the ferry's horn and rings the bell. The band plays a cheerful tune. 'Hooray!' The villagers cheer and clap as she docks. Captain Cow waves her hat at them.

'My fellow villagers, let's welcome the *Tinker Bell*

to Firefly Island!' shouts Mr. Horse, and they all clap and cheer even louder. 'Tomorrow we'll have her official launch. But today you can go aboard to see what a wonderful ferry she is!'

The villagers roam all over the ferry, admiring her shiny brass fittings, fresh paint and sparkling glass. 'She is a beauty', Nolo thinks. 'It's going to be wonderful to launch her with her new name tomorrow!' He is so proud, he could burst!

Launching the *Tinker Bell*

3 FEBRUARY

Tweedle-toot-toot! Boom! Boom! Everybody is back at the dock for the *Tinker Bell* launch. The band is playing and the sparkling ferry bobs gently in the chilly water.

'It's your big day, Nolo! Congratulations!' cries Mr. Horse, the mayor, giving him a pat. Nolo can hardly breathe, he's so excited. Mr. Horse climbs onto his soap box. 'My fellow villagers, welcome to this wonderful celebration', he begins. 'Have you ever seen a more beautiful ferry?'

'No! Never!' answer the happy villagers.

'Then let's launch her! I hereby name you the *Tinker Bell!*' Mr. Horse grabs a bottle of fizzy water wrapped in a cloth. He leans back and swings it hard against the bow of the ferry.

Smash! The bottle breaks inside the cloth! Bubbles spray all over, just as he planned.

But Mr. Horse keeps moving in the same direction. He can't stop! Mr. Horse flies straight off the dock and into the icy water!

'Oooh!' cries the crowd.

Captain Cow throws a lifebelt on a rope. 'Quick! Grab it, Mr. Horse!'

In a moment he's safely on the *Tinker Bell*'s deck, dripping wet. Captain Cow wraps him in a blanket. The villagers watch in silence as they hold their breath. Suddenly, Mr. Horse bursts out laughing. Somebody cries, 'Let's give our wet Mayor a cheer too!' The band plays, Captain Cow blows the ferry's horn, and everybody yells, 'Hip-hip hooray!'

Nolo thinks, 'What a wonderful day. I want to be the captain of a ferry when I grow up!'

February

4
FEBRUARY

Home Music Night

'It's music night tonight!' Zig Zebra calls to her twin, Zag.

Their family loves making music. Zig grabs her flute and Zag her trumpet. Mummy sits at the piano and Daddy is at his drums.

'Here's the Zebra Family Band!' he laughs.

'What shall we start with tonight?' asks Zag.

'How about a march?' suggests Mummy.

'Yes! How about Number 42?' asks Daddy, flipping through his music book.

They never call the songs by name, just the page number. Soon they all have page 42 open.

'One, two, three, four', counts Mummy, and they're off! They play with lots of energy, and when they finish they're quite out of breath.

'Didn't we sound good?' asks Zig.

'Definitely darling', answers Mummy.

'I'd like to sing. How about 23?' asks Zig.

'Oh yes! Here we go!' says Daddy.

Zig wiggles around like a rock star but she sings really badly!

'She sounds like a donkey braying, or a zebra braying, I think', laughs Zag at her own joke. Still, Zig loves it and she takes a bow at the end.

'You really are something special!' laughs Daddy, winking at Mummy. 'I'm not sure zebras were born to sing, but you are enjoying it. Good try!'

'You just don't know good singing when you hear it!' Zig giggles. In her mind, she is a star!

5
FEBRUARY

Ivan the Invisible

Just like every other day, Ivan Monkey is busy in his laboratory.

He loves science, but his experiments never go the way he hopes. He's a mad scientist.

'How can I become invisible, so nobody can see me?' he wonders. 'Maybe I need to be covered with something that's invisible?' He thinks hard. 'Now, what is invisible around here?' he murmurs. 'Air, perhaps? No, that won't work!' he says. Minutes pass.

'Aha! Dust! You can hardly see it at all!'

So he runs around his lab, collecting dust. 'Quite a pile, more than I expected. Mmm, now what?' he thinks out loud. 'Aha! Glue! I'll cover myself in glue and roll in all this dust'.

To test if his experiment has worked, he goes to visit Hoopla Hippo's family, next door. He knocks on their door. Hoopla's mummy opens the door, looks out, looks him over and steps back, partly closing the door again.

'Ahem', he says. 'Can you see me?' he asks.

'I can see something, but I can't tell WHO you are. Are you related to Ivan? You look a little like him, but sort of fluffy'.

'Oh dear', Ivan mutters. 'It's me, Ivan, but I was trying to become invisible'.

'Oh, Ivan, I see', she says kindly, knowing him well. 'I'm afraid you are just very, very dusty today!'

Mystery Footprints

6 FEBRUARY

Bouncer Brachio is walking in the woods. 'It must have been quite wonderful in ancient times, when the giant brachiosauruses lived here', he thinks.

'Now there are none left – except for my family – and we've become much smaller. We're mini-dinos!' he smiles to himself. Suddenly, he sees a *huge* brachio footprint in the snow.

'How can that be? No!' He studies it, his heart racing. 'Have the ancients come back?' he whispers. He looks around nervously, but sees nothing moving. It's silent in the woods. Now Bouncer is scared. His heart is pounding.

'I'll quickly get Daddy', he exclaims and he hurries home. 'Daddy, Daddy, Daddy! You have to come and look! The ancient giants have come back! It's unbelievable!'

'Really?' Daddy smiles. 'You have to show me. This is exciting news!' Soon Bouncer and his daddy are back in the woods, peering at the giant footprint in the snow.

'Hmmm', says Daddy. 'It certainly is bigger than our feet'. He puts his own foot inside the print. There's lots of room to spare.

'What do you think?' asks Bouncer, excited.

'I… I think I know', says Daddy. 'But you won't like my answer. I walked along this path yesterday. I think that's my own footprint. When the sun shines on footprints, it melts the edges, and they get bigger and bigger'.

He smiles at Bouncer. 'So I certainly am older than you, but I'm not one of the ancients. Sorry!'

Bouncer laughs. 'Good OLD Daddy! I was sure the ancients were back. The joke is on me!'

They head off home, making new, small tracks.

Cooking Club

7 FEBRUARY

It's Cooking Club day. Hoopla Hippo and his friends enjoy watching Hoopla's mummy in the kitchen. She loves making things, and they try to do what she does. Most of all, they love eating what they make.

'We're going to make a bunny salad today', Hoopla's mummy says. They all look puzzled.

'Here's what you do. First, take some nice green leaves to make the bunny's nest',

She puts a few lettuce leaves on her plate.

'Then, you take half a pear – that's the bunny – and you put it in its nest. Now, you use two raisins to make the bunny's eyes'.

She pops two raisins into the pear, and the bunny suddenly has tiny dark eyes!

'He's winking at me!' says Hoopla, laughing.

'These almonds make his ears', says Mummy Hippo, then she uses a small marshmallow for the bunny's tail and a red cherry for its nose.

'Do you think you can do the same thing?' she asks. 'Yesss!' they answer. There's a flurry of arms and hands reaching for things.

'Oops!' cries Hoopla, as his bunny slips off his plate and slides across the floor. He chases it, but he slips on the pear and falls on his back.

Everyone bursts out laughing.

'Hoopla! Is your pear bunny trying to get away from you?' laughs Slye Snake.

'I'm afraid he's a squash now!' And Hoopla laughs at his joke with his crazy hippo laugh.

'HOOO, HO-HO-HO-HO!'

'HOOO, HO-HO-HO-HO!'

Slye Needs Glasses

8 FEBRUARY

Slye Snake and Baabra Sheep are looking at a big book in Baabra's house. Its pictures tell the story of a brave mouse who tricks a cat.

'I like the buttons on the mouse's shirt', says Baabra. 'What's so good about them?' Slye asks.

'The little mouse faces on them', smiles Baabra.

Slye brings the book closer, squints and says, 'Oh, now I see what you mean'.

Baabra looks at her friend in surprise. 'You couldn't see them before?'

'No. I can't see that well', Slye says sadly.

'You're joking!' exclaims Baabra.

She picks up a deck of cards, walks across the room and holds a card up.

'What's on this card?' she asks.

'I don't know. I can't see it', Slye replies.

Baabra walks closer. 'Tell me when you can', and at last Slye cries, 'It's a chicken!'

By now Baabra is standing right next to Slye.

'Gosh, you really do have a problem', Baabra says. 'I think you need glasses'.

'Maybe you're right. We snakes can't see very well', Slye says thoughtfully.

'We've got to do something about that', says Baabra, taking charge of her friend. 'We'll go to Dr. Henny's office tomorrow morning'.

Slye smiles happily. It would be nice to see properly.

Dr. Henny's Clinic

Sly Snake and Baabra Sheep visit Dr. Henny's clinic. 'What seems to be the problem Slye?' she asks gently.

'I don't think I can see properly', Slye says. 'Things that are far away are sort of blurry and even small things that are close to me are sometimes difficult to see. Do you agree, Baabra?'

Baabra nods and tells Dr. Henny about the mouse's buttons in the picture book and the card with the chicken on it.

'I'm sorry to hear about your problem Slye', Dr. Henny says kindly. 'But I'm certain we can sort it out easily. Let me have a look'.

Dr. Henny checks Slye's eyes. She looks into them with a little flashlight. Then she asks Slye lots of questions.

'Yes, Slye', she says finally. 'You do need glasses'.

'Told you so!' laughs Baabra.

'I'll get the glasses made on Big Island', says Dr. Henny. 'They will be on the *Tinker Bell* ferry when she arrives this time next week. Just pick them up and come back to see me'.

'That's all I have to do?' asks Slye, amazed.

'Yes', answers Dr. Henny. 'We'll make sure they fit you properly. But you'll be able to see properly straight away Slye', smiles Dr. Henny.

'Really? You mean, just like that, no more problems?' asks Slye.

'Yes, Slye', smiles the doctor. 'You're going to love it. What shape of frames would you like?'

'Round', answers Slye, 'definitely round!'

Slye can't wait for the *Tinker Bell* to arrive next week!

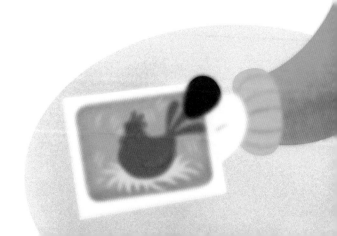

February

The General Store

10 FEBRUARY

Grandad and Bouncer Brachio are going shopping at Mr. Ptera's general store today.

It's a wonderful place, packed with food, clothes, tools, paint – in fact, almost everything! Mr. Ptera loves solving problems for the villagers.

He smiles as they come in, greeting them all warmly. 'Good morning, all of you Brachios! How can I help you today?'

'Let's see, Bouncer', Grandad says, looking over the gardening section. 'I have lots of tools, but we probably should get you a pair of gardening gloves – digging and weeding can be hard on your hands'.

They find a small pair for Bouncer. He grins.

'And I bet you'd like your very own trowel'.

'What's a trowel?' Bouncer wants to know.

'Here's one. You use it to dig holes to plant things in, and then to dig them up later'.

'That would be wonderful', grins Bouncer, digging in the air with the trowel Grandad hands him.

'Do you need string?' Mr. Ptera asks helpfully.

'String?' Bouncer can't imagine why.

'Yes!' laughs Granddad. 'You'll see soon enough what we will use it for', he tells Bouncer.

'I never thought that gardening would have so many mysteries', declares Bouncer.

'How about a sweet?' asks kindly Mr. Ptera.

'Oh, yes!' Bouncer says. 'Cherry, please!'

A Bright Pink Card

11 FEBRUARY

Bouncer Brachio is at the post office. He turns the little arrow on the post office box lock to point to 1, then 5, then 7. The door pops open.

A bright pink card! That means Mrs. Trico, the postmistress, has a package for him.

'Good morning, Bouncer', she says as he hands her the card. She ducks below the counter and comes up with a small box. She reads the label and says, 'I think somebody is going to plant a garden this spring!'

'Yes, my grandad is going to teach me how to do it', Bouncer answers proudly.

'You'll have lots of fun', she smiles, handing Bouncer the box.

'It feels empty!' he laughs, shaking it

'Seeds don't weigh very much, you know', Mrs. Trico explains. 'It's amazing how such tiny things can produce such big, delicious vegetables and beautiful flowers'.

'Well, I hope mine do, anyway!' Bouncer nods, and he's off to Grandad and Grandmother's farm. Grandad sees him coming up the path and comes outside to greet Bouncer.

'They came! They came!' yells Bouncer, running as fast as he can.

'Brilliant!' answers Grandad. 'Let's see!'

They go inside – but we'll have to wait to learn what they find inside the box.

12 FEBRUARY Making Valentine's Cards

Hoopla Hippo and Nolo Giraffe are busy making Valentine's cards.

'I like Valentine's Day', declares Hoopla, colouring a beautiful card for Baabra Sheep.

'Me too', answers Nolo, cutting some coloured paper to glue onto one he's making for his mummy and daddy.

'It makes me feel nice to show I like someone', Hoopla continues, studying his card for Baabra.

'Yes, and I feel very good when I get one too!' laughs Nolo. 'I hope somebody thinks about sending me one!'

They glue, colour, cut and sprinkle glitter on their cards. The piles of finished Valentine's cards grow higher and higher.

'Now, don't look at what I'm doing', warns Hoopla, hiding the one he's working on now. It's for Nolo.

'Hmmm. Why not?' asks Nolo sweetly, as if he doesn't know the answer. He's busy making a Valentine's card for Hoopla too.

At the end of their card making afternoon, they pull out a heap of envelopes. 'Mummy, can you help us?' Nolo asks.

'Of course!' she answers. Nolo's mummy writes the names they want on each envelope. Hoopla and Nolo put their beautiful cards into the envelopes. And then the finishing touch – into each envelope they drop a tiny little sweet.

They pop some sweets into their own mouths when they have finished. It was a lot of work, but it was a lot of fun too!

'Now I can't wait for Valentine's Day. Just two days away!' says Hoopla, licking his lips.

February

Planting the Seeds

13 FEBRUARY

Bouncer Brachio and his grandad are planting some of Bouncer's garden. It's still cold outside, but Grandad has made some plans.

'Today we'll plant your lettuce plants indoors so they get a head start', he explains. 'The other seeds go into the ground once the weather gets warm'.

'What about those mystery seeds?' asks Bouncer. He remembers his grandad had ordered some seeds that he won't tell Bouncer about.

'You'll just have to wait and see what comes up', laughs Grandad.

Grandad has filled some flat planting boxes with earth. They gently water the boxes and let the water drain through.

'Now scatter the seeds like this', Grandad says, showing Bouncer how. He sprinkles seeds on the earth. 'Let's cover the seeds with just a little more earth', Grandad says.

They put plastic film over the boxes to keep them moist so that the seeds can start to grow.

'I'll put these boxes by the window so they get gentle sunlight every day. And I'll make sure they don't get dry', promises Grandad.

Bouncer has been thinking about delicious salads and buttery beans as he's been working. 'It's fun playing with the earth while you think of eating', he laughs. 'But won't you tell me about those mystery seeds? Please?'

Valentine's Day

14 FEBRUARY

It's Valentine's Day! All over Firefly Island the villagers are busy delivering their cards, flowers and gifts.

'Happy Valentine's Day!' they call to each other. Hoopla Hippo and Nolo Giraffe started early and have finished their deliveries quickly.

'Let's see if you have any', Hoopla says to Nolo. They hurry over to Nolo's house and find a pile of Valentine's cards and a tiny box at Nolo's door.

'Let's see if you have!' grins Nolo, and they take Nolo's pile over to Hoopla's house. There's another little pile of Valentine's cards at Hoopla's door.

'Let's open them', Hoopla says, so in they go. They pile their Valentine's cards and boxes on the kitchen table.

'Gosh!' exclaims Nolo, opening his box first. 'It's from my Mummy and Daddy! Look! A tiny racing car! *Vrooom-Vrooom!*' he growls.

'And look at this!' cries Hoopla. He pulls a skipping rope out of his box. 'I can train just like the people on TV do!' he says.

They settle down to look at all the cards, eating the sweets inside them as they go. At the end of the afternoon, both friends are feeling a little sick. All the sweets have disappeared into their tummies. 'I love Valentine's Day', moans Nolo.

'Me too. I can't wait for next year', sighs Hoopla, patting his sore tummy!

February

Hoopla Pays for His Fun

15 FEBRUARY

'Ouch!' cries Hoopla Hippo. It's the middle of the night and he has a tummy ache. It keeps getting worse and worse.

Mummy hurries into his bedroom and asks, 'Is your tummy still upset? I think you ate too many Valentine's day sweets Hoopla'.

'Don't say that word please', groans Hoopla. 'What word?' asks Mummy, puzzled.

'Sweets. I don't want to think or hear about anything sweet for the whole of the year!' protests Hoopla. He burps.

'Maybe next year you shouldn't eat all your sweets in one go', says Hoopla's mummy, with a wise smile. She rubs his tummy gently and it starts to feel better.

Hoopla falls asleep. In the morning, he gets up and goes to the kitchen.

'Oh dear, seeing food makes me feel ill!' he moans. He goes back to bed and sleeps.

By lunch time his tummy is back to normal.

'I think I can eat a little now', he says to his mummy with a smile. 'What was I thinking? I should have stopped. Still, those sweets were really delicious', he thinks.

'I've made you some soup', says Mummy. 'That's good for you when you aren't feeling well'.

What a shame she wasn't there to give him advice yesterday, during his Valentine's day feast!

Slye Gets Her New Glasses

16 FEBRUARY

Tooooooooot! Captain Cow blows the *Tinker Bell's* horn to tell the villagers she's arriving. Who's waiting to meet the ferry today? Slye Snake and Baabra Sheep are so excited, they can't stop jumping and jiggling. Soon Captain Cow comes ashore and hands them a little package. 'Here you go, Slye', Captain Cow says. 'Thank you very much!' cries Slye.

They run as fast as they can to Dr. Henny's office. 'Let's see what they have made for you Slye', says Dr. Henny, unwrapping a beautiful pair of glasses. 'Try them on', she continues. Slye holds the glasses over her eyes. 'Amazing! Everything is so clear now!' she cries.

Then she stops. 'Do I have to hold them up like this all the time?' she asks Dr. Henny, a bit worried. 'I thought about that after I saw you last week', laughs Dr. Henny.

'Since snakes' ears and noses don't stick out, we do have a little problem making your glasses stay on. But I think I have found the answer!'

Dr. Henny takes an elastic band out of her pocket and attaches it to the glasses. Then she puts them on Slye. She tightens the elastic a little at the back, so the glasses stay snuggly in place.

'Hey presto! Now you can see better all day long. Just don't forget to take them off at night', she teases, and she gives Slye a friendly pat.

Slye looks up, down, from side to side, and slowly turns around, staring at everything in Dr. Henny's office. 'The world is even more beautiful than before, now that I can see well', smiles Slye.

The Hideout Test

17 FEBRUARY

The friends have all gathered at the Hideout. It is a little hut in the woods that their parents made just for the youngsters and its tiny door is too small for grown-ups.

Zig and Zag Zebra need to pass a test before they can go inside.

'I'm a little scared', whispers Zig to Zag.

'Me too', Zag whispers back.

'Let's get started', says Nolo Giraffe, taking charge. 'Here's your test. You have to hold your breath longer than Hoopla does'.

The zebras blink worriedly. They know hippos can stay under the water for a long time.

'Start when I count to three', Nolo says. 'One, two, THREE!'

Hoopla, Zig and Zag take deep breaths and then stop breathing. Their eyes get big. Suddenly Hoopla bursts out laughing.

'HOOO, HO-HO-HO-HO!'

'HOOO, HO-HO-HO-HO!'

'I couldn't stand it!' he gasps.

'Zig and Zag', Nolo smiles, 'You have passed the test! Now then, do you promise you will never tell anyone the secret password?'

'Yes', says Zig, nodding nervously.

'Yes', says Zag. The twins look very serious.

'Good. The secret password is... *underpants*!'

Everybody laughs and laughs, especially Zig and Zag. Then each of them crawls inside.

February

18 FEBRUARY

What Do You Want to Be?

Baabra Sheep, Slye Snake, Zig Zebra and her twin sister Zag are having a tea party at the Zebra family's house. Slye asks all her friends, 'What do you want to be when you grow up?'

Baabra knows. 'A postmistress, like Mrs. Trico. I would love to see people smile when they get letters in their post office boxes'.

Zig, who likes books, says, 'I want to have a gift shop, like Mrs. Brachio, and sell books and presents. And read stories to children'.

Zag, who loves being outdoors, says, 'For me, running the camping ground, like Mr. Brachio does, would be perfect. What about you, Slye?'

Slye giggles. 'I want to be a mayor, like Mr. Horse. I would make speeches every day!'

Zig and Zag's mummy comes in with biscuits.

'Thank you Mummy', smiles Zag. They help themselves and munch away happily.

'What have you been chattering about?' Mummy asks. They tell her about their dreams. Mrs. Zebra claps her hands. 'I think that's wonderful!' she says. 'Would you like me to ask if these grown-ups would let you go to visit them for a morning, so you can see what their jobs are really like?'

'Yes!' answers everyone. 'That would be really fun!' Baabra says. 'I hope they say yes! I can't wait to get started!'

19 FEBRUARY

Chilly and Hotta's Café

It's really cold today. Nolo Giraffe, Bouncer Brachio and Hoopla Hippo are going to the café for some hot chocolate.

'Come in from the cold!' welcomes Hotta Toucan. She comes from South America, where coffee and cocoa beans grow in the warm summer sun.

'Have a seat', adds Chilly Penguin. He also comes from South America, but from a place where the weather is much, much colder.

'What would you like? Hot chocolate or ice cream?' Chilly asks. The friends shiver, laugh and order hot chocolate.

'Why did you decide to live here, Hotta? Isn't it

awfully cold for you?' asks Nolo. Hotta smiles. 'When Chilly and I met, we fell in love and got married. We came to Firefly Island on our honeymoon. We liked it so much here that we decided to stay and we opened our café. We love making snacks, coffee and hot chocolate in the winter and delicious ice cream in the summer. We are so happy here, even in the winter!'

'Guess what!' Chilly says as he brings their steaming cups. 'We're going to have a baby!'

'That's wonderful!' say the friends.

'Have you picked a name yet?' asks Nolo.

'Yes – but we're not telling', Hotta beams. 'You'll find out soon'. What can it be...?

Ivan's Floating Experiment

20 FEBRUARY

Ivan Monkey would love to be able to float in the air, like a feather or a snowflake. 'Hmmm', he mutters, scratching his chin. 'What can I use to make myself float?'

Looking around his lab, he spots a box of soap powder, and an idea goes PING in his head.

'Soap bubbles float in the air. Can I use them to make myself float?' he wonders. He stirs soap powder with water and begins whipping it up. Soon he has a bowl full of bubbles. He scoops the bubbles up and starts putting them under his arms so he can float. They pop and dribble down his sides.

'Faster, faster!' he cries, speeding up. But the bubbles keep popping. Ivan is not rising off the floor yet, so he goes even faster. Soon he is completely soaked, and the soap bubbles sliding down his body are making a puddle on the floor. 'Something is going wrong', he murmurs.

His doorbell rings. When Ivan opens the door, he sees Hoopla Hippo, his neighbour. Hoopla looks surprised and stammers, 'Oh... Ivan... my mummy has baked some biscuits and we wanted to share some with you... Were you having a bath?'

Ivan looks at all the soapy water dripping off his body. 'Um. Yes. Hoopla. Exactly. Thank you for the biscuits. See you later!'

Sometimes it's really difficult to explain to people what your dreams are all about!

Grandmother Brachio's Glasses

21 FEBRUARY

Grandmother Brachio loves to read the morning paper while she sips a cup of hot tea. 'I'm really looking forward to today's paper. It has a puzzle in it. It's good for my old brain to get some exercise', she chuckles.

She boils the water and gets out a teabag and a cup. When her tea is ready she settles down in her rocking chair.

'Ah!' she says. 'My reading glasses! Now where did I put them?'

She gets up and starts looking. 'They must be in the kitchen', she murmurs. But they aren't.

'They aren't in the bathroom either. Or in my bedroom. Where could they be?' she asks herself.

'Did I leave them at the post office yesterday? Or at the café? No, I had them last night when I read my bedtime book', she says to herself.

Grandad Brachio hears her and comes into the room. 'Anything wrong, dear?' he asks.

'I just can't find my glasses anywhere', she replies.

'Can't you?' Grandad smiles. 'What about these?' He gently takes her glasses from her hair and hands them to her.

'Oh! Hee-hee-hee! Silly me!' Grandmother giggles like a little girl.

'I'll get you a neck chain for them, and then you'll never lose them again dear', smiles Grandad fondly. He loves her very much!

Two Wiggly Teeth

22 FEBRUARY

The Zebra twins, Zig and Zag, are not talking as much as usual today. Each of them is losing their first baby tooth. They are so busy wiggling their loose teeth with their tongues that they don't have much time to talk. After sitting for a while on the sofa in their living room, busy wiggling, Zig finally says something. 'I wonder if mine will fall out before bedtime tonight. Then I can put it under my pillow and the tooth fairy will take it and leave me a present!' She goes back to wiggling.

'Me too', is all Zag has time to say.

More time passes.

'Zig and Zag! Come to dinner!' calls their mummy. They go to the table, sit down and start to eat.

'It hurts a bit when I chew', complains Zag.

'I know, Zag. I remember what it's like. Your tooth will come out when it's ready. Just chew on the other side tonight', Mummy smiles.

Suddenly Zig squeals and then holds up a baby tooth for everyone to see. 'It's out!' she cries.

Zag feels sad. She carries on wiggling her tooth until it's almost bedtime. Suddenly Zag squeals, 'Yippee!'

'Oh look! It's so little!' she cries.

Now both sisters have teeth to leave for the tooth fairy. Will the tooth fairy come?

The Tooth Fairy's Gifts

23 FEBRUARY

Zag Zebra wakes up first this morning. She pokes her tongue into the hole that her baby tooth popped out of last night.

'It's a special day!' she cries.

She jumps out of bed and sweeps her pillow away.

'Look! The tooth fairy came!' exclaims Zag.

Her twin sister Zig is just seconds behind her.

'There's something for me too!' Zig laughs.

Two little perfectly wrapped boxes!

Quickly the twins pull off the ribbons and tear off the wrapping paper. Each one finds a small black telescope and a little card.

'Oooh!' Zig and Zag say at the same time.

'I can't believe she could take my tooth away and leave me this without waking me up. How can she do that?' asks Zig excitedly, waving her telescope around.

'I don't know, but it's really wonderful that she does', answers Zag, putting her telescope to her eye and peering out the window. 'Look! I can see the ferry boat arriving! This is brilliant!'

The twins take their presents and cards to show their parents. Mummy reads the message on each card out loud. It's the same for each twin.

The tooth fairy writes, 'I am very happy that you have taken such good care of your teeth. That is why I have left this very special present for your first tooth. When your others pop out, I will leave you smaller presents'.

'Congratulations, and keep on brushing!'

'Yes, we will!' nod the twins.

'Hurry Zag', calls Zig. 'Let's eat breakfast as fast as we can. I can't wait to show our telescopes to our friends!'

'And the holes where our teeth used to be!' giggles Zag, showing hers to everybody.

February

Mud Pies

24 FEBRUARY

'Baabra, could you play with Lammie while I hang our washing out to dry in the garden?' asks Baabra Sheep's mummy this morning.

'Of course, Mummy', answers Baabra. 'Come on, Lammie, let's make mud pies!' she laughs.

'Mud pies!' echoes Lammie, wriggling happily. He has no idea what they are.

They go outside. Baabra finds two pie tins, two little plates and two shovels in their sandpit.

'Right Lammie, let's go and find some really delicious mud', she calls. Lammie trots along happily, singing 'Mud, mud, mud!'

Baabra shows Lammie how to scoop up mud with his shovel, then put it on the pie plate. He's not very good at it, and spills lots of mud on his curly white fleece, but he tries hard.

Before long they each have a lovely mud pie. Baabra cuts two slices with her shovel, putting each one on a little plate.

'Now Lammie, this is pretend pie. We don't eat it!' she warns. Then she pretends to take a bite of her slice and says, 'Yummy!'

Lammie does not understand, but he laughs and crows, 'Yummy! Yummy! Yummy!'

He puts the mud pie in his mouth.

'Yuk! Phooey!' he says, and he starts spitting. Mummy comes running.

'Oh my goodness! Don't put that in your mouth!

That's mud!' she groans. But Baabra and Lammie are laughing and having so much fun that she can't be grumpy. 'Come inside and let's get cleaned up', she says, laughing herself!

Puzzling Playtime

25 FEBRUARY

Nolo Giraffe and Hoopla Hippo are playing together.

'What shall we play?' Nolo asks.

'Anything is fine', smiles Hoopla, holding his hands behind his back.

'How about blocks?' asks Nolo.

'Oh. How about something else?' asks Hoopla. 'I played with blocks at home yesterday',

'What about my train set?' offers Nolo.

38

He points to the shiny black engine and the colourful string of carriages behind it.

'Well…' considers Hoopla.

Nolo sees Hoopla isn't that keen on trains today.

'We could colour!' urges Nolo, getting a little bit upset with Hoopla's fussiness.

'I suppose we could', says Hoopla. He sighs.

'Hoopla, what's wrong? You don't seem to want to play with anything today', says Nolo.

Hoopla grins. 'I just wanted to see how many things you could think of. I was only teasing. How about this?'

Hoopla brings a brand new puzzle out from behind his back.

'You joker!' laughs Nolo. Soon they are busy putting the puzzle pieces together. Hoopla really can be a rascal sometimes!

Jokes and Riddles

26 FEBRUARY Hoopla Hippo's mummy is reading a book of jokes and riddles to Hoopla at bedtime.

'What runs but cannot walk?' she reads.

Hoopla screws up his face and thinks hard. 'Hmmm. Let's see. A turtle can walk, but it can't run. So that's the wrong way around'.

'Good try, though it is not an animal', Mummy replies, giving Hoopla a little help.

Hoopla looks at the ceiling, as if he is hoping for an answer to fall out of the sky.

'That's even harder', he says. 'I give up'.

Mummy smiles and says, 'It's a river. A river is always running but it can't walk!'

'Gosh, you're right!' smiles Hoopla. He's planning to try out this riddle on his friends.

'Would you like to hear a joke now?' Mummy asks.

'Yes!' smiles Hoopla.

'What did one wall say to the other?'

Hoopla looks at the walls in his bedroom, wondering what they could want to talk about.

'I can't guess, Mummy', he says, really curious.

'Meet me at the corner!' Mummy laughs. Hoopla laughs with his crazy hippo laugh.

'HOOO, HO-HO-HO-HO!'

'HOOO, HO-HO-HO-HO!'

Now he's got a riddle and a joke to tell his friends. He can't wait!

February

Playing Statues

27 FEBRUARY

All the friends are at the Hideout. Hoopla Hippo has already stumped them with his riddle and made them laugh with his joke.

'Let's play a game now', suggests Baabra Sheep. Everybody agrees.

'Do you know how to play statues?' asks Zag Zebra. Only her sister Zig does. It's a game they played in their old country. Zag likes games where you move a lot.

'Here's what you do. I'm the statue maker. I grab your paw and swing you around and around, really fast. Then I let go. You'll get dizzy, but you have to freeze like a statue right away'.

'I twirl everybody like that, until you've all been turned into statues. The first statue who moves has to be the new statue maker. Do you want to try?' The friends can't wait. Zag picks Nolo Giraffe first, spins him around and then lets go. He lands on his bottom with his feet in the air!

Next comes Baabra. She ends up rolling over and over, finishing up on her side.

The rest of the friends end up in funny positions all over the place, laughing and laughing. It's impossible to stay perfectly still!

Zag the statue maker walks around the statues, watching. Nolo's legs wobble.

'That's it! Nolo's the statue maker now', laughs Zag, and they all get up to play again!

Leap Year Leaping

28 FEBRUARY

'Tomorrow is February 29th! Time for the Leap Year Competition!' Nolo Giraffe tells all the friends at the Hideout this morning. Zig and Zag Zebra look puzzled, since they are new to Firefly Island.

'Every four years we get one extra day in February. It's called Leap Year. This is one of those years. Here on Firefly Island, but only on February 29th, we have a competition. Everybody tries to leap – or jump, or spring, or whatever – as far as they can. The competition is tomorrow. So let's start practising!'

Nolo marks out a starting line a short distance away from the sandpit nearby.

'I'll be the marker', Slye Snake says, so she scratches a leaping line at the edge of the sandpit. The friends line up. One by one, they run fast from the starting line to the leaping line. Then they try to jump as far as they can. Slye marks the spot where they land in the sand. 'Bravo!' she cries for each jump.

Some of the friends are terrific jumpers, and some are just not built for this sport. But it's so much

fun trying to make the best possible jump, that everybody loves it.

By now everybody is full of sand and out of breath. 'See you tomorrow!' calls Nolo, and he trots towards home, leaving a little trail of sand as he goes. Who will win the competition?

 ## The Leap Year Competition

The whole village has turned out for the Leap Year Leaping Competition! Mr. Horse, the mayor, stands on his wooden box and makes a speech.

'Welcome to the Leap Year Leaping Competition! This only happens every four years, so it's an exciting day. I will be the marking judge. Please pick a number and then we can begin!'

Each of the villagers, old and young, picks a slip of paper out of a jar. The number on the slip tells them the order in which they can all jump.

'It's wonderful that everyone has a different jumping style', explains Baabra Sheep to Zig and Zag Zebra'. 'My family has very bouncy jumpers. The Brachio, Trico and Hippo families have… um… a hard time getting off the ground! The Snakes make everyone laugh. They wriggle to the leaping line and then shoot through the air like an arrow. And the villagers with wings, like Chilly Penguin, Hotta Toucan, Roota Rooster, Dr. Henny and even

Mr. Ptera, can jump really far!'

Now it's Nolo's turn. He runs as fast as he can, then tucks his front legs up and pushes off with his back ones. He lands with his feet in four different directions and falls on his bottom.

'That is the best jump so far!' cries Mr. Horse.

But here comes Zig and Zag's daddy, Mr. Zebra. He's never heard of a competition like this but he's determined to do his best.

He gallops to the leaping line and then just *sails* through the air, landing a bit farther than Nolo's landing marks.

'The winner!' exclaims the Mayor, and everybody cheers.

The newest villager is this Leap Year's Leaping Champion!

March

Picking a Present

'Tomorrow is Bouncer Brachio's birthday', Baabra Sheep tells the friends at the Hideout today. 'He says that we are all invited to his party!'

'I wonder what we should give him', says Slye Snake, squinting her eyes.

'How about a card that says we will help him clean his room?' laughs Hoopla Hippo. He knows how messy Bouncer can be.

'That's no fun', groans Nolo Giraffe.

'Let's go to Mr. Ptera's store and have a look for something', Baabra Sheep says, smiling. She likes making her friends happy.

The friends cycle to Mr. Ptera's general store. It has everything anybody could ever want, from food and clothes to tools and toys.

'What does Bouncer like?' asks Zig Zebra.

'He and his grandad are planting Bouncer's own garden', remembers Zag Zebra. 'Farmer Bouncer! Just imagine that!'

'That gives me an excellent idea', Slye exclaims. 'Follow me!'

The store fills with laughter as the friends pick their gift. Finally, Slye says, 'This is the one'.

Mr. Ptera wraps the gift up and ties a beautiful green ribbon around the box.

Can you guess what it is?

Bouncer's Surprise

The next day, the friends are at Bouncer Brachio's house for his birthday party.

The friends are singing:

Happy Birthday to you!
Happy Birthday to you!
Happy birthday dear Bouncer,
Happy birthday to you!

Slye Snake gives Bouncer the big box.

'Look Bouncer, we have brought you a present', she exclaims.

'Ooh! What can this be?' he laughs, shaking the big box. 'I can't guess what's inside'.

He opens it and smiles. 'Wonderful! Now I really am Farmer Bouncer!' He takes out a big, floppy straw hat and puts it on. He looks perfect! Everyone claps and cheers.

'Thank you everybody!' he laughs.

'Come to the table', calls Bouncer's mummy.

The friends sit down. Bouncer's mummy comes in from the kitchen with a big cake and a birthday crown. Bouncer swaps his hat for his crown.

'Look at that! My garden!' Bouncer cries as the cake is put in front of him.

His mummy has made a cake that looks just like a little garden. She has made all kinds of vegetables out of icing. They each get a big slice of the 'garden', and it tastes wonderful!

March

3 MARCH
The First Picnic of the Year

The Zebra family is going for their first picnic of the year on Firefly Island.

'It's sunny, so it's picnic time!' says Daddy. Zig and Zag bounce along the path to the picnic shelter. The leaves have just opened on the trees and the woods smell wonderful.

'Hello, Mr. Trico', they call to the park ranger. He waves and says, 'You're the first ones having a picnic this spring. You'll find lots of firewood around here for your cooking fire'.

Mummy lays out the picnic blanket and unpacks the basket. The twins collect wood and Daddy Zebra builds a lovely fire.

'Look at that!' Daddy is proud of his little camp fire. He cuts some fresh forked sticks so that they have pointed ends. 'Now put a sausage on your stick and turn it slowly over the fire until it gets brown', Daddy explains to the twins.

'Oh no!' says Zig, as her sausage catches fire and drops into the burning wood.

'No problem, Zig. Just be more careful with your next one', says Mummy. Soon everyone has a nicely browned sausage. They pop them into rolls and tuck in.

'Delicious!' they cry.

'I love eating outdoors in the early spring sunshine', says Mummy.

'A fine first picnic!' says Zag, and Zig agrees.

4 MARCH
Playground or Ferry?

The friends are sitting in the Hideout this afternoon, trying to work out what to do.

'Let's go to the playground', says Hoopla Hippo. He loves the slide.

'Or we could meet the ferry', says Nolo Giraffe. 'It comes every afternoon when the little hand on my watch points to the number four. Do you remember I won the competition by naming the *Tinker Bell*?' he asks proudly.

'YES!' they all shout. 'You keep telling us!'

'Why can't we go and meet the ferry today, and then play at the playground tomorrow?' offers Baabra Sheep, who likes everyone to get along. The friends all agree. This way everyone gets what they want.

At the dock, Nolo Giraffe cries, 'There's the *Tinker Bell!*' Her motor throbs and waves roll off her as she chugs toward Firefly Island.

Captain Cow docks the ferry.

Mr. Ptera, the general store owner, is standing on the dock, waiting for something. Captain Cow hands him a tall box. 'Your kites have arrived, just in time for the kite flying season', she smiles. 'Kites!' exclaim the friends.

'Yes, kites', smiles Mr. Ptera. 'We'll have a kite sale in three days. I hope you can pop in!'

'Yes! Definitely! Wonderful!' shout the friends. Hurray! It's almost kite season again!

At the Playground

Hoopla Hippo wakes up smiling today. The friends are going to meet at the playground.

He chatters about the slide with his mummy and daddy during breakfast.

'It's sooo high and scary when you climb up to the top', he says, looking at the ceiling. 'And then you have to sit down and let go – and WHOOOSH! Away you go!'

'And the wind flies by my ears and tickles my tummy', he chuckles, and then really laughs. 'HOOO, HO-HO-HO-HO!'
'HOOO, HO-HO-HO-HO!'

Hoopla roars, patting his tummy. His mummy smiles and gives him a quick hug.

'I'm glad it's so much fun for you. Would you like to take a bag of biscuits along to share with your friends?'

'Oh, yes please!' Hoopla grins. He gets his jacket and hat while Mummy puts the biscuits in a bag.

At the playground, Hoopla spots his friends on the slide. Everyone is laughing, screaming and having a wonderful time.

He runs to the slide and waits for his turn to climb up. When he gets to the top, he yells as loudly as he can, 'Long live Hoopla, King of the Universe!'
'HOOO, HO-HO-HO-HO!'
'HOOO, HO-HO-HO-HO!'

Hoopla laughs loudly. 'This is tickling my tummy!' he yells as he zooms down the slide.

'Slides are always just as much fun as you remember', he laughs.

'The biscuits are yummy too!' adds Baabra.

March

She takes her stethoscope and listens carefully to the egg.

'A nice strong heartbeat!' she says, patting Hotta and smiling at Chilly. 'I think your chick will be pecking out of this shell very soon'.

'We can't wait, but I suppose we'll have to', sighs Chilly as he gently wraps the egg in its warm blanket again.

'See you soon! Thanks for the check-up!' they call as they leave Dr. Henny's clinic and walk back to their café.

Can you guess what the baby's name will be?

A Baby is Coming

6 MARCH

Chilly Penguin and Hotta Toucan are very happy. They are going to have a baby chick soon!

They close the café so they can take their egg to Dr. Henny for a check-up.

'How are the proud mummy and daddy?' the doctor asks when they arrive at the clinic.

'We are fine, thank you. Of course, we are very excited about having a baby!' exclaims Hotta, gently unwrapping a fluffy blanket that covers a large egg.

'And we have finally picked a name we both love', beams Chilly.

'Oh, really?' smiles Dr. Henny. 'What is it?'

'We thought we'd keep it a secret until our chick hatches', Hotta laughs, 'but that really is hard!'

'Well, we'll all know soon', says Dr. Henny.

Kite Sale

7 MARCH

Today is the Great Kite Sale at Mr. Ptera's general store. The villagers love to fly kites, so the store is packed with shoppers. And kites!

'Young or old, everyone gets excited', laughs Mr. Ptera. 'You need to have a new kite every year'.

'I think I'll have that box kite with yellow stripes', says Roota Rooster. 'Or maybe that one over there? It looks just like a beach umbrella!'

Hotta Toucan picks out a golden butterfly kite. 'We can fly it now, and then hang it over our baby chick's crib after it hatches', smiles Hotta.

Baabra Sheep and Nolo Giraffe both go for the same kite. It's beautiful, with an odd shape and three long, shiny tails. They look at each almost as if a fight is going to start. Baabra thinks for a second, then lets go of the kite.

'You can have it', she smiles. 'I like that one that looks like a squid even more'.

'Don't forget strong new string!' Mr. Ptera says again and again to the villagers as they pay.

By late afternoon, most of the kites have gone home with their new owners. Mr. Trico comes in. He works out in the woods, which means that he can't shop early in the day. He falls in love with a kite that looks like a dragon.

'I'm so happy nobody else bought him earlier', he grins. 'He's going to fly superbly. Now all we need is a good breeze!'

Kites over Firefly Meadow

8 MARCH

Today, the villagers have gathered at Firefly Meadow. The weather is sunny and luckily there is a good breeze. The friends are carrying their kites and string holders and they chatter excitedly. Hoopla Hippo runs across the meadow to make his kite go higher and higher. 'Look! Look!' he shouts to Baabra Sheep.

'That's high! You are an excellent kite flyer!' she shouts back.

Nolo Giraffe is getting his new kite into the air and doesn't see Hoopla coming his way. Hoopla is galloping now, his eyes on his kite.

'Watch out, Hoopla!' Baabra yells, but it's too late. Hoopla crashes into Nolo and the friends tumble to the grass.

'Ow! Ow! Ow!' Nolo groans. He is squashed under Hoopla, who is rather heavy.

'HOOO, HO-HO-HO-HO!'

'HOOO, HO-HO-HO-HO!'

Hoopla laughs. He is laughing so hard, he can't get up. Luckily, Nolo is slender, and with his long legs, he crawls from under Hoopla.

The other friends start to laugh, watching Nolo and Hoopla get tangled up in string.

And two beautiful new kites land on the far side of the meadow as the two friends untangle themselves.

The kite season has started perfectly!

Hiccups

9 MARCH

Zig and Zag Zebra are laughing like mad.

Zag has the hiccups and she can't stop them. They come every couple of seconds and each time she hiccups, the twins start laughing all over again.

'Hic!' goes Zag.

'Ooh!' Zig squeals, and the two of them practically fall down with laughter.

'I can't stop! Hic!'

Zag tries to cover her mouth, but nothing she does can manage to stop her hiccups.

'Hic!' There she goes again.

'Oh Zag, you've got to stop!' gasps Zig.

'I don't know how to! Hic!' Zag struggles to reply.

Zig has an idea. She suddenly fixes Zag with a really serious stare. 'Look into my eyes', she orders.

Zag looks hard at Zig.

'BOOO!' yells Zig.

Zag jumps in fright, her eyes opening wide.

'Did it work?' Zig asks, patting her twin.

'I don't know', answers Zag doubtfully. 'I have to wait a second to see if it… Hic!'

'Oooh!' giggles Zig. 'It didn't!'

The twins are laughing harder than ever.

'Oh, Zag, you've got to stop! I can't laugh any more. My tummy hurts!' Zig finally says.

'I don't know what to do!' Zag says.

A moment later though, in a quiet voice, she says, 'Guess what? I think they're gone!'

Shopping for Mummy

10 MARCH

Slye Snake is going shopping for her mummy at Mr. Ptera's general store. Her shopping list is a little strange. Because she can't read yet, her mummy has drawn pictures of all the things to buy!

'Let's see', she whispers. The first drawing is of six eggs. She goes to shelf where the eggs are and picks out a box of them. Slye makes sure there are six inside and puts it in her shopping basket.

The next one is easy – a loaf of bread. She picks her favourite kind, with lots of raisins.

'What's next?' Ah, two apples. She picks out the two prettiest ones.

'What's this?' she asks next. Mummy has written the number two, and then a word. Why did she do that, instead of drawing it?

Slye goes over to Mr. Ptera and says, 'Good morning Mr. Ptera. Could you please help me? I can't read this word'.

Mr. Ptera smiles and says, 'Of course, Slye! Let me see'. He pulls his glasses from the top of his head and looks at the list, then grins at Slye.

'You're going to like this. That word is sweets, so your mummy is giving you a treat!'

Slye giggles and picks out one really sour lemon drop and one crunchy chocolate bar.

Do you think she will wait until she gets home before she eats them?

Whooo Was That?

11 MARCH It is night and Baabra Sheep is nearly asleep. A soft wind is blowing outside her window and the moon is shining brightly. Shadows from the tree branches outside her window rise and fall on the wall. She likes watching them as she goes to sleep.

All of a sudden a dark shape flutters and lands on one of the branches.

'What in the world is that?' Baabra asks.

The shape is quite big and very dark. It stays where it landed, rising and falling as the branch moves in the wind.

'Who-who-who-whooooo!' Baabra hears a strange cry just outside her window.

'Who-who-who-whooooo!'

'It must be the shape, crying like that. But what is it?' Baabra asks herself.

'I know my window is closed, so I'm safe', she whispers, to stop herself from being afraid.

Still, she wants her mummy and daddy here. She runs to their bedroom.

'Mummy, Daddy, come quickly! There's a monster out there!' she hisses in the dark.

They jump out of bed and run to her room. Daddy looks at the wall, then out of the window.

'Baabra, you are really lucky!' he exclaims. 'Your visitor out on that branch is a beautiful owl! An owl brings you good luck!'

'Really?' Baabra asks doubtfully. 'I wish it would go and bring somebody else good luck tonight!'

March

12 MARCH

And What do You Want to Be?

Nolo Giraffe, Bouncer Brachio and Hoopla Hippo are talking about what they want to be when they get bigger.

'Did you hear that Zig and Zag Zebra's mummy is going to help us visit people who have jobs we'd like to have when we're grown up?' asks Nolo. 'That means we need to pick some sort of job'.

'I love food', laughs Hoopla, 'so maybe one day I can really learn to cook. Then I could work in a café, like Chilly Penguin and Hotta Toucan!'

'For me', answers Nolo, 'if I could choose anything, I'd be a ferry captain like Captain Cow. She has a really brilliant job. I bet it's hard to dock the ferry without crashing into the dock!' He makes a loud crashing sound.

Bouncer has been thinking hard. He is very kind hearted and he's finding his gardening project with Grandad Brachio a lot of fun. He enjoys seeing his baby plants growing up healthy.

'I'm not sure yet. Some kind of helping job? Maybe I could be a doctor, like Dr. Henny', he says.

He surprises himself, and the others too, when he says this.

'Let's go and tell Mrs. Zebra and see what happens', says Nolo. 'It will be fun, no matter what!'

So they jump on their bicycles and head off to the Zebra home.

13 MARCH

Bubble Trouble

Lammie Sheep is supposed to be having a sleep. But he's not.

He saw a piece of chewing gum on his mummy's desk today and he took it. 'I can't have gum, except when Mummy says I can', he thinks, snuggling into his pillow.

Nevertheless, he pops it in his mouth. It tastes sweet and quickly becomes soft and chewy. He falls asleep.

Later Lammie wakes up. He wants to get up, but he can't lift his head from his pillow!

'Help! Help! Mummy, help!' he yells, and starts crying and struggling to lift up his head.

Mummy comes running into his room. She looks at Lammie and starts laughing.

'Oh, Lammie, did you take that piece of bubble gum from my desk?' she asks.

'Sorry Mummy!' Lammie sobs.

'Well, it fell out of your mouth when you were sleeping and has stuck your wool to your pillow!' Mummy laughs again. 'Let's get you unstuck'.

Mummy gently pulls the pillow away from Lammie's curly hair. The gum stretches and finally breaks. But there's still a lot of it stuck in his hair.

'Come with me to the kitchen', Mummy says. 'First I'll put ice on the gum. When it's frozen, I

50

can break it away from your hair'.

In a little while she says, 'Now there's only a little bit left'. She rubs peanut butter on the chewing gum, and in a while it slides off.

'Now into the bath with you! You smell like a sandwich', she smiles. Lammie's glad she isn't cross. He's really learned his lesson!

Grandmother Brachio's Birds

14 MARCH

Grandmother Brachio loves the colourful birds that come to the bird feeder at her house. Today she puts on her jacket, picks up the bucket of bird seed, and goes out of her front door. The birds fly away, but perch nearby.

'Don't go too far', she laughs. 'Soon your feeder will be spilling over with delicious seeds!' The birds look as though they can hardly wait.

A gentle breeze is blowing today. While Grandmother fills the feeder, she hears a *BANG!* behind her. She quickly turns to go back inside.

'That noise must have been my door blowing closed', she says to herself. The door has locked itself tightly shut.

Grandmother pats her jacket pocket. 'Oh, no!' she cries. 'My keys are in the house. I've locked myself out!'

'What am I going to do? Grandad is out all day today, so he can't help. Dear me!'

Just then Bouncer arrives. She explains her problem. He thinks for a moment, and then says, 'Wait here a moment Grandmother'.

In a few minutes Bouncer opens the front door from the inside, saying, 'Ta-daaaaa! Welcome home!'

'How in the world did you get inside?' asks Grandmother.

Bouncer laughs. 'On my way to visit you, I saw that your kitchen window was open, so I just wriggled in and got your keys'.

'Oh, silly me! What a helper you are, Bouncer!' laughs Grandmother, and she hugs him.

March

They put stickers all over each other, laughing like mad, until all the stickers have been used.

Now two, very sparkly and colourful young zebras are laughing and pointing at each other.

'Let's look in the mirror', cries Zig.

'Yes!' hoots Zag.

They trot to the mirror and admire their work.

All of a sudden Mummy Zebra comes in.

'My goodness!' she cries, then laughs. 'What have we here? It looks as though the circus has come to town!'

She gives the twins hugs and takes a picture of them to send it to their family, far away.

15 MARCH

Zig Zag Stickers

Zig and Zag Zebra are at home today. Paper, crayons and a giant sticker book cover the table.

They are using stickers to add sparkles and bright colours to their drawings

'Your picture is better than mine', sighs Zig.

'No', says Zag. 'I think yours is wonderful'.

Zag can see that Zig isn't very happy. She grabs a sticker and puts it on Zig's forehead. 'There! That shows you are a great artist!'

Zig laughs, chooses a different sticker, and puts it on her sister's forehead.

'You are a great artist, too!' she giggles.

Zag picks out another sticker and Zig does the same.

16 MARCH

Nolo Can't Talk

Nolo Giraffe is not feeling well. He doesn't feel all that poorly, but he has lost his voice.

'You have a throat infection', Dr. Henny says, when Nolo's mummy brings him to the clinic.

'You need to keep quiet, sip lots of warm drinks and try to breathe in a lot of warm, moist air, like in the shower. Then you will get better quickly', Dr. Henny says, patting Nolo's arm.

'---- ---- ---- ----', Nolo tries to answer, but he can only make funny whispery sounds.

'And don't try to talk, Nolo, because that will make it worse', adds Dr. Henny.

Nolo feels silly not being able to speak. But he

knows he has to do what Dr. Henny says.

On the way home he spots Slye Snake. 'Hello Nolo', Slye calls. Nolo nods. 'Do you want to cycle up to the Hideout this afternoon?'

Nolo points to his throat, then makes signs as if he is having a sleep.

'Pardon?' Slye asks. 'Why the hand signals?'

Nolo laughs, but no sound comes out.

'Nolo has to rest until his throat is better', his mummy explains. 'So the bicycle ride will have to wait a little while'.

'Oh, I see', Slye smiles. 'Get well soon Nolo!'

Nolo smiles and waves, croaking 'Bye-bye!'

Borrowed Book

17 MARCH Baabra Sheep is having a wonderful bubble bath. She is looking at a beautiful, big picture book that she has borrowed from Zig and Zag Zebra, while she soaks in the warm soapy water.

'I wish I could be that princess', she says to her mummy, who is putting away clean towels. Baabra has spotted a princess with curly hair.

The book is quite heavy, and when Baabra points at the princess, it slips into the water.

'Oh, no!' Baabra cries, trying to get the book out of the water as quickly as she can. But it's too late. The whole thing is under water now.

'Mummy. Help!'

Baabra's mummy peers into the bath. 'Oh, Baabra, you didn't bring that book into the bath, did you?' she says, shaking her head and pulling the book out of the water.

Baabra sobs, 'It's Zig and Zag's book! I really am in trouble now!'

'I do think you have a problem', says Mummy sadly. 'Let me get you out of the water and dry you off. Then we'll see what we can do'.

Soon Baabra is in bed. Mummy snuggles beside her. 'What if we bought a new book for Zig and Zag?' Baabra asks.

'I think that's a really good idea', Mummy smiles, patting Baabra's curls. 'You can do that tomorrow!'

'Thanks, Mummy', murmurs Baabra sleepily.

March

Making Things Right

18 MARCH

The next morning, Baabra remembers the disaster of the book in the bath. She still feels dreadful as she eats her breakfast.

Mummy helps her to get ready to go to Mrs. Brachio's gift shop to buy a new book for Zig and Zag Zebra.

'Here's some money', Mummy says.

'I'm really sorry, Mummy', Baabra answers, ready to cry again.

'You can help me with some work today to pay for the new book', suggests Mummy.

'Oh good!' nods Baabra, and she's quickly off on her bicycle to the gift shop.

She buys a book like the one she dropped into the bath. It may even be prettier! Back at home she and Mummy wrap the book up like a present.

Baabra tells her mummy what to write on a card, and then she goes to Zig and Zag's house.

'I'm so sorry', Baabra says to the twin zebras. 'I dropped your book in the bath and ruined it, so I have got you a new one. I hope you like it. I'll never take a book into the bath again!'

Zig and Zag open the package and really love the new book.

'But Baabra, you don't have to feel so sorry', laughs Zig. Zag nods. 'Our auntie bought each of us a copy of the book you borrowed. So we still have a dry one!'

Roota's Big Pounce

19 MARCH

Roota Rooster is strutting around in his garden.

His little dark eyes are focused on the ground, looking for worms and insects.

He wanders over to a pile of leaves.

'This is always a good place to find nice juicy worms', he says.

His stomach is rumbling!

'I'll scratch around and see what I can find'.

Soon he's stirred up the pile so much that he can't even see his own feet.

He tilts his head to one side, staring down and watching for the slightest movement. 'There's a worm! Got you!' he cries, jabbing at the spot with his beak where something just moved.

'Owww!' he yells.

Roota has jabbed his own claw, underneath all those leaves!

It really, really hurts.

He hops around on his good foot for a while, then gently tries to put his injured foot down. But it hurts too much.

'Doctor Henny needs to look at this', he mutters. He flaps and hops his way to Dr. Henny's clinic. She's saying goodbye to Mr. Horse when Roota arrives.

'What's wrong, dear?' she asks her husband.

'I thought my claw was a worm', Roota confesses, with a funny look on his face.

'Oh, Roota, you didn't!' laughs Dr. Henny. 'Let me have a look'.

She sees that it's not too serious. She gives him a little peck on the cheek and bandages him up.

'What a rooster you are!' she laughs.

20 MARCH Mr. Horse's Megaphone

Mr. Horse, the mayor, is twitching with excitement. The *Tinker Bell* has just arrived. Captain Cow docks the ferry carefully. Then she calls to him. 'Ahoy there, Mr. Horse! We have a package for you!'

'I know!' shouts Mr. Horse. 'It's my megaphone!'

'Why do you want a really big phone?' asks Slye Snake, who is standing nearby.

'It isn't a big phone', smiles the mayor. 'It's called that but it is something different. When you speak into it, it makes your voice louder'.

Slye knows how much Mr. Horse loves making speeches.

'Oh, I understand', she says. 'You have your soapbox to stand on so that everybody can see you. Now, with your megaphone, everyone will certainly be able to hear you!'

'Exactly', smiles Mr. Horse happily.

Captain Cow steps off the *Tinker Bell* and hands Mr. Horse a funny-shaped package. He tears the wrapping off and admires his new megaphone.

'Isn't it beautiful?' he asks, stroking it.

'It certainly is', grins Slye.

'Here', he says, smiling at Slye, 'give it a try. You are my speech coach, after all!'

Slye puts the small end of the megaphone to her mouth and in an official sounding voice, says, 'Attention! Attention! Mr. Horse's new megaphone has arrived!'

It is really loud and doors and windows fly open as all the villagers lean out to see what is happening.

'I think it works!' laughs Mr. Horse.

'It certainly does', answers Slye. 'I can't wait to REALLY hear your next speech!'

March

A Garden Plan

21 MARCH

Bouncer Brachio and his grandad are planning the garden. They are eating Grandmother's yummy homemade vegetable soup, and seed packets cover the table.

'The weather is getting warmer. Let's imagine this table is your garden. Where shall we plant each sort of seed?' Grandad asks.

'Does it matter where they go?' asks Bouncer, puzzled.

'Well, we don't want the tall plants to make shadows over the short ones, because then they won't grow quickly enough', Grandad says.

Bouncer looks at the pictures on the packets. 'Corn and beans look very tall. Lettuce is very short. I think beet and carrots are sort of medium, and tomatoes are bigger', he says.

'You are right!' exclaims Grandad. 'So let's put the lettuce in the front row. Then a row of beet and a row of carrots, and then a row of tomatoes'.

'And the giant corn and beans go at the back!' giggles Bouncer.

'That looks perfect to me', Grandad says, rubbing his hands as if he wants to get to work. 'Tomorrow we will start planting!'

Bouncer's Garden Gets Planted

22 MARCH

Bouncer Brachio is already at Grandad's house this morning. He's got a spade to help turn the earth over and break up clumps. 'I'm all ready, Grandad!' he says.

Garden tools, seed packets, sticks and string are scattered all over Bouncer's garden.

'Can you remember where everything goes?' asks Grandad.

Bouncer thinks of his kitchen table garden from yesterday. 'The corn and beans go at the back', he says proudly.

'Exactly right, Bouncer! We can move your baby lettuce plants out here next week, and plant your tomatoes later, when it's warmer', explains Grandad. 'Now we put small sticks in the ground. Then we tie strings between them', he says. 'Take a little stick and draw a line in the earth beside each string', he says.

'Now we sprinkle the seeds inside your lines, and cover them up with earth', says Grandad.

Once all the seeds have been planted, they put the empty seed packets onto the sticks to show what's growing there.

'Now, let's give the seeds some water', Grandad continues. They are ready!

'I can't wait until the plants come up', laughs Bouncer, and he gives Grandad a big hug.

56

23 MARCH

Ivan's Key

Ivan Monkey is working on a problem. 'I need something to hide the key to my house in. What can I use?' he asks himself.

He looks around his lab and spots a coconut.

'Hmmm', he says. 'I could put my key in the coconut and leave it by my front door. No one would guess a key is hidden inside!'

He grabs a saw. 'I'll cut a hole that's just big enough for my hand. Then I'll pour out the coconut water', he says. And he does exactly that.

'I'd better make sure that it works', he thinks, so he drops his house key into the hole.

'Now I just reach in and get it', he whispers, but when he grabs the key inside the coconut, his hand is too big to come out. His hand is stuck inside the coconut!

'Oh, no!' he cries, hopping around, trying to free his hand. But it is really stuck.

A little later he knocks on the Hippo family's door. Hoopla opens it. He starts laughing when he spots the coconut on Ivan's hand.

'Can I help?' he asks, trying to stop laughing.

'Umm, yes', says a miserable Ivan. 'Can your daddy pull this off?' he says, pointing to the coconut. 'My hand and key are stuck inside'.

Hoopla blinks. 'Have you tried letting go of the key?' he asks. 'Your hand will be smaller'.

Ivan lets go of the key. His hand slips out of the coconut. 'Oh Hoopla, thank you!' he cries.

24 MARCH

Testing, Testing...

Mr. Horse, the mayor, is thrilled with his new megaphone. The only problem is that he can't really practise using it. He's been whispering into it inside his house, and it makes his whispers really loud. But he wants to see what will happen when he makes a real speech.

'I'll walk over to the fire tower and call up to Mr. Trico', he says to himself. 'That way I won't disturb the villagers'.

So he walks through the woods to the fire tower, his megaphone slung over his back. When he gets there, he can just make out Mr. Trico, high up on

58

Cozy Hatches!

25 MARCH

Chilly Penguin and Hotta Toucan are really excited! They have been keeping their egg warm and this morning they heard a tapping noise coming from inside the shell. *Tick-tick-tick! Tick-tick-tick!* they hear.

Chilly puts a wing around Hotta. 'It won't be long now before we see our chick', he smiles.

'I really can't wait!' answers Hotta, beaming up at him.

Tick-tick-tick! the sound comes again.

Suddenly Chilly and Hotta see a tiny crack appear in one spot on the shell. The chick is starting to break through! The chick pecks away for a while, then rests a little. Then the pecking starts again.

By now there is a quite a hole in the shell. Slowly, the tiny beak inside makes the hole bigger.

'Good work! Keep it up!' encourages Chilly.

'I would like to help it break the shell open, but it's best when a chick does it alone', whispers Hotta. Now they can see the chick's face – and suddenly a tiny head pops out! Soon the chick is outside the shell, wobbling around. It's a girl and she has Chilly's colouring, but Hotta's big bill. She's really pretty!

'Oh, Cozy, I'm so glad to see you', croons Hotta. That's the chick's name. They've been keeping it a secret. 'You are the most beautiful chick in the world', sighs Chilly, the proud new father.

the lookout tower, peering around with his binoculars. 'Hello there!' Mr. Horse bellows into his megaphone.

Mr. Trico jumps and turns suddenly, pointing his binoculars at Mr. Horse.

'I'm trying out my new megaphone!' he shouts. Mr. Trico lets his binoculars hang from their strap and waves violently. He must be answering, but Mr. Horse can't hear him.

'How are you today?' thunders Mr. Horse politely. Mr. Trico seems to be nodding silently. He looks down at Mr. Horse again through his binoculars. 'Ah. We have a problem here. He can see and hear me, and I can see him, but I can't hear a word he is saying', reflects Mr. Horse.

'Well, have a good day!' he roars, and Mr. Trico waves goodbye.

'Perhaps I should get a second megaphone?' Mr. Horse asks himself, as he wanders home. 'At least I know this one works!'

March

Zebra Confusion

'Let's play house', says Slye Snake to Zig Zebra. They are in Slye's bedroom. Zig's twin sister Zag is out shopping with their mummy.

Zig nods and says, 'Yes! I'll run home and get my tea party things', and she's off.

Slye throws a blanket over a table to make the house. Then she puts the children – a teddy bear and a doll – inside it.

Slye's mummy calls out, 'Slye, you've got company!' and Slye goes to meet Zig.

'Couldn't you find your tea party things?' she asks, seeing her friend has nothing with her.

'What tea party things?' the little zebra asks.

'What do you mean, what tea party things?' asks Slye, confused.

'I'm sorry, Slye, I don't know what you mean', answers her friend, also confused.

Just then Slye's mummy calls, 'Slye, you've got more company!' and Slye goes to the door, really confused now. There stands another little zebra with a box of tea party things.

'Oh! Now I understand!' Slye laughs. 'Zag came over while you were gone. I thought she was you! I didn't know why she didn't have her tea party things, and she didn't know what I was talking about! Anyway, come in, Zig! Let's all play house!'

Cozy's Welcome Party

Hotta Toucan and Chilly Penguin have invited the villagers to visit their café today to celebrate the birth of their new chick, Cozy.

'What a lovely name', says Mr. Horse, the mayor, who is the first to arrive.

'We thought it would be nice to find a name that makes us think of Hotta's warm homeland and my cold one', Chilly explains. 'When it's not too hot, and not too chilly, it's just Cozy!' answers the proud daddy, beaming at his chick.

'Feed me! Feed me!' cheeps Cozy. It's the only thing she knows how to say so far.

Hotta and Chilly have made all kinds of snacks and drinks for the villagers who visit. The visitors bring little presents for Cozy.

'Oh, she's gorgeous', sighs Grandmother Brachio. She and Grandad give Cozy her very own scrapbook, so that she can record things all through her life.

The Zebra family arrives. Zig and Zag can't believe how tiny Cozy is. They give her a bright red ball with bells inside.

'Cozy, when you roll this ball you can make your own music', says Daddy Zebra. 'We love making music. We hope you will too!'

All afternoon the villagers come. They stay for a chat and a snack. It's a very happy day.

'Feed me! Feed me!' cheeps Cozy to each one. She opens her mouth wide.

Chilly pops a tiny piece of food into Cozy's beak, and she gobbles it up.

'You'll be a big bird soon if you like to eat so much', laughs Hotta. And it's true, she will!

Scary Faces

28 MARCH

All the friends are at the Hideout, talking about what to do.

'I'm tired of doing the same old things all the time. Like going to the playground or playing hide and seek', complains Hoopla Hippo.

'What if we painted our faces to make ourselves look really scary?' asks Nolo Giraffe. 'I saw some brilliant pictures in a book!'

'Yes! That sounds really good', says Hoopla. All the friends perk up.

'But where can we find face paint?' asks Slye Snake.

'What if we borrowed our mummies' makeup?' asks Hoopla.

'Excellent idea!' replies Slye. 'Let's meet at the Hideout tomorrow. Bring your mummies' makeup and mirrors along'.

'I will bring my book with the scary face paintings', promises Nolo.

'Do we have to keep this a secret', asks Hoopla, and they all agree they should. What an exciting day it will be!

March

Red Faces

Baabra Sheep feels a bit scared about borrowing her mummy's makeup to paint her face. Will Mummy be cross?

Nevertheless, Baabra quietly packs her mummy's makeup kit and a little mirror into her own backpack, and cycles to the Hideout after breakfast. The friends are already there, waiting for her.

'This is my book with scary faces', Nolo Giraffe says, showing them his book. The friends start drawing jagged red lines on their faces. Then they add dark circles and white lines.

'Now what?' asks Bouncer Brachio.

'How about a parade through the village?' asks Hoopla. They agree, and off they go.

As they walk in a line through the street, some villagers stop and stare and some laugh. Then they meet Hoopla's and Baabra's mummies. 'What have you done to your face?' Hoopla's mummy cries when she spots the strange parade.

'Have you used my makeup?' Baabra's mummy asks. She doesn't look happy.

'Go home at once and wash your face, right now. Tomorrow you will stay indoors as a punishment', Hoopla's mummy continues.

'Baabra', her mummy explains sternly. 'I'm cross, because you took things that belong to me without asking. If you had asked, I would have said yes. But you must learn to ask. You need time to think about what you've learned today'.

'Yes, Mummy', Baabra answers, feeling dreadful. She goes home and heads off to the bathroom to wash her face.

A Lesson Learned

Each of the friends have to stay at home today. They need to think about the mistake they made yesterday, taking their mummies' makeup without asking first.

Baabra Sheep gives her mummy a hug and begins to cry when she comes to the breakfast table.

'I'm sorry Mummy', she sniffles. 'I should have asked you if I could use your makeup'.

'Can you imagine how you would feel if I just took your dolls away one morning, without asking you

first?' asks Mummy gently.

'I'd feel sad, but I'd also be angry. They are my dolls, not yours', says Baabra.

'Exactly. So you must always ask if you would like to use someone else's things. Most of the time you will find out it's fine and then there's no problem at all'.

Baabra nods and gives Mummy another hug. Mummy smiles at her and says, 'I can see you've learned your lesson. Tomorrow you can play with your friends again'.

Baabra spends the rest of the day looking at books and playing with her little brother, Lammie. She's a little quiet, but she's glad that she can see her friends tomorrow.

The Puppet Show

There's a puppet show at the gift shop today!

The villagers love puppet shows. They crowd into the shop, chattering and laughing. The youngsters sit in the chairs in the front rows, and their parents and other villagers sit behind them.

The curtain on the puppet theatre is closed, but you can hear lots of whispering and giggling behind it. Now and then it bulges out a little.

'I can't wait to see this', Zig Zebra says to her twin sister Zag.

'Me too. I wonder what it will be about. I hope there's a princess and a prince, and maybe a dragon!' Zag sighs.

Mr. Horse, the mayor, stands up on his soapbox and says, 'Ahem! Ahem!' until the villagers go quiet. He doesn't need his megaphone today, but he wishes he could use it.

'My dear fellow villagers, welcome to today's puppet show. Today's show is called *The Princess's Rescue*. I hope you enjoy it!'

He steps down off his soapbox and the curtain slowly opens. In a few minutes everyone feels as if they are in the castle where the princess lives. The dragon is scary and breathes smoke, but the prince saves the princess and they live happily ever after. The villagers clap long and loudly at the end.

'That was fantastic!' crows Zag.

'And the prince and princess were so romantic', sighs Zig.

There's ice cream for everyone now. A good day!

April

The Bicycle Mystery

1 APRIL

Bouncer is rushing his breakfast.

'I want to be first at the Hideout this morning', he tells his mummy. 'We're going to cycle to the camping ground for a picnic lunch!'

'I'll make you a sandwich', Mummy smiles. He grabs his lunch, and runs to the garden shed to get his bicycle.

'What?' he exclaims, surprised. Where is his bicycle? There's a different one where it should be!

'That's Nolo's bicycle', he says, shaking his head. Since his bicycle is missing, he gets on Nolo's and pedals off to the Hideout.

All his friends are there, talking excitedly.

'I don't understand it', Zig Zebra is saying. 'Our bicycles have gone. But in their places we found Slye Snake's and Baabra Sheep's ones!'

The same thing has happened to everybody. Nobody can solve this mystery.

'Well, we all have our own bicycles back', says Bouncer, taking charge. 'So let's get going!'

At dinner, Bouncer tells his mummy and daddy about the bicycle mystery. They look at each other and burst out laughing.

'Don't you know what day it is, Bouncer? It's April the first – April Fools Day! All the mummies and daddies swapped your bicycles around last night!'

'No!' cries Bouncer. He had no idea grown-ups could be so cunning and so funny.

Happy April Fools Day!

Grandmother Brachio's Party

2 APRIL

It's Grandmother Brachio's birthday, but she has forgotten it. Grandad has planned a surprise.

'Let's go for a walk, Grandmother', Bouncer says, winking at Grandad, and off they go.

While they are gone, the villagers get busy.

'We'll blow up the balloons', says Zig Zebra, and she and Zag start puffing.

'We'll decorate the garden', says Slye, and she and the other friends put coloured flags everywhere.

Mrs. Hippo has baked a wonderful cake.

Hotta Toucan and Chilly Penguin arrive. 'We have ice cream and cold drinks from our café', they say. Soon everything is ready.

'Time to hide!' exclaims Grandad, as excited as if he was four years old. 'They're coming back from their walk. Everybody hide!'

Bouncer and Grandmother come round the corner. 'My goodness, what's this?' exclaims Grandmother. 'It looks as if someone's having a party here!'

'Happy Birthday!' all the villagers cry, and they pop out from their hiding places.

'Whose birthday is it?' Grandmother asks.

'It's yours, dear! Did you forget?' Grandad smiles.

'Oh, silly me, I did! What a wonderful surprise', laughs Grandmother. What a happy day!

 Job Visits

The friends have gathered at Zig and Zag Zebra's house.

'I know each of you have an idea about what you want to be when you grow up', Mummy Zebra says, 'so I asked some grown-ups if they would let you visit them to see what their jobs are like'.

'That's wonderful!' exclaims Bouncer Brachio. 'I want to be a doctor. So can I work with Dr. Henny?'

'Yes, Bouncer', smiles Mummy Zebra. 'And Nolo, I think you want to work with Captain Cow'.

'I've been thinking. I've decided I don't want to ever grow up', Hoopla Hippo suddenly says.

'Really?' they all say, surprised.

'Yes. I love playing and eating and laughing all day! Why would I want to go to work?'

'You're so funny!' crows Zig. 'You should be a clown!'

'Yes! I can see it already: Hoopla the clown!' laughs Nolo. 'I bet you will become very famous!'

'And very rich!' Hoopla adds, liking the idea.

'And we can come and visit you in your big house with lots and lots of toys!' squeals Baabra Sheep.

'And I'll be your personal ferry boat captain!' Nolo adds, with a bow.

'And I'll take care of you when you're ill', Bouncer adds.

'HOOO, HO-HO-HO-HO!'

'HOOO, HO-HO-HO-HO!'

Hoopla starts laughing. 'And you'll be so famous that everybody will know you are coming when they hear your laugh', Zig giggles.

April

Hoopla's Job Visit

Hoopla Hippo loves to cook and eat, so today he is going to work with Chilly Penguin and Hotta Toucan at their little café.

'We're so glad you can join us', Hotta says when Hoopla arrives. Chilly shows Hoopla the kitchen and the giant freezer that you can walk into.

'Better put on that jacket, Hoopla. It's extra cold in there!' chuckles Chilly. 'I love it!'

'Look at all the ice cream!' Hoopla exclaims, his breath making a cloud in the frozen air.

'Would you like to serve Mrs. Trico now?' Hotta asks, giving him a cup of tea to take to her.

'Thank you, Hoopla!' smiles Mrs. Trico.

Snnnrrr! Snnnrrrr! Snnnrrrrr!

'What's that?' Hoopla asks himself, turning to look. It's Roota Rooster! He's snoring away at his table.

'Mr. Roota!' Hoopla calls, shaking his wing. 'Wake up! Wake up!'

'Nhhhmmm!' Mr. Roota wakes up suddenly. 'Is it time? Is the sun up yet?' he murmurs.

'Roota, you are in Hotta's café. The sun rose hours ago!' Hoopla giggles.

'Hoopla, as you see, sometimes funny things happen in our little café!' Hotta laughs.

'Yes, but it seems like a wonderful job! Thank you!' Hoopla answers. 'Have a good day, Roota!'

Cleaning Up

Bouncer Brachio is in trouble.

His room is a disaster. Dirty clothes are scattered all over the floor, with toys and books all mixed in.

His mummy comes in and silently stares at the mess. Then she takes a deep breath and says, 'Bouncer, after breakfast please tidy up your room. This is NOT alright!'

Now, after his breakfast, he's sitting on his bed, looking at the piles of things.

'Yes, it's true. I really don't like this mess, but I don't like cleaning up either', he grumbles.

Daddy pops his head in and whistles in amazement. 'Goodness! How can you live like this, Bouncer? How do you find things?'

Bouncer shrugs. 'I dig around until I find them. I just don't like cleaning up', he whines.

'I have an idea', says Daddy. 'I'll set the timer on my watch for five minutes. You clean as fast as you can until I say stop. Let's see how much you can do in that time, yes?' asks Daddy with a smile. 'Here we go: one, two, three – GO!'

Bouncer flies around his room, shoving dirty clothes into his hamper, putting books on the shelf and throwing toys into his toy chest. He has finished before Daddy's watch alarm bell rings.

'Amazing! You did it!' cries Daddy, sweeping Bouncer off his feet in a big hug.

'That wasn't bad at all', grins Bouncer.

Mr. Horse's Hair

Mr. Horse is starting to lose his hair and he really doesn't like it. He has heard about some magic oil that you can put on your head to make your hair grow back. He ordered some last week and it should be on the ferry coming from Big Island today.

'Hello, Mr. Horse', says Nolo Giraffe, who loves to watch the ferry arrive. 'Going to Big Island?'

'No, there's a package for me on the *Tinker Bell* today', he answers, a little shyly.

'Oh, what is it?' asks Nolo curiously.

'Um, some hair oil', replies Mr. Horse.

Nolo looks at Mr. Horse's head and sees that there's not a lot of hair left there.

'Do you need much of that?' he asks, not noticing that Mr. Horse is feeling bad.

'Well, it's special hair oil. It's supposed to… to make your hair grow back', stammers Mr. Horse,

turning a bit red in the face.

'Oh, I see', answers Nolo, beginning to understand and suddenly feeling sorry. 'I… umm… I hope it works!' Nolo says.

'And me!' answers Mr. Horse, patting down what is left of his hair in the breeze.

Just then Captain Cow blows the *Tinker Bell's* horn and the ferry docks.

Captain Cow shuts off the engine. Then she hands Mr. Horse a little package, and says, 'For you!'

Mr. Horse hurries home to try the magic oil out on his head.

'I really hope it works for him', Nolo thinks, shaking his head as he watches Mr. Horse trot off.

April

Big Island Cinema Day

7 APRIL

Baabra Sheep and her mummy are going to Big Island to the cinema.

'Let's go!' Baabra yells as the *Tinker Bell* chugs away from the dock. 'What kind of film is it?' Baabra asks.

'It's a funny cartoon about insects', Mummy explains.

'Sounds wonderful!' cheers Baabra.

Soon they land on Big Island and walk to the cinema. They buy their tickets.

'Mummy, could I have some popcorn please?' Baabra asks sweetly.

'Of course!' Mummy answers.

The lights dim and the cartoon starts. Everybody laughs and claps. The insects get into all kinds of silly trouble. Then… BANG goes a balloon on the screen. The young panda sitting next to Baabra is so scared that he throws all his popcorn up into the air. It comes down and covers him completely!

'Oooh!' cries Baabra. She starts laughing at the way he looks.

'You look just like a sheep!' she whispers.

The panda whispers back, 'But I can eat my fleece!' He sweeps the popcorn back into his cup and pops some into his mouth, smiling.

'That was wonderful! I really loved it!' Baabra exclaims when the lights come on again.

'Lots of surprises!' laughs the little panda.

Not So Funny

8 APRIL

Hoopla Hippo has been learning more things from his joke and riddle book. He's got one for Mr. Horse. Nolo Giraffe told him that Mr. Horse is losing the hair on his head and that he bought some magic oil to help it grow back.

'Hello, Mr. Horse', Hoopla the joker says, when he sees him in front of the post office one morning. 'I have a funny joke for you'.

'Oh, good, Hoopla. I love funny jokes', smiles Mr. Horse. 'How does it go?'

'A horse walks into the doctor's office. He says, 'Doctor, Doctor, I'm going bald. I need something to keep my hair in'. The doctor looks at the horse, and answers, 'How about a paper bag?''

Hoopla laughs at his joke. He's told it so well. He looks at Mr. Horse, hoping to hear a loud laugh.

But Mr. Horse isn't laughing. He is rubbing the top of his head, looking embarrassed.

'Ah, that's really funny, Hoopla', Mr. Horse says weakly. 'I'd need to get going now', he adds, and he hurries into the post office.

'Oh no', thinks Hoopla. 'I think I've really hurt Mr. Horse's feelings. He must feel upset about his hair falling out!' Hoopla goes inside too.

'Mr. Horse, I'm really sorry', Hoopla says.

'That wasn't very kind of me'.

Mr. Horse smiles, relieved.

'Do you know what? Just saying that you're sorry really does make it all better. Thanks, Hoopla'.

He pats Hoopla's head.

'Nice hair, by the way!' he adds, and they both laugh!

Crash-Bang-Boom!

9 APRIL

The friends are at the Hideout this afternoon.

'I have to go home now', Nolo Giraffe says. 'My aunt and uncle are coming over from Big Island to have dinner with my family'.

He leaves. But in a second he's back again.

'Look outside!' he exclaims. 'A storm's coming!'

They rush outside. Tall white clouds fill the sky. Below them, black clouds are piling up.

'See that sort of dark, foggy curtain in the sky?' asks Nolo. 'That's rain falling'.

'Is it coming this way?' asks Baabra Sheep.

'I think so. Those tall white clouds are called thunderheads, and they can mean a thunder storm is coming', says Nolo.

'Ooh, I'm afraid of thunder and lightning!' says Zig Zebra. Zag nods nervously.

'Let's get going!' cries Bouncer Brachio. 'I don't want to get wet!'

They jump on their bicycles and race for home.

Nolo gets to his house just as his aunt and uncle are ringing the doorbell.

'Hello, Nolo!' they say as he arrives, and they each give him a hug. Then a huge flash of lightning and a crash of thunder make them all jump. It begins to rain heavily.

'Let's get inside!' Nolo yells.

His mummy opens the door and says, 'Home sweet home! And just in time! Welcome!'

April

Mr. Ptera's Cellar

10 APRIL

Mr. Ptera must put some groceries into the cellar at his general store. He opens the squeaky door and turns the light switch on. Nothing happens.

'The light bulb must have blown', he mutters. 'Oh, well, I'll just have to do it in the dark', he adds.

Krrr! Krrr!

'What was that?' he asks himself.

Krrr! Krrr!

'There it is again! What can it be?' Mr Ptera wonders, slowly going downstairs.

Krrr! Krrr!

Suddenly he hears a fluttering sound. He freezes.

Krrr! Krrr!

Something brushes by his head.

'Whoaaa!' he screams.

He thunders up the stairs and slams the door shut. He is safe in his shop.

'What's wrong, Mr. Ptera?' Baabra Sheep asks. She gives Mr. Ptera a worried look.

'There's something in my cellar', he cries, breathing hard. 'Could it be a ghost?'

'I don't think so', Baabra says bravely. 'I don't really believe in ghosts. It sounds like you do, though'.

'No, not me, not really', says Mr. Ptera a little weakly.

'I'll come back tomorrow with my torch and we'll see!' Baabra says, patting Mr. Ptera's arm.

Baabra and the Ghosts

11 APRIL

The next morning Baabra Sheep comes back to Mr. Ptera's store with a big torch. 'Hello again, Mr. Ptera', she says cheerfully.

'Good morning, Baabra', answers Mr. Ptera eagerly. 'I'm so glad to see you. I don't want to go down in that cellar alone again'.

Together, the two go down the dark stairs.

Krrr! Krrr!

'There it is', Mr. Ptera whispers.

Krrr! Krrr!

'Mr. Ptera, you certainly do have a mystery guest. What could it be?' Baabra whispers.

Something white flashes through the air and sweeps by them.

'Yikes!' Baabra cries.

'Whoaaa!' Mr. Ptera exclaims.

They both are trembling with fear.

'What was that?' Baabra whispers. Baabra swings the beam of her torch over the shelves of groceries.

Krrr! Krrr!

'Look!' she cries, as the light lands on something white, high up on the top shelf. Tiny black eyes blink in the light.

Mummy pigeon is looking down at them from her nest. Three chicks peak out around her.

'Oh, you scared us!' Baabra gasps, relieved. And she and Mr. Ptera both start laughing.

April

Joke Numbers

12 APRIL

Ivan Monkey is feeling bored. He doesn't want to work in his laboratory, but what else is there to do?

'I need to think of something fun to cheer myself up', he says to himself. 'Jokes might work…!'

But jokes are funnier when you share them.

Ivan has an idea. He writes down five funny jokes he knows. Beside each one he writes a number. Then he goes next door to Hoopla Hippo's house. It is built right next to Ivan's house.

'Hoopla, I feel as though I need a few laughs', he explains. 'These are my favourite jokes', and he tells Hoopla each one.

'Oh, they are *sooo* funny!' laughs Hoopla.

'I'm glad you like them', chuckles Ivan. 'Now I have a favour to ask you. Every now and then, would you please knock on the wall between your house and mine? You can knock once or twice, or three, or four or five times'.

'Of course, but why?' asks Hoopla. He can't imagine what Ivan is thinking.

'Because when you do that, I'll think of Joke Number One, or Joke Number Two – or whatever number of times you knock. And then I'll have a laugh!' exclaims Ivan delightedly.

'That's fun! I'll be happy to do that', Hoopla promises. Later, Hoopla taps three times on the wall and he hears Ivan laughing away!

A Flag for the Hideout

13 APRIL

The friends are at the Hideout. 'What can we do to have some fun?' asks Slye Snake. She's feeling a little grumpy today.

After a while, Nolo Giraffe says, 'I think we should have a flag by the door'.

Hoopla Hippo looks at Nolo thoughtfully. 'Can we make one all by ourselves?'

Everyone lights up. 'Yes!' they cry!

'What colour should it be?' asks Zig Zebra. 'I like red!'

'I like blue', says her twin sister Zag.

'Brown!' 'Green!' 'Yellow!' 'Purple!' Everybody has a different favourite colour.

This could be a problem. The friends sit and think for a while.

'Ha! I have an idea', says Nolo suddenly. 'Each of

us can find a piece of cloth in our own favourite colour. We can sew all of the pieces together to make our flag. Then we'll have a flag that stands for every one of us. It will be our Friendship Flag, and the sign of our Hideout!'

'That's wonderful', shouts Slye and all the friends clap excitedly.

'My mummy can help us with the sewing', Hoopla Hippo offers.

'I'll ask my daddy to help us find a flagpole', Nolo adds.

'What a brilliant plan', laughs Zig.

'I can't wait to get started!' giggles Zag.

'A Friendship Flag for all of us!' adds Bouncer Brachio.

And now, Slye doesn't feel grumpy any more!

Camp Opening

14 APRIL

Bouncer Brachio is busy today. His daddy runs the camping ground on Firefly Island. Bouncer is helping his daddy make sure everything is ready for the summer.

'The opening party is tomorrow, and I can't wait', Daddy says to Bouncer.

'We've got lots of firewood for bonfires and cooking', he murmurs, checking it off his list.

'The dock has been painted and the signs along the paths are all new. What else is there?'

'Is the supply shop ready?' asks Bouncer.

'I think so. Why don't you check it?' asks Daddy.

That makes Bouncer feel important.

Bouncer walks around the shop. It sells things that people need when they are camping, like food, matches and warm clothing.

'Something is missing here', he thinks.

He can't work out what it is.

He pokes around some more. His stomach is growling. It's snack time.

Suddenly Bouncer runs to Daddy. 'You forgot to order something important for the supply shop', he says proudly.

'Oh, really?' asks Daddy, surprised.

'Yes! Snacks!' laughs Bouncer.

'Gosh! You're right!' chuckles Daddy. He writes a note on his list. 'We'll get some in time, I promise!'

Daddy gives Bouncer a pat.

Bouncer grins. He likes helping.

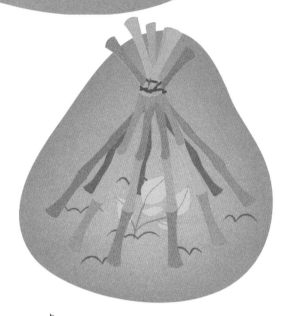

Bouncer's Bean Teepee

15 APRIL

Bouncer Brachio and Grandad are working in the garden.

'Look at that!' Bouncer cries, spotting tiny green leaves poking out of the rich, dark soil.

'Everything is coming up now', chuckles Grandad.

'Today we'll make a teepee tent for your beans'.

'I can't wait to see that', Bouncer says.

'Now for your bean teepee', smiles Grandad.

Last month they drew a circle near the back of the garden, and poked holes in the ground around the circle. They planted two bean seeds in each hole. Grandad points to nine, tall bamboo canes he has brought along.

'Bouncer, stick each cane into the ground, just outside the tiny bean plants', he says. Grandad takes some strong string from his pocket. 'I'll tie

the tops of the canes together. See that? It makes a teepee!' he exclaims.

'Your beans will climb up these poles and soon you'll have a leafy tent to hide in whenever you want!' chuckles Grandad. That's amazing!

Zig's Job Visit

16 APRIL

'Goodness, you're an early bird – I mean, an early zebra!' Mrs. Brachio laughs, as Zig Zebra prances into the gift shop this morning.

'I'm glad I can help you today', replies Zig. She would like to have a gift shop one day.

'Let's start with a little tour before we get too busy', Mrs. Brachio says.

'Here are the toys and books. And there are the biscuits, the postcards, the flowers…'

'You have so many things!' exclaims Zig.

'Here are some new things that came on the ferry yesterday', Mrs. Brachio says.

Zig opens boxes and puts shiny new toys and big books on shelves.

The shop door opens and closes and a little bell tinkles.

'Can you please put price stickers on these puzzles?' asks Mrs. Brachio.

Zig nods.

There's loud laughing behind some shelves.

'Zig, could you please ask our guests over there to

quieten down?' asks Mrs. Brachio.

Zig's eyes get big. She goes to the corner.

It's Zag Zebra and Baabra Sheep!

'Hello', laughs Zig Zebra, greeting them.

'We've come to have a look at how you're doing', replies her sister.

They all giggle again.

'Could you please be a little quieter? You are disturbing the other customers', Mrs. Brachio asks. But by now she is giggling too. So, the four of them are laughing.

'It's such fun helping in a gift shop!' grins Zig.

A Miserable Day

17 APRIL

Zig Zebra is feeling grumpy. Everything is going wrong. She's pouting in her room.

Her twin sister Zag comes to Zig and asks cheerfully, 'Would you like to play school?'

'No!' harrumphs Zig.

Zag looks at her in shock. Zig is usually so cheerful!

'Just go away. I don't want to play', Zig says.

Zag sees this is no time to talk and leaves.

Zig picks up her doll and throws her across the room. But her doll hits a statue she made out of clay. It breaks on the floor.

'Oh, nooo!' Zig wails, and she bursts into tears.

Mummy Zebra and Zag come running.

Mummy gathers Zig in her arms and holds her

gently until Zig gets calmer.

'Nothing is going right today! I don't want to play! I was mean to Zag! And then I threw my doll! And I broke my statue!' she sobs.

'There there. We still love you', soothes Mummy. 'You know what you've done is wrong. Let's clean this up and start the day all over again'.

Zag pats her back.

'I'm sorry', Zig whispers, starting to smile.

Things are looking better already.

75

The Sewing Lesson

'Mummy, can you teach me to sew?' Hoopla Hippo asks.

'Of course, but why do you want to learn?' she asks, surprised.

Quickly Hoopla explains about their flag.

Mummy nods and smiles. 'It sounds like a wonderful idea, Hoopla. Let's start now!'

She gets out her sewing box and lots of pieces of fabric.

Then she threads a needle for each of them.

'Sewing is simple', she says. 'You hold your needle like this, and the fabric in the other hand', Mummy explains, showing Hoopla.

'Take care – the point of the needle is very sharp!' she says.

'Okay', says Hoopla, with wide eyes.

'Just poke the needle into the fabric. Good. Now push its point up and out of the fabric a little further along'.

'Owww!' he yells a moment later. 'I pricked myself! I'm bleeding!' and he sucks his little finger.

'Oh Hoopla, didn't I just tell you that the needle has a sharp point?' she laughs.

'But it hurts!' he whines.

'Come here. I'll kiss it and make it better', his mummy smiles.

'You did say it was sharp', Hoopla laughs.

After a few more not-very-good stitches, he gets much better.

'I didn't know it was so easy to sew!' he grins, stitching away.

Mummy gives him a quick hug. 'You are doing really well! Now let's look through my bag of scraps find you a nice piece of something purple'.

Hoopla's favourite colour, of course!

Grandmother's Surprise

Grandmother Brachio has planned a little surprise. Grandad loves chocolate, so she bought him a big piece this morning.

She's unpacking her shopping bag in the kitchen. 'Eggs in the refrigerator, flour on the shelf...' she talks to herself a lot.

'Now where can I hide this?' she asks herself when she comes to the piece of chocolate.

She sees the oven. 'I'll just pop it in there. He'll never find it!' Grandmother smiles.

Towards the evening, she comes back to the kitchen to start cooking supper.

'I'll start by baking the potatoes', she says to herself. She turns the oven on to warm it up for the potatoes.

She hums a little tune as she works, thinking about how happy Grandad will be when she gives him the piece of chocolate.

'Time to put the potatoes in the oven', she says. She opens the oven door. There's big puddle of melted chocolate at the bottom.

'Oh no!' she cries. Grandad rushes into the kitchen, thinking she might have hurt herself. When he sees what's happened, he bursts out laughing and gives her a hug.

'Oh, silly me!' she smiles weakly. 'Sorry!'

'Don't worry, dear! It's the thought that counts', he says. 'Now let's clean this up!'

20 APRIL

Bouncer's Shadow Puppets

It's Bouncer Brachio's bedtime.

'Daddy, when you were little, did you play games when you were falling asleep?'

Daddy thinks, then answers, 'Yes. I used to make shadow puppets on my wall'.

'What are they?' Bouncer asks, curious.

'I'll show you', Daddy answers. He puts his hand up so it makes a shadow on the wall. 'Look, there's a dog!' he says. 'Woof! Woof! And here's a rabbit'. He shows Bouncer how to make two floppy ears and a head with his hand. Now there are two rabbits on the wall, one big and one small. Bouncer's little one jumps up high, right over the big one!

Bouncer laughs. 'I'm a good bouncer', he squeaks in a rabbit voice.

'Or how about a swan?' Daddy says, making its head and bill with one hand and arm, and the swan's feathers with his other hand.

Suddenly the swan bites Bouncer's shadowy little rabbit's ear.

Daddy growls, 'I'm a hungry swan, looking for a rabbit sandwich!'

'EEEK!' giggles Bouncer, as he and Daddy have a swan and rabbit battle on the wall.

Bouncer is getting sleepy now. 'I think I'd better tuck you in now', laughs Daddy, and he gently puts both of Bouncer's arms under the covers and kisses his nose goodnight.

Things of Beauty

21 APRIL

It's spring cleaning time on Firefly Island. While the mummies clean their houses like mad, the children secretly collect things their mummies want to throw away. They are all gathered at the Hideout, with big boxes full of their treasures.

'We can make some beautiful things with this rubbish – I mean, these things', Baabra Sheep says.

'You're right', Nolo Giraffe agrees. 'Let's use them to make things to decorate the Hideout!'

'Yes!' Bouncer Brachio joins in with the idea.

'Let's use these old plates and make the entrance to our Hideout a bit more difficult for grown-ups to enter', Nolo suggests.

'Yes! So it is just for us alone and nobody else can enter. Of course, unless they know the password', Bouncer replies.

'And that's only us', Baabra giggles.

Fairly soon, they have used all the things to change their entrance.

'That's perfect!' says Zag. She puts the last touches on the door that she's been painting.

They crawl through the smaller door and gather inside. They look around admiring their little work of art.

'This so much more cosy!' Baabra whispers, snuggling up to Zag.

'Nolo is a genius', they shout together and they all start giggling!

Lammie's Cycle Lesson

22 APRIL

Today's a big day for Baabra Sheep's brother, Lammie.

'Ride bicycle!' he yells. He is just a toddler, but he's going to learn to ride his bicycle.

'It's not a bicycle, exactly', Daddy explains. 'Bikes have two wheels. Lammie's has four, with big wheels in front and back and two extra, small wheels in the back too. They help him from falling over.'

'Okay, Lammie, let's get you on the seat', Baabra says and lifts Lammie onto the bicycle.

Lammie is happy just ringing the bell and going 'Brrr-ooom! Brrr-ooom! Brrr-ooom!', so he doesn't

move!

'Lammie', Baabra giggles, 'you don't push both pedals at the same time!'

Daddy says, 'Let's each take one of Lammie's feet. You push down, then I will, until Lammie gets the feeling of how it should go'.

Ever so slowly, Lammie starts pedalling on his own, with his tongue sticking out a little.

'Brrr-ooom! Brrr-ooom! Brrr-ooom!' he crows, as he finally gets going faster and faster. He loves it!

'Lammie! The wall! Turn now! Turn now! Oh, Daddy, help!' Baabra yells. But it's too late. Lammie crashes into the wall, his bicycle tips over and he falls.

BAAM!

Lammie isn't hurt, luckily.

'Hee-hee-hee!' he giggles, lying on the ground.

'You need to watch where you're going!' Baabra laughs.

'You will have to practise a lot! You will tip over on a bicycle!'

Dressing-Up Day

It's been raining all day and Zig and Zag Zebra are bored. Their mummy has an idea.

'Why don't you explore the loft?' she smiles. 'Try opening the old chest by the window. You can play with whatever you find in it'.

In seconds they are in the loft. The rain patters on the roof, right over their heads.

'I wonder what's inside it', Zig whispers, opening the chest.

'Is it from a pirate ship?' asks Zag.

'Ohhh!' the twins say in one breath.

The chest is full of beautiful dressing-up clothes! In a flash they pull out all sorts of things.

'Look at these dresses!' cries Zig, holding one up to see if it fits. It does.

'And look! Hats, capes, boots… and fancy parasols!' breathes Zag.

They find more things in the bottom: crowns, scarves, gloves and sparkly jewellery.

'Ooooh!' cries Zag, trying on a ruby red gown, black cape and long black gloves.

'I'm a queen!' shouts Zig, twirling in her crown, yellow gown with sparkles, and tottery high heels.

They look at themselves in a dusty mirror in the corner.

Zag sighs, 'What a treasure, even if it's not a pirate chest!'

Talent Show is Coming!

24 APRIL

Slye Snake sees a new poster on the news board next to the Firefly Island Post Office.

'Hello, Mr. Ptera', she says, as he walks by. He runs the general store.

'Hello, Slye', he answers. 'What's happening?'

'There's a new poster', Slye says, pointing. 'What does it say?'

'Firefly Island Talent Show', reads Mr. Ptera. He reads on, and then tells Slye what it's about.

'There will be a talent show soon. Anybody who wants to can sign up and do anything that's fun for people to watch. The best acts will win a prize', he says.

'Can I do something?' Slye is curious.

'I'm sure! I hope you win!' laughs Mr. Ptera.

Slye walks home, thinking. Wouldn't it be fun if her friends were in the show?

She tells them all about it when they meet later that day at the Hideout.

'Oh, that would be fun!' exclaims Zig Zebra. 'Our family plays music together!'

'And I could do some magic tricks', says Slye, hoping she can work something out.

The youngsters decide to ask their families to sign up for the talent show.

'Even if you don't win, it's going to be a lot of fun, and a super night!' exclaims Zig, and they all agree.

Double Trouble

25 APRIL

Hoopla Hippo is playing in his garden, pretending to be the bravest of knights killing the most dangerous dragon.

'I'll use this piece of wood as my sword. Mummy's clothes-peg bag is the huge dragon', he says aloud to himself.

'Take that! And that! And that!' yells Hoopla, stabbing at the bag as it swings wildly on the clothes line.

Smack! Smack! He sends the dragon flying. But... his hand slips on the wooden sword, and a huge splinter sticks into his finger.

'Owww!' cries the knight, and he runs inside.

Mummy Hippo is making lunch.

'What in the world?' she exclaims as Hoopla comes roaring in. 'Oh, dear, a splinter!'

'Waaah!' Hoopla howls, while she gets tweezers, some disinfectant and a sticking plaster.

'Now please sit still, Hoopla. In a minute this will be out', she says calmly.

Hoopla squeezes his eyes shut. Mummy holds his hand in hers. 'Take a deep breath', she says, and he does.

Zip! It's out! But Hoopla jumps so much when it comes out that the splinter slides right out of the tweezers and… right into Mummy's hand!

'Owww!' she cries. Hoopla stares.

Luckily she can get it out right away. But what a strange thing – one splinter hurting twice!

Rainbow

26 APRIL

It's raining lightly. Nolo Giraffe is on the dock, watching Captain Cow dock the *Tinker Bell*.

She waves at Nolo and toots the horn.

'Hello Nolo', she calls out. 'How are you? Do you want to come aboard for a minute?'

'Yes! Yes!' Nolo cries. He rushes up the ramp. Just as he gets to Captain Cow, she points at the sky.

'Look at that! A rainbow! You can see the beautiful colours: red, orange, yellow, green, blue, indigo and violet'.

And it's true. In the sky over Big Island, there is a huge, perfect rainbow.

'Oh!' whispers Nolo. 'It's like a bit of magic in the sky', he says.

'Oh yes. It really is pretty', agrees Captain Cow.

'You know, they say there's a pot of gold at the end of the rainbow. So I'd better hurry back to Big Island and see if I can find it!'

'Really, Captain Cow?' asks Nolo. 'I wish I could find one. If I did, I would have enough to buy my very own ferry! I wish I had one just like the *Tinker Bell*'.

'She certainly is beautiful, isn't she?' laughs Captain Cow. 'I hope you find your pot of gold really soon. In the meantime, why don't you pull this?' she asks.

Nolo pulls down on a rope and the ferry's horn blasts across the island. 'Holy cow! I mean, er… sorry!' Nolo is embarrassed.

'No problem! See you soon Nolo!' calls Captain Cow, firing up the engine as Nolo runs back to the dock and waves.

Warm Milk

27 APRIL

'May I please be excused?' asks Slye Snake at the end of lunch.

She wants to play with her friends.

'Finish your milk, Slye, and then you can', answers Mummy Snake, smiling.

'But it's got warm', Slye moans. There's just a tiny bit left in her glass.

'A second ago you... you drank almost all of it', says Mummy.

'I don't like that last bit in my glass', moans Slye. Her mouth is a thin, straight line.

'Slye, we don't want to waste food. Please drink it up, or you won't get to play this afternoon', says Mummy firmly.

Slye knows the milk isn't really warm. She gulps it down, making a face just for fun.

'Next time, drink until the last drop is gone', Mummy says, smiling at Slye's stubbornness. Mummy had to do the very same thing when she was little. So she knows all about it!

Fruit Pizza

28 APRIL

'Today we'll make fruit pizzas', Hoopla Hippo's mummy says.

'Fruit pizza?' the friends buzz.

'I know all about pizza, but I have never heard of a fruit pizza', says Slye Snake, curious.

Mummy Hippo puts a sugar biscuit, as big as a small plate, in front of each of them.

'That's the pizza base', she says. 'Spread the pizza base with this soft, sweet cream cheese'.

'This stuff tastes fantastic!' cries Hoopla, tasting a bit. He just loves to eat!

'Hoopla, stop it! Wait until it is finished!'

'Now all you do is pick out your favourite fruits and decorate your pizza', Mummy continues.

'I like strawberries and bananas', laughs Slye. She

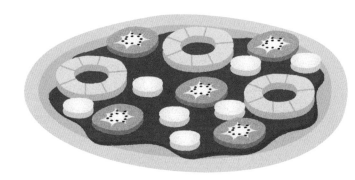

has put her pieces in circles.

'For me, it's kiwis!' giggles Nolo giraffe. He has put his kiwis in lines. He adds a few pieces of pineapple for extra colour.

'I like anything and everything!' Hoopla laughs tasting some more cream with his finger.

'Now eat them up!' laughs Mummy. She pours juice for everyone.

They admire their pizzas, then take big bites!

Mr. Horse's Race

29 APRIL

Mr. Horse is in his pyjamas in bed, reading his favourite magazine. The magazine is all about horse races. It's filled with pictures and stories of the winners.

'What an exciting life those race horses have', he murmurs to himself, turning out his light and snuggling into his pillow.

In moments he is sound asleep.

He dreams that he's a race horse at the World Championships.

Bang! goes the starting pistol, and he's off! He gallops as fast as he can, jumping over hedges and pools of water, hearing the other horses catching up with him.

'Faster! Faster!' he cries.

The crowd is shouting and clapping for him.

'Come on, faster!' he shouts to himself.

His heart pounds, and his legs stretch to take long strides. He's puffing and snorting.

'That's the way! Now just get to the finishing line!' he exclaims, seeing it coming towards him. His hooves thunder on the race track.

He wins! 'Yippee!' he yells 'I am the new World Champion race horse – and he falls out of bed with a thud.

'What a race!' he says, tangled up in his blanket. 'I won!' And he feels as if he did!

Grandad's Mystery Plant

30 APRIL

Bouncer and Grandad Brachio are gardening. Let's check our mystery plant', Grandad says, going to the back of the garden.

'I'm dying to know about that mystery plant', Bouncer says to himself.

'Look. It's up!' cries Grandad.

Bouncer runs to take a look. 'It's just a small leafy plant', Bouncer says.

'Can you tell what it is now?' Grandad asks.

'No, but I can see something round and orange coloured', Bouncer says, pointing at a branch.

'You're so clever! But I won't tell you! You'll have more fun this way', grins Grandad. 'Let's give it some water, so it can grow some more', he continues.

Bouncer gets the watering can and sprinkles the plant with water. He loves helping things grow! He wonders to himself, 'What could the mystery plant be?'

Can you guess?

May

Lammie's Choo-Choo

1 MAY

Lammie Sheep is looking at a picture book about a train full of toys.

'Choo-choo! Choo-choo!' he says.

He has an idea.

'Choo-choo!' he says again. He gets to work.

'Hrrrrmf! Hrrrmf!' he grunts, putting the kitchen chairs in a row.

'Choo-choo! Choo-choo!' he chants.

He runs to his room, grabs a doll and runs back to the kitchen.

'Dolly! Choo-choo!' cries Lammie as he puts her on the second chair.

Lammie runs to his room again for his teddy bear.

'Teddy! Choo-choo!' he laughs, putting Teddy on the next chair.

He bustles back to his room and gets his stuffed monkey.

'Monkey! Choo-choo!' he exclaims, plopping monkey on the last chair. That's the guard's van.

Lammie climbs up on the first chair, the engine. He's the train driver!

'Tooot! Tooot! Choo-choo-choo-choo-choo-choo!' he yells.

Mummy peeks in. 'Gosh, Lammie!' she exclaims. 'Your train is right on time!'

Mr. Trico's Tower

2 MAY

'It's tower day!' yells Slye Snake when she wakes up today.

She gets dressed, eats breakfast and rushes off. Mr. Trico, the park ranger, has invited the friends to climb to the top of his watch tower. The friends walk there, chattering away.

'There it is!' cries Hoopla Hippo. The path leads to the tall wooden tower. Mr. Trico waves to them from way up in the sky.

'Come on up!' he calls. 'You've got 200 steps to go! Good luck!'

The friends start climbing, laughing and joking. By the time they get to the top, everyone is puffing. Mr. Trico smiles. He climbs the steps every day.

'Gosh!' is all they can say, looking out.

'I can see Big Island!' cries Zig Zebra, pointing her new telescope at it.

'I can't see anything', Slye says, puzzled.

'Wait a second', Zig says, 'use my telescope! Isn't it wonderful up here?' she beams.

'I still can't see much', grumbles Slye.

Suddenly, Zig takes a good look at Slye.

'Of course not, Slye! You forgot to put on your glasses this morning!' she giggles.

Slye slaps her head. 'Oh dear! I was in such a hurry to get here!'

'You'll just have to come back another time', Mr. Trico laughs.

'*WITH* your glasses!' the friends yell together.

May

Night Adventure

Baabra Sheep wakes up in the middle of the night. She goes to the bathroom.

'I wonder what the living room looks like in the dark', she thinks. 'I'll just tiptoe downstairs'.

Moonlight streams in through the curtains.

'Gosh! Everything is black and white. I can't see any colours', she murmurs.

The furniture looks ghostly and strange.

'It's not so pretty in the dark', she says, feeling a little lonely and a bit scared.

'I want to go back to bed'.

She turns to go upstairs and suddenly sees a tall, pale shape in the doorway.

'A ghost!' she cries and starts shaking with fear.

'I am NOT a ghost', answers a familiar voice.

It's Daddy, in his dressing gown.

'What in the world are you doing down here in the middle of the night?' he asks. He hugs her to calm her down.

'I wanted to see what the living room looked like', Baabra whispers, trembling.

'It's not as nice', Daddy nods. 'Let's get back to bed. The sun will rise soon. Then everything will be pretty again'.

He carries Baabra to bed and tucks her in. 'Pleasant dreams', he whispers. But she's already fast asleep!

Hoopla the Juggler

Hoopla Hippo is learning to juggle scarves with Daddy.

'Start with the blue scarf, Hoopla. Throw it straight up and catch it in one paw', Daddy says, showing him how.

'I did it!' Hoopla cries.

'Let's try two scarves now', Daddy says. 'Hold one in each paw, then throw each one straight up. Catch them with the same paw'.

Hoopla throws them. He grabs one and then the other as they float down.

'Excellent!' cries Daddy. 'Now a harder trick. Throw just one, then turn around and catch it'.

'Here goes!' laughs Hoopla, throwing and spinning. He misses.

'Once more!' he cries, throwing the scarf higher and spinning again.

'Blow! One more time!' he cries. He catches it!

'Oh!' yells Hoopla, wobbling around. 'I'm dizzy! Everything is moving!' He sits down with a thud. Daddy laughs and helps him up.

'You're doing well! Now for a difficult trick. Throw one scarf a bit across your body and throw the other a bit to the other side. Catch each one with your other paw'.

Hoopla throws one scarf, then the other. They both land on his head!

'HOOO, HO-HO-HO-HO!'

'HOOO, HO-HO-HO-HO!'

Daddy laughs and pulls the scarves off Hoopla's head.

'If you watch the places where you want each scarf to go, it's easier'.

Hoopla gives it another try, and it works!

'Wonderful, Hoopla!' Daddy says, clapping. Hoopla takes a bow and gives Daddy a hug.

What's Going On?

Grandmother Brachio is standing in front of her wardrobe, looking at the clothes inside.

'What did I come here to get?' she asks herself. 'I really have no idea!' She knows she wanted to get something from the wardrobe before she goes shopping. 'I wonder what it was?' she whispers. 'Oh, well, it can't have been that important'.

She gets her shopping bag, grocery list and purse. Then she sets off walking.

'I like shopping at Mr. Ptera's general store', she thinks. 'He always has lots of good food'.

Suddenly she trips over something.

'My goodness, I almost fell!' she says to herself. 'What shall I buy? Oranges, and milk, and – my goodness!' she cries, as she stumbles again.

'What's going on here?' she asks herself.

She looks down at the path. No, it's fine.

Suddenly she realises. 'I forgot to put on my belt! So my skirt keeps falling down! And I keep tripping on my own skirt!' She chuckles.

'That's what I wanted from the wardrobe – my belt!' she says. She bunches up her skirt and heads back home to get it. 'Silly me!' she giggles, shaking her head.

Cozy's New Word

6 MAY

'Feed me! Feed me!'

It's a new thing Chilly Penguin and Hotta Toucan's chick Cozy can say.

Hotta is teaching Cozy to feed herself.

'Feed me!' chirps Cozy.

'Here are some seeds you can eat all by yourself, Cozy', says Hotta.

She puts some on the tray of Cozy's high chair.

'Feed me! Feed me!' Cozy squawks, even louder.

She stares at the seeds with her little eyes.

Hotta points to the seeds and says, 'You're big enough to feed yourself now, Cozy'.

Cozy pecks at the seeds. They fly everywhere. She pecks again. This time she gets one.

'Feed me! Feed me!'

'You're doing really well, honey'. smiles Hotta. 'Try again'.

'Feed me! Feed me!' replies Cozy.

'These look really yummy, Cozy', Hotta says, pointing again.

Cozy goes peck-peck-peck at the seeds and gets a few this time.

'Well done!' smiles Hotta.

'Feed me! Feed me!' cheeps Cozy.

But she knows how to eat by herself now. She's already peck-peck-pecking away!

The Zebra Family Band

7 MAY

Daddy Zebra comes home from work.

'Guess what?' he says to the family. 'There's going to be a talent show in our village! Should we sign up to play a song?'

'You mean all four of us?' asks Zag.

'Of course. Why not? The Zebra Family Band. How does that sound?' asks Mummy.

'I vote yes!' cries Zig.

'Me too', Zag exclaims.

'Let's do it!' say Zig and Zag together, and everybody laughs.

'And we could all dress up in the fancy clothes we found in the attic', says Zag.

She and Zig loved doing that, when it was raining the other day.

'Splendid idea!' Daddy says. 'But it's all girls' clothes up there. I don't want to wear a dress!' Daddy laughs.

Mummy thinks for a second and then says, 'I could make something'.

'Yes! A pirate costume!' Zig yells.

'We'll see about that', Daddy says shyly.

'Let's play some tunes first and pick the one we want to do for the show', Zag exclaims.

Which one will they choose?

Mother's Day

8 MAY It's dawn on Mother's Day. The friends plan to pick wild flowers in Firefly Meadow. Then they'll make beautiful bouquets and give them to their mummies when they wake up.

'Hoopla, you're late again!' calls Nolo Giraffe as Hoopla Hippo arrives at last.

'We're all here now', Nolo announces. 'Let's go!' They hop on their bicycles and ride off.

The meadow is full of brightly coloured flowers nodding in the breeze.

'My mummy loves yellow', says Baabra Sheep, picking lots of bright yellow buds.

'Mine loves violets', answers Slye, and she heads to a spot that's full of them.

'My mummy loves all sorts of flowers', Bouncer whispers as he picks one flower after another. And another… and another….

The friends work quickly. Before the sun is fully up, they've each made a beautiful bouquet.

Except Bouncer, the gardening expert. He has picked so many flowers, he can't carry them!

'I'll help', Baabra Sheep laughs. She takes a bunch to carry for Bouncer. 'You certainly picked a lot. I'm glad you left a few!'

'My mummy will love them', grins Bouncer.

And off home they go.

What lovely Mother's Day gifts!

Home Sweet Home

9 MAY

The friends are all in the Hideout today.

'Do you miss your old home?' Slye Snake asks Zig and Zag Zebra. 'I think I would', she adds, a bit sadly. 'I mean, I know I would'.

'We miss our old friends', Zig replies.

'But you have us now', Bouncer Brachio points out, smiling.

'Oh yes! You are all wonderful', laughs Zag. 'We love playing with you. We've learned lots of fun new games from you'.

'And you taught us your game of Sardines', Nolo Giraffe smiles.

'We have never lived on an island or gone on a ferry before. And we've never seen snow!' adds Zig.

'Where we used to live, we had to move around a lot, looking for water', Zag explains. 'But here we have it right inside our house'.

'And it's all around the island', Zig giggles, pointing in every direction.

'That must really be different. I can't even imagine a very dry place', answers Slye slowly.

'Do you know what's best about living here?' asks Zig, and everyone shakes their heads.

Zag grins. She knows what's coming.

'Everybody shares. So… we brought a big bag of sweets today!' Zig laughs.

She tears open the bag and gives each friend a big pile.

'Yum!' they cry, and start chewing contentedly.

Beauty Sleep

10 MAY

It's bedtime. Mr. Horse is in his pyjamas, brushing his teeth.

'I've put a few drops of that magic hair oil on my mane every night for some time now', he says.

He stares closely at his mirror, turning his head this way and that.

'I *think* my hair is growing back', he murmurs happily.

'Well, here's tonight's treatment', he says, sprinkling a few drops of the magic oil on his mane and rubbing it in. He goes to bed. Soon he's almost asleep. But he has an idea.

'Maybe I should put a little more magic oil on. Wouldn't that make my mane grow faster?'

He goes back to the bathroom and sprinkles a little more on.

Then he climbs back into bed.

But once again, just as he's falling asleep, he sits straight up.

'Maybe just a little more', he mutters. Off he goes to the bathroom again.

Then he shuffles back to bed.

'Hmmm. Now I can really get my beauty sleep', he smiles, and in a few minutes he's snoring away.

And what does he dream about? He's the beautiful horse that Zorro the bandit, rides in the films. With a long, flowing mane, of course!

Dreams Come True

'What a wonderful night's sleep!' cries Mr. Horse.

'And that dream I had! Gosh, I was superb. As fast as lightning, clever and handsome. The best horse in the world. And Zorro is terrific!'

He stretches. 'I'll have breakfast at Hotta Toucan and Chilly Penguin's café', he thinks to himself.

He walks to the café, whistling a happy tune.

Chilly calls out, 'Hello, Mr. Horse!' as he comes in. 'The usual?' he asks, and Mr. Horse nods. Chilly gets a cup of coffee and bowl of cereal with bananas and brings them to Mr. Horse.

'You look as though you are feeling really healthy these days', he says to Mr. Horse, smiling.

'Well yes, I am', answers Mr. Horse, 'but why do you ask?'

'Oh, I was just noticing that you seem to be… a lot more hairy', Chilly says gently.

'Really? Can you see a difference? I've been using a little magic oil to make my mane grow thicker. It was getting a little thin', Mr. Horse blushes, touching it. He suddenly freezes.

Mr. Horse jumps up and runs to look at himself in a mirror on the wall.

'My gosh! Look at me! My mane! It's magnificent!' he cries, giving it a shake.

'It looks as though your oil really *is* magic', chuckles Chilly.

'It's a dream come true!' crows Mr. Horse.

May

Weather Machine

12 MAY

'A weather machine could make the weather sunny at any time', daydreams Ivan Monkey, staring out the window. 'What makes a warm, sunny day?' he asks himself, frowning.

'Aha!' he cries. 'The sun! So I need to make an extra sun and warm it up in here first!'

He grabs a yellow balloon. Quickly he fills the balloon with helium gas. It gets huge and rises up to the ceiling. 'Perfect!' he yells.

Then he turns the heating in his house up as high as it will go.

He is soon getting terribly hot and sweaty.

'Perfect! Just like an ideal August day!' he thinks.

But as it gets hotter and hotter, he starts to feel dizzy. Suddenly he falls off his stool and lands on his head on the floor!

Hoopla Hippo is walking past and hears a crash. He rushes into Ivan's house.

'Ivan! It's burning hot in here!' he cries.

Ivan struggles up. 'I'm… I'm fine, but I can see lots of stars', he murmurs, rubbing his head. 'I was making warm, sunny weather. Look', he adds, pointing to the yellow balloon.

Hoopla smiles. Ivan is not making any sense, but that's perfectly normal.

'I think you'd better come outside and get some fresh, cool air', Hoopla says, smiling.

'You've almost fried yourself to a crisp!'

Sweet and Crunchy

13 MAY

Bouncer Brachio is working in his garden with Grandad. 'It's getting warm outside. Your garden will start growing quickly now', Grandad says.

'And look – you can pick your first lettuce'. Grandad points to them. 'The leaves are big enough to pick!'

They fill a basket with them. 'I could eat the whole basket', Bouncer says. He is hungry.

'Look Grandad! My beans are climbing up my teepee!' crows Bouncer, looking around. 'They've grown halfway to the top already!'

'You'll be sitting in the shade in there soon', answers Grandad.

Next to the beans is the mystery plant. It is growing fast too.

'Gosh. Look at those big leaves. And the orange flowers. Please tell me what it is', pleads Bouncer.

'You'll know before long', Grandad says. 'Today you need to pick off all the flowers except one. That flower will use all the energy the plant makes to

grow big and strong'.

That seems strange to Bouncer, but he does it.

'Let's go in and taste your lettuce', Grandad says. So they head off to the kitchen.

Grandmother washes the leaves and lets them dry. 'Would you like to make rolled lettuce?' she asks. Bouncer nods happily.

He sprinkles a little sugar on a lettuce leaf and rolls it up. Then he pops it in his mouth.

'Yummy! Crunchy and sweet!' exclaims Bouncer. 'My very first lettuce is just like sweets!'

Bouncing Tummies

14 MAY

Nolo Giraffe and Hoopla Hippo are at Nolo's home, playing on his mummy's computer.

'Let's play bouncing tummies', Nolo says.

'What's that?' asks Hoopla.

Nolo explains. 'It's like tennis. You move so that the ball bounces off your tummy, back to the other player. You get a point each time you bounce the ball off your tummy'.

'That sounds like a good game!' says Hoopla. 'It should be lots more fun than computers', he adds. He jumps off his chair and rubs his hands.

'I will be brilliant at this', laughs Hoopla, waving his hands and patting his round little tummy.

'Come on Nolo, I'm going to beat you', he chuckles. Nolo looks confused. 'I need to explain something',

he says uneasily.

'Just play, Nolo', teases Hoopla, 'you know you're going to lose!'

Nolo stares at Hoopla with big eyes. He doesn't know what to say.

'I have a secret weapon!' laughs Hoopla, and he pats his tummy again.

'Sorry Hoopla, but we play it here', Nolo says, pointing to the computer.

'So you mean it *is* a computer game?' Hoopla asks. Nolo nods.

Hoopla begins his hippo laugh.

'HOOO, HO-HO-HO-HO!'

'HOOO, HO-HO-HO-HO!'

'Oh Hoopla, you are funny!' laughs Nolo.

book and flips through the pages again.

'There are pictures inside now!' Slye exclaims. She can't believe her eyes. Mummy must be a real magician!

'Now I'll make them disappear again', Mummy says. '1, 2, 3! Abracadabra!' She flips through the pages once more, and sure enough, the pictures have all gone! Slye is speechless.

'How do you do that?' she wants to know.

Her mummy smiles, then carefully shows Slye how the magic trick really works.

'Slye, if you practise a little, you will amaze the villagers at the talent show', Mummy says. 'Let's find you a magician's hat, too!'

Slye begins to practise. It's not really hard.

She hopes she can keep the magic trick a secret!

Slye's Magic Trick

15 MAY

Slye Snake is really excited! Her magical colouring book came in today's post. Slye picked it up at the post office. Mummy is helping her learn how to do a magic trick with it. Slye wants to do the trick in the talent show that's coming soon.

Mummy has read the instructions and does the trick first so that Slye can enjoy it.

'Here's a colouring book. But it's blank inside!' Mummy says, turning the blank pages. 'So I need your help. Think hard about the colouring book pictures that we want to put in it, Slye'.

Slye thinks hard, scrunching up her face.

'1, 2, 3! Abracadabra!' cries Mummy. She taps the

Snack Kebabs

16 MAY

Mrs. Hippo is holding the cooking club in her kitchen today. All the friends are there.

On the table they see bowls filled with pieces of cheese, bananas, grapes, strawberries and other fruit. And a plate of biscuits.

'What are we making?' asks Slye Snake. 'I'm really hungry!'

'I thought we'd make snack kebabs', says Mrs. Hippo. She brings out a packet of wooden sticks. They look like giant toothpicks, with points at both ends. She gives each friend a stick.

'This is really easy and fun to do', Mrs. Hippo says.

'Pick out some fruit and cheese'.

The friends each choose their favourites.

'All you do is put a piece of fruit on the stick. Then add some cheese, and then another fruit, more cheese, and so on', Mrs. Hippo says, showing them how to do it.

The friends poke their sticks through the fruits and cheese. Each kebab is different!

Slye jabs her wooden stick into her hand.

'Ow!' she cries. 'It doesn't hurt, really', she laughs.

'Now, please help yourselves to some biscuits. I'll get some plates and juice for you', Mrs. Hippo says, getting busy.

They all start eating and chattering.

'They're delicious!' exclaims Slye happily.

Bubble Painting

Baabra Sheep and Lammie are blowing bubbles. Lammie loves the bubbles flying through the air.

'Bub-bles! Bub-bles!' he laughs. He blows into his bubble wand. A beautiful shiny bubble floats up into the air.

'Watch this, Lammie!' whispers Baabra.

She dips her wand into the bubble mixture and holds her arm out straight. Then she twirls around. A whole string of bubbles flies away.

Lammie tries it too.

'Bub-bles! Bub-bles!' he sings.

Mummy Sheep comes over with a big piece of paper and two tiny bottles of food colouring. She sticks the paper on the wall of the garden shed.

'What are you doing, Mummy?' asks Baabra.

'I thought you two might like to bubble paint', says Mummy. She opens one little bottle and lets several drops of red food colouring drip into Baabra's jar of bubble mixture. She opens the other and drips a few drops of blue into Lammie's.

'Now blow a bubble so it bursts on the paper', Mummy says, smiling.

Baabra and Lammie do that. When their bubbles pop, they leave bright spots of red and blue on the paper.

'Amazing! A pretty painting, Mummy!' cries Baabra.

'Bub-bles! Bub-bles!' laughs Lammie.

May

Walking on Water

18 MAY Ivan Monkey has started a new experiment. 'I really wish I could walk on water', he says to himself.

'How can I do that?' he wonders, looking around his laboratory.

In the distance, he hears a deep horn blowing. The *Tinker Bell* ferry is arriving at the Firefly Island dock.

'Hmmm', says Ivan to himself. He's had an idea!

He gets to work. Soon he's built two small wooden boats. Each one is just big enough for him to put one of his feet in. Straps hold the tiny boats onto his feet, like giant shoes.

'Could I walk to Big Island?' Ivan asks himself.

Clump! Clump! Clump! Clump! he goes, walking to the harbour in his new boat shoes.

Ivan clumps his way to the dock and stands on the edge, looking down into the water.

'Here goes! I'm walking on water!' he cries, waving at Captain Cow.

Ivan steps off the dock. He makes a huge splash. Then he starts to sink, until he's standing up to his neck in the chilly water.

'Help! Help!' he cries.

Captain Cow throws him a red and white lifebelt tied to a rope. She pulls and pulls.

Before long Ivan is on the *Tinker Bell*, dripping wet and shivering, but safe.

'Welcome aboard, Captain Ivan', she laughs.

Who's Who?

19 MAY It's raining hard. Much too hard to go out to play.

Zig and Zag Zebra don't mind. They are in their loft, digging into the chest of dressing-up clothes.

'Let's get dressed up and see if Mummy can tell who we are!' says Zig.

'Brilliant!' answers Zag.

'I'll wear this bandit's mask over my nose and forehead', Zag says. 'And this red cape and these tall boots. I'll wave this sword around'.

'You look super!' exclaims Zig. 'I'm going to be a mysterious queen', she says, putting a sparkling crown over her ears. She pulls on a fancy long dress and a pair of long black gloves.

'Your Majesty!' cries Zag, and she swishes her cape and bows to Queen Zig.

'Right, let's go and find Mummy', says Queen Zig. She and Zag the bandit go downstairs.

'Good afternoon, Madam', says the bandit to Mummy.

'Good afternoon, sir', replies Mummy.

Mummy curtseys to Zig. 'And good afternoon, your Majesty'.

'Guess who we are!' orders Queen Zig.

'Well, are you also known as Zig? And are you also known as Zag?' she smiles.

'Oh! How do you know?' they ask.

'A mummy just knows these things', answers Mummy. She hugs them both.

'How about some milk and biscuits?'

'Baabra! Did It!'

'Mummy! Mummy!' Baabra Sheep and baby Lammie yell. A puddle of milk is spreading across the kitchen table.

Mummy Sheep turns from the stove.

'What's wrong?' she asks. Then she sees the mess. Her eyebrows go up.

'Baabra! Did it!' cries Lammie, pointing wildly at the puddle and Baabra.

'I did not!' exclaims Baabra, drawing herself up in a huff.

'Baabra! Did it!' wails Lammie.

'Now settle down, both of you', says Mummy calmly.

Mummy looks at them. 'One of you did this. And I know who. So please tell me the truth this time'.

'I didn't do it!' cries Baabra.

'Baabra! Did it!' yells Lammie furiously.

'Lammie, I know that you spilled your milk', says Mummy. 'That can happen. But it's not nice to say that Baabra did it'.

Lammie looks at Mummy. His lips quiver and tears drip from his eyes.

'You see, Lammie, the milk from your glass points to you. So I think you knocked your glass over. Is that what happened?'

Lammie gulps. 'Lammie... Lammie... Did it', he sniffles.

'That's alright', Mummy smiles. 'Next time, just tell me what really happened'.

Lammie nods. Baabra sighs in relief.

May

Choosing Costumes

21 MAY

Tomorrow is the Firefly Island talent show.

The Zebra family is in their loft. It's time to pick out costumes.

Mummy tries on a shiny red dress and puts a sparkling crown on her head.

'What do you think?' she asks, twirling around.

'Beautiful!' Daddy exclaims, giving her a kiss.

'I have made something for you', she says, smiling. She puts a pirate's hat on Daddy's head. Then she gives him a black patch to cover one eye.

'Blow the man down!' he bellows. He looks in the mirror.

'Gosh! I'm a pirate drummer!' he laughs. 'Yo-ho-ho!' he growls.

Zig puts on a blue soldier's uniform with shiny silver buttons and braid. 'I've got my outfit', she announces.

'I want that one', Zag says crossly.

'I found it first!' replies Zig.

'Now, now. There are lots of other things here', says Mummy gently. 'Look at this, Zag'.

She wraps a mysterious black cape around Zag, and adds a pointed witch's hat.

Zag loves it. 'Wonderful. Now I've got mine too!' she exclaims, grinning.

'Then we're all ready for tomorrow!' laughs Daddy.

Talent Show Night

22 MAY

It's Talent Show night and the whole village is watching the show.

It's been a wonderful evening!

'And last is Hoopla Hippo', Mr. Horse booms. The crowd claps and cheers.

Hoopla comes on the stage and takes a bow.

'Here goes!' he says.

He's been practising really hard for his juggling act. He has decided to balance china plates on sticks.

He balances one, two, then three plates on the sticks, sweating with nervousness. It's really very difficult! The crowd goes wild. 'Come on, Hoopla! Come on, Hoopla!' they chant.

Hoopla slowly adds a fourth, then a fifth plate.

Suddenly, Hoopla feels as if he's going to sneeze.

'Oh, no!' he thinks. The plates fly everywhere.

Aaah-aaah-aaah CHOOO! he explodes.

All the plates crash to the stage and shatter in a million pieces.

Ooh! Goes the crowd.

Hoopla freezes, then wipes his nose, takes a bow and cries, 'Ta-dah!', as if it's all part of his act. The crowd cheers again!

'I think we have a winner, don't you?' yells Mr. Horse, and the crowd says in one voice, 'Yes!'

And Hoopla wins the Talent Show!

May

Slye's Secret is Out

23 MAY

Nolo Giraffe can't stop thinking about Slye Snake's colouring book trick. How did it work?

'Please show me, Slye!' he begs.

'A magician never tells', Slye says. But she's proud of her trick and she likes Nolo. She smiles.

'Alright Nolo. You have to use a magical colouring book', she explains, showing him.

In her book some pages are blank, and some pages have colouring pictures on them. 'I got it from a magic shop', says Slye.

'Now look at the edges of the pages Nolo', she says, pointing.

The blank pages have a little bit cut off. They don't quite come to the edge of the colouring book. The pages with pictures are normal, just as wide as the cover.

'When you want to show the blank pages, you put your thumb here', Slye explains, fanning the book's pages. Nolo sees only white pages.

'When you want to show the pictures, you put your thumb here', she says, fanning again. As if by magic, Nolo sees only the pictures!

'Can I try?' asks Nolo. He's clumsy at first. 'It's really difficult to slide your thumb to the right place and then fan the pages', he says.

'I had to practise my trick with Mummy until I got good at it', Slye explains.

Nolo nods. 'I want one of these books too!'

In a Minute!

24 MAY

Nolo is playing on his mummy's computer.

'Nolo, can you please lay the table for dinner?' Mummy calls from the kitchen.

'In a minute, Mummy', Nolo calls back.

He carries on with his computer game.

Minutes pass.

'Nolo, I need you to lay the table now', says Mummy, standing beside Nolo.

'Yes, Mummy… just let me finish this… game… and…' Nolo's voice fades as he clicks the mouse furiously.

'Nolo. Look at me', says Mummy sternly.

Nolo blinks and turns to look at Mummy.

'What have I been asking you to do?'

'Ummm… to clean my room?' asks Nolo helpfully.

'No. To lay the table. It's dinner time, and we usually eat from plates, not a bare table', Mummy says. She's tapping her foot impatiently now.

Mummy's upset, even if she is joking a little.

'I'm sorry, Mummy. I just wanted to finish my game first'. Nolo really does feel sorry.

'I understand that', says Mummy, 'but if you can't find time do your chores, then no more computer time for you this week. Do you understand?' she asks.

'Watch me!' Nolo cries, jumping off his chair. He runs to the kitchen, grabs plates, forks, knives, spoons and glasses, and lays the table in record time!

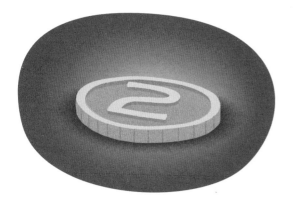

Disappearing Coin

25 MAY

Hoopla Hippo loved Slye Snake's magic trick. He's learned one too.

'Ladies and gentlemen', he begins, bowing to the friends in the Hideout. 'Please watch the shiny coin in my hand', and he waves it around.

'I will magically make it disappear, simply by rubbing it on my elbow', Hoopla says.

He rubs it on his left elbow.

The coin drops on the table in front of him.

'Uh-oh', he says, and his friends groan.

He picks the coin up with his right hand and puts it in his left hand. Then he puts his right hand to his ear, as if he's listening to something, and rubs his right elbow.

'Abracadabra! Alakazoom!' he cries.

He opens both hands – empty!

'Amazing! Fantastic!' the friends yell.

'How did you do that?' asks Slye Snake.

'I'll show you how, if you promise not to tell any grown-ups', Hoopla whispers. They all lean forward. 'I made it look as if I moved the coin to my left hand, but I really kept it in my right hand. Then, when I put my hand to my ear and rubbed my elbow, I dropped the coin down the back of my shirt. It's easy when you practise it a lot', he says proudly.

'It really looked like magic to me', laughs Slye. 'I hope I can learn to do it as well as you did!'

Hail Storm

26 MAY

The weather has been hot for a whole week.

Now, tall, white clouds are moving in fast.

'Gosh, those are monster clouds', says Baabra Sheep, playing at the playground.

'I bet it will rain', answers Zig Zebra.

The clouds race closer. Raindrops start pitter-pattering down.

Then it really starts to pour down. 'Under the tree!' cries Baabra.

Suddenly they hear a new swishing sound.

'Look! Little white stones are falling!' cries Zig. Her twin, Zag, runs out from under the tree to get one of them.

'Look! They're not stones! They're ice!' yells Zag over the roar of the storm.

They all dash out, pick up small, round balls of ice, and run back under the tree. Everybody is puffing.

'Ouch! That stuff stings!' laughs Zig. They pop the ice into their mouths.

'Wassh ish dat?' asks Zig, her mouth full of little balls of ice.

'We call it hail', Baabra says. 'It doesn't happen often, just sometimes, after really hot weather'.

'I've never seen anything like it', Zag says.

'Look, it's piling up! Like snow!' yells Baabra.

The hail stops. The ground is white now. The friends leave the tree and start sliding around on the hail. They scoop it up and throw it at each other.

'Firefly Island has some really strange weather', laughs Zig. 'But I love it!'

Not Fun at All

27 MAY

The hail storm was not all fun.

'My poor garden', wails Bouncer Brachio. The hail has broken leaves off his vegetables. Some have been pounded into the earth.

'We'll do our best to help them get better', Grandad replies. They start cleaning up.

In the village, Hotta Toucan and Chilly Penguin are trying to put up the sun umbrella outside their café. The wind had blown it over during the hail storm.

'I never saw anything like this where I came from!' says Hotta, amazed.

Chilly laughs and says, 'I've seen plenty of hail. But yesterday's storm was bad'.

Ivan Monkey is looking at his rowing boat in the harbour.

'My poor boat. The hail took off all its paint!' The bright red paint that covered the inside of the boat has completely gone.

Mr. Ptera is standing outside his general store. He had a pretty, striped awning over the front door.

'Look at that', he says to Mr. Horse, the mayor. 'The hail has torn it to shreds'.

'It looks almost as though it's kite day at your shop', answers Mr. Horse, as the pieces of cloth flap in the breeze.

Captain Cow blows her horn as the *Tinker Bell* ferry docks in the harbour.

'Our shiny brass bell got damaged by the hail', she says, showing Mr. Horse. 'The hailstones have made little dents in it. But it still sounds fine', she smiles, clanging it.

'Then things will back to normal before long', says Mr. Horse, glad that all the problems can be fixed. It's just difficult to believe that little pieces of frozen water can do so much damage to so many things!

Dr. Henny's Lesson

28 MAY

'La-la-la-LAAAH-la-la-la!'

Zag Zebra hears a strange sound while walking past Dr. Henny's clinic.

'Somebody's really ill!' she thinks. She peeks in.

'La-la-la-LAAAH-la-la-la!'

Dr. Henny is standing on her desk, singing like an opera star. She can't see Zag.

'La-la-la-LAAAH-la-la-la!'

'Ahem!' Zag clears her throat. Dr. Henny jumps, sees Zag, and flutters down off her desk.

'Oh, hello, Zig – or Zag?' she says. 'Wait. You're Zag – you're wearing pink', she babbles, acting nervous.

'I heard you and thought I'd say hello', Zag smiles.

'I just started singing lessons', Dr. Henny chuckles. 'I'm really awful, but I do love to sing. And I can practise here'.

'That's brilliant! Well, I've got to go', says Zag.

'She sings even more badly than Zig!' thinks Zag, laughing to herself.

May

29 MAY — Red-Light, Green-Light, 1-2-3

The friends are playing in Firefly Meadow. 'Let's play *red-light, green-light, 1-2-3*', says Nolo Giraffe.

'Yes!' 'Wonderful!' 'Who's IT?' they ask.

'I'll be IT the first time', Nolo declares.

He trots to one end of the meadow. The friends head off to the other end.

'Here goes!' Nolo calls, and he turns his back to them.

'Red-light, green-light, 1-2-3!' he yells.

All the friends scramble as fast as they can towards him. They freeze as he turns around.

But Hoopla Hippo wobbles and falls over. Nolo points to him, laughing. 'Hoopla, I caught you moving!' he cries.

Hoopla trudges back to the starting line.

Nolo turns his back again. 'Red-light, green-light, 1-2-3!' he yells.

They all run quickly towards Nolo. Zig Zebra is getting close to him when Nolo turns back. She slides and falls over. 'Got you, Zig!' he cries. Zig shakes her head and walks back to start all over again. Her twin, Zag, prances with excitement.

'Red-light, green-light…' Nolo yells.

'Got you!' yells Zag, tagging Nolo.

'I won! I won!' she cries.

'Yes, you did', grins Nolo. 'Now you're IT!'

30 MAY — Lammie's Flower Bites!

Lammie Sheep is in love with flowers this summer. He spends hours in the Sheep family's garden.

'Pretty! Pretty!' he says, over and over.

Sometimes he picks a few to give to Mummy. But today he's just looking.

'Flower! Flower!' he whispers. He sticks his black nose right into one of the yellow flowers and sniffs in its smell.

'Yummy! Yummy!' he cries happily. Then he goes on to the next flower.

A bright red flower has just opened this morning. Lammie stands still and spends a minute just looking at it.

He leans over to sniff it. Right in the centre, he

spots a tiny black and yellow creature moving around. It's working busily away. What could it be doing?

'Furry! Furry!' he whispers. The creature is black and yellow. It looks to Lammie a little bit like a tiny, funny-coloured sheep.

Lammie leans closer to sniff the beautiful red flower.

Zzzinggg!

'Owww!' wails poor Lammie. His nose feels as though it's on fire!

Tears stream out of Lammie's eyes as he runs off to find Mummy Sheep.

'Lammie! What in the world has happened to you?' cries Mummy when he finds her.

She sweeps him up in a big hug.

'Flower! Bite!' wails Lammie.

'Oh dear, did you get stung by a bee?' she soothes. She puts cream on it to make it feel better. 'Mummy! Good!' he sighs.

Joke Book

Hoopla Hippo has learned a new set of jokes to tell the friends when they gather at the playground today.

'Nolo, what animal makes the most of his food?' Hoopla asks the young giraffe.

'I have no idea', Nolo answers.

'A giraffe. A little food goes a long way!' laughs Hoopla, pointing at Nolo's neck.

'Oh, that's terrible!' laughs Nolo.

'Slye, what comes into the house through the keyhole?' he asks Slye Snake.

Slye frowns. 'Wait, wait. Let me think', She's quiet for a moment. Then suddenly her face lights up.

'The key!' she cries.

'Right! Well done!' exclaims Hoopla.

He leans over and whispers something to Bouncer Brachio.

'Bouncer, what's that carrot doing, growing out of your ear?' sounding like a grown-up.

Bouncer pats his ear and pretends to be surprised.

'I don't know! I thought I planted cauliflower!' Bouncer replies. And Hoopla cracks up, laughing at his own joke.

'HOOO, HO-HO-HO-HO!'

'HOOO, HO-HO-HO-HO!'

All the friends fall down laughing. The jokes were funny, but Hoopla's laugh is even funnier.

June

Scavenger Hunt

The Brachio family has gone to the camping ground early this morning.
It's a beautiful spring day.

'Here come the villagers!' Bouncer yells as they start arriving with their picnic baskets.

'Welcome to our camping ground opening party, everyone', Bouncer's daddy calls. 'To get started, let's have a scavenger hunt!'

He gives each family a list of things to find and a bag to collect them in.

'Off you go!' Mr. Brachio cries. 'The first family to find all the things on the list will win a prize!' The families all scurry off.

'Let's see. A stick with two branches', reads Hoopla Hippo's mummy.

'Three different leaves', reads Bouncer's grandad.

'One black and one white pebble', reads Zig and Zag Zebra's daddy.

The camping ground is full of villagers hunting for all these things. Cries of 'Found it!' and 'Got it!' and lots of laughter fill the air.

'Where can we find a piece of string?' asks Baabra Sheep. 'It's impossible'.

'Here! Here!' yells baby Lammie, waving his dummy, tied to his buggy with string.

'Hooray! My hero!' laughs Baabra. 'Now we've got everything on our list!'

'The Sheep family wins!' cries Mr. Brachio. 'This delicious cake is yours!'

'Lammie, you won for us!' giggles Baabra, and everybody laughs and cheers.

Heads and Tummies

The friends are playing at the playground. Dr. Henny walks by and waves.

She calls out, 'How are you all today?'

'Fine!'

'Super!'

'Wonderful!'

They all burst out laughing.

'Are you sure?' Dr. Henny asks.

She walks closer. 'Maybe you'd better check'.

'Can you pat your heads and rub your tummies today?' Dr. Henny continues.

The friends look surprised.

Then they all start laughing again, but they are puzzled.

'What can she mean? Is she joking?' Hoopla asks himself.

'No, I mean it!' she smiles. 'Let's see. You have to do both things at the same time'.

One by one the friends start trying.

'This is really difficult', giggles Slye Snake. 'If I start by patting my head, then I can't help but pat my tummy!'

'And when I rub my tummy, I can't help rubbing my head', chortles Hoopla Hippo.

Nolo Giraffe has been silently trying. His tongue sticks out a bit as he tries.

Suddenly he cries out, 'I can! I'm doing it! Look!'

It's true! Nolo is patting his head and rubbing his tummy, with a big grin.

'Well done, Nolo!' Dr. Henny calls to him.

One by one the friends manage to do this strange thing. They know by now that Dr. Henny is joking with them.

Meanwhile, Dr. Henny is trying not to laugh at the playground full of youngsters looking silly. But it *is* hard.

Give it a try. Can you do it?

The Sculpture Garden

3 JUNE

The villagers of Firefly Island meet every month with Mr. Horse, the mayor. They tell him how things are going on the island. Tonight they are meeting in the library.

Bouncer Brachio's mummy has brought one of her famous chocolate cakes. Everybody gets a big piece.

'Delicious!' cries Mr. Horse. He says, 'Welcome, everyone. What is on your minds?'

Mrs. Brachio says, 'I've been thinking about that big grassy area next to our school. We could make a sculpture garden there'.

'What's that?' asks Roota Rooster.

'It's a garden full of statues. A sort of outdoor museum you can visit and enjoy any time you like', explains Mrs. Brachio.

'What would we put there?' asks Mr. Zebra.

'Why don't we let our youngsters decide. They have good imaginations', answers Mrs. Brachio.

They all nod yes and smile.

'We all agree, it sounds excellent. I'll ask the youngsters tomorrow', promises Mr. Horse.

'Now let's have another piece of that cake!' crows Roota, and everybody laughs.

June

Tracing Day

4 JUNE

Mr. Horse explains the sculpture garden idea to the friends. They love it! It makes them feel really important.

'Well, what can we put in this new garden?' Baabra Sheep asks the friends.

There is a silence while everybody thinks hard.

'I've got an idea. What if we make wooden statues that look like each one of us?' asks Nolo Giraffe. 'Wouldn't that be good?'

'Yes!'

'Definitely!'

'Excellent!'

'How could we do it?' asks Slye Snake.

Mr. Horse gets excited. 'I have an idea', he says. 'We'll trace the shapes of your bodies on this paper. Then we'll cut flat pieces of wood to match the paper, and paint the wood to look like you!'

'Gosh!' they cry. They start tracing each other's shapes on big sheets of paper.

'Ooh, that tickles!' giggles Baabra Sheep as Bouncer Brachio traces under her chin.

'Nolo I had no idea your legs were so long!' laughs Slye Snake, slithering along the ground and tracing around them.

When the tracings are finished, Mr. Horse takes the pieces of paper and goes off to cut the wood.

'Meet me by the school tomorrow morning so that we can paint your statues!' he cries.

'Yes!' the youngsters reply. 'See you then!'

Painting Day

5 JUNE

The whole village is ready to paint and set up the sculpture garden.

Mr. Horse, the mayor, has cut nine pieces of wood to match the tracings of the youngsters.

'Welcome, everyone!' he cries. 'Please pick a statue and paint it so it looks just like the youngster. Let's get started!'

With lots of laughing and some spilled paint, the villagers work on the wooden figures. They have a snack while the paint dries.

'Now let's plan where the statues will go', says Mr. Horse. 'Baabra, will you please stand there?'

And one by one the youngsters each go and stand where their statues will be.

'How does that look?' Mr. Horse asks. Everybody thinks it looks perfect!

'Then we'll put the statues where they belong', Mr. Horse says, directing the daddies.

They hammer strong sticks into the ground to keep the statues in place.

At last all the work is done.

Everyone gathers in front of the new sculpture garden and applauds.

It looks brilliant. There's Hoopla Hippo, Bouncer Brachio, Nolo Giraffe, Baabra Sheep, Lammie Sheep, Slye Snake, Zig Zebra, Zag Zebra and even Cozy, the new chick.

The sculpture garden is perfect!

The Secret

6 JUNE

Baabra Sheep is playing at Zig and Zag Zebra's house today. But they are bored.

'Mummy', Zig says, 'we don't know what we want to do. Do you have any ideas?'

Mummy Zebra is making a fruit salad. She looks at her bowl full of fruit and smiles.

'Would you like to learn how to make invisible ink?'

'Yes!' the three youngsters exclaim.

'Good. Go get your water colour brushes, some white paper and also some cotton buds', she answers.

Soon they are back with their supplies.

'Now squeeze the juice from this lemon', Mummy Zebra says, cutting it into pieces.

They squeeze the juice into a saucer.

'Now dip your cotton buds or brushes into the juice, and draw a picture on the paper'.

Baabra draws a funny face. Zig makes a house. Zag draws a doll.

Once the juice has dried, they can't see anything on the paper at all.

'Mummy, it's certainly invisible ink now', laughs Zig, 'but what do we do to be able to see it?'

Mummy Zebra leans close to the three youngsters and whispers the secret that makes the ink appear.

'Don't tell anyone!' she warns, and they all giggle.

June

Magic Pictures

7 JUNE

Of course, on this fine sunny morning, the three friends can't wait to share their secret. They are all in the Hideout.

'Look at this', Baabra Sheep says.

She, Zig Zebra and her twin sister Zag show the others the pieces of white paper.

'What is there to see?' asks Hoopla Hippo.

'Nothing at the moment, but there really is something to see. It's drawn with invisible ink!' whispers Baabra mysteriously.

'Then how can you see the drawing?' asks Nolo Giraffe, puzzled.

Slye Snake picks up one of the pieces of paper and walks out in the bright sunlight. She holds it close to her eyes.

'I can't see a thing', she mutters. She keeps on staring at the paper, wondering what the secret could be.

'Wait a minute!' she says to herself. 'Is that a picture, just starting to appear?'

In a little while the picture becomes clearer. It's a house, painted in light brown. With every passing minute the picture becomes clearer.

'It must be the sunlight that makes the invisible ink turn brown!' Slye exclaims. Soon the friends are laughing at the other drawings.

Then they all rush home to make their own invisible ink pictures!

Nose Balancing

8 JUNE

Nolo Giraffe really wants some sweets.

'Perhaps if I learn to do a trick, Mummy will let me have some', he thinks.

He looks around. 'I wonder if I can balance that ruler on my nose?'

He stands the ruler on his nose and lets go.

Plop! The ruler wobbles and falls off.

'This is really difficult!' he says to himself.

He tries again. He keeps his body under the ruler this time. It stands up longer, but then falls to the floor. Again.

'Getting better!' he cheers. 'Keep trying, Nolo! Those sweets are almost yours!'

Nolo keeps trying. He starts to feel how to keep the ruler standing up on his nose.

'Hmm. When I watch the top of the stick it works better!' he says a moment later.

Before long, Nolo can keep the ruler standing up balanced on his nose for ages.

'I'm going to try Mummy's big ruler', he decides. He finds it and puts it on his nose so it's standing

110

up in the air. 'Here goes!' he thinks.

'Amazing! This long ruler is even easier than my short one!' Nolo can't believe it.

'Nolo, what on earth?' says his mummy, coming into the room.

Her son is waltzing around the room with a long ruler balanced on his nose. 'You clown! How do you do that?'

Nolo takes a bow. 'I'll teach you how, if you give me some sweets!' he grins.

Sore Nose Sniffles

Baabra Sheep is looking at a picture book in the waiting room outside Dr. Henny's office. She has the sniffles.

Dr. Henny comes out and says, 'Hello, Baabra! How are you today?'

Baabra sniffs and says, 'I don't feel very well. My nose is runny. And it hurts from blowing it and wiping it so much'.

'Poor you', says Dr. Henny. 'Come in'.

They go inside Dr. Henny's office. Baabra jumps up on the examining table.

'We'll check everything', Dr. Henny says. She looks at Baabra's throat and in her ears, and listens to Baabra's heartbeat.

'You have a good, strong heart', Dr. Henny says, smiling at Baabra.

'And I have good, strong eyes too', answers Baabra, laughing a bit.

'That's true', replies Dr. Henny.

'Yes', says Baabra. 'I love that picture book in your waiting room'.

'I'm glad you do', says Dr. Henny. 'It looks as though you only have the sniffles, so please stay in bed today and tomorrow. Drink lots of warm drinks and put this on your nose so that it won't hurt so much', she says, handing Baabra a tube of cream. 'These will help too. They are extra soft', Dr. Henny says. She hands Baabra a special box of tissues, decorated with stars and rainbows. 'Now get to bed. You can borrow that picture book too!'

Baabra smiles. 'That's the best medicine ever!' and she heads off home to bed.

111

June

Ivan Goes Fishing

10 JUNE

Ivan Monkey loves going fishing, even if he doesn't catch anything. And that's just as well, because he doesn't catch fish very often. He has a little rowing boat that he keeps in the harbour of Firefly Island.

'It's a fine day to go fishing', he chuckles to himself as he gets into his boat this morning. 'I'd better wear a hat. The sun is bright and warm'.

Ivan quickly rows his boat out to the deeper water. He starts fishing, enjoying the fresh air and sparkling water.

All of a sudden he feels a hard tug on his fishing line.

'A fish! A fish!' Ivan cries.

'It must be a huge one', Ivan says a moment later. 'It's almost pulling me into the water!'

He brings the fish closer to the boat. Now he can see it in the water.

'My goodness!' Ivan yells. 'It's gigantic!'

Suddenly, his fishing line snaps. The fish has gone.

'Oh, no!' he cries. He thinks hard, then draws a big, black X on his boat. 'I'll get you tomorrow!' he says. Do you think he will?

A Big Disappointment

11 JUNE

Ivan Monkey is dancing a little jig on the dock as the sun rises this morning. He barely slept last night.

'I've got to catch that giant fish again!' he whispers to himself, rubbing his hands.

Ivan has invited Mr. Horse, the mayor, to come along with him. Here comes Mr. Horse now.

'I'm really excited', Mr. Horse says. 'I brought my camera along just in case!'

Ivan has already loaded his things into his rowing boat. Mr. Horse puts in his fishing rod, lunch bag and camera.

'I really hope you can find that giant fish again', Mr. Horse says.

'Me too', laughs Ivan. 'Let's go!'

'Where did you catch your giant fish?' the mayor asks as they row out of the harbour.

Ivan smiles a little shyly.

'I did something to show me just where it is. So that the fish will be easy to find'.

'Really? How can you be sure where it is?' asks Mr. Horse, surprised.

'It's very simple, really', Ivan says proudly. 'I painted this X right where the fish was when my line broke', he says, and he points to the big, black X drawn on side of his boat.

Mr. Horse blinks, then smiles. 'Ivan is a mad scientist, after all', he thinks.

'Good luck!' he says, gently shaking his head.

112

June

Jumping Team

12 JUNE

'Oh blow! I'll try again!' puffs Hoopla Hippo. He got a skipping rope for Valentine's Day. He had forgotten all about it, but now he's trying to learn to skip with it.

'Right. Here goes', he says. He twirls the rope up over his head.

'Oh no!' he cries again, as it catches on his bottom.

'My backside is just too big!' he cries, 'But I'm definitely going to learn to skip'.

Nolo Giraffe and Slye Snake come past.

'What are you up to, Hoopla?' asks Slye.

'Skipping. Or more to the point, trying to', Hoopla answers grumpily.

'What's the problem?' asks Nolo.

'I stick out too far at the back and the rope can't get round me', Hoopla says, a little embarrassed. Slye feels sorry for Hoopla.

'Let's try it this way Hoopla', she says. She takes one end of the rope and gives the other end to Nolo to hold.

'Okay, Hoopla, stand beside the rope, then when I say JUMP, just jump', Slye orders.

'Turn the rope with me', she tells Nolo. The rope makes a huge circle in the air.

As it comes toward the ground, Slye yells, 'JUMP!' and Hoopla jumps over the rope.

'Jump! Jump! Jump! Jump!' Slye chants.

'Look! I'm doing it!' yells Hoopla. Then he trips on the rope and falls in a heap.

'Oh blow!' he cries, but he's smiling.

'I did it!' he says. 'Thanks to you friends!'

A Green Teepee

13 JUNE

Bouncer Brachio is in his garden.

'Gosh! Everything has started to get really big!' he exclaims.

'It's amazing how fast things grow, isn't it?' laughs Grandad Brachio.

'Look, Grandad. The corn is really getting tall', Bouncer cries.

He measures his corn plants against his leg. 'They are already up to my knees, and it's only the middle

114

of June', he laughs. 'It will be knee high by the start of July', Grandad says.

'You have short knees', he continues, 'but you will have corn to eat before long'.

'And here – look at this! My teepee!'

Bouncer points at the leafy green teepee. His string bean plants are curling around the poles that make it a teepee shape.

'I'm going in', he laughs, and he wiggles in.

'It's nice and cool in here', comes a voice from inside the teepee. 'I'm going to stay in here for a little while', Bouncer says.

Bouncer looks around his teepee. The sunlight is soft and a little green inside. Small insects buzz around the bean vines.

'I'm sure you like living here', he says to the insects. He breaks off a string bean and chews it.

'Mmm, yummy, even if it is raw! I'll pick some for lunch', he decides.

Later, Bouncer's grandmother cooks the beans, and yes, they are even more delicious!

Father's Day Secret

14 JUNE

Bouncer Brachio is busy with a secret project. Father's Day is coming, and he's making a lovely present for his daddy.

'I've almost finished Mummy', says Bouncer proudly, waving a colourful picture.

'That looks lovely!' says Mummy.

'I've put everything in it', Bouncer says proudly. 'Daddy is standing there in the camping ground. And there's the sun, trees, a campfire and tents. And, of course, me!'

'Now you can take your picture to the post office', Mummy says. She slides the picture into an envelope, writes an address on it, and gives Bouncer some money. He puts the money in the envelope and then skips to the post office.

'Mrs. Trico, can you please send this for me?' he asks the postmistress.

'Of course, Bouncer', she smiles. She gives Bouncer the stamps he needs.

'I like the taste of the stamps', he grins.

'Looks like something important!' Mrs. Trico says. She gives Bouncer a wink.

'Yes! And it's a secret!' he replies. 'But I'll tell you. It's a picture. Someone is going to put it on a t-shirt for Daddy for Father's Day'.

'Oh, he's going to love that', smiles Mrs. Trico. She puts the envelope in the post bag.

Bouncer skips back home.

He can't wait for Father's Day to arrive. His daddy will be so happy!

June

Flood

'Help! Help! Emergency!' yells Ivan, running to Mr. Horse's house.

'What's wrong, Ivan?' Mr. Horse calls out.

'There's a flood on the road!' cries Ivan. 'I think the fire hydrant is broken!'

'I'll come straight away', cries Mr. Horse. 'Just let me get my toolbox and I'll be right there!'

They run to the centre of the village, where they find that water is gushing out of the fire hydrant.

'Oh no. What a mess!' cries Mr. Horse.

He runs to the fire station and turns on a loud siren.

Weee-uuu! Weee-uuu! goes the siren.

Villagers come running from everywhere. They are all volunteer fire fighters.

'Where's the fire? Where's the fire?' they shout.

'It's not a fire! It's water!' yells Mr. Horse back. 'I think a pipe has broken!'

He turns off the siren.

'We've got to turn the water off!' someone says.

Mr. Horse digs around in his toolbox and comes up with a big, heavy wrench.

'Unnngh! Unnngh!' he grunts, turning a knob on the hydrant.

'Well done, Mr. Horse', calls Ivan as the water slows down to a little trickle.

'We'll have to repair it properly tomorrow, but this will do for today. What a mess!' Mr. Horse sighs. There's water everywhere!

Boat Race

The friends loved all the excitement over the fire hydrant flood yesterday.

'Look, it's still running!' says Slye Snake as they meet at the hydrant.

'And it's making a little river!' calls Nolo. He picks up a stick and sends it floating down the stream.

'Let's have a boat race!' says Slye. 'Everybody get a stick or something that can be your boat!'

They find sticks and leaves nearby.

'Right, let's say this is the starting line. We'll put our boats in a row and see which one gets to the harbour first', Slye says.

The little boats bob gently as they float down the stream.

'Mine's winning!' cries Baabra Sheep.

'Mine's catching up!' Hoopla Hippo crows.

They walk along the stream, cheering for their own boats.

Suddenly all the boats slow down.

'What's going on?' complains Baabra.

'The water isn't moving as quickly any more', Hoopla says, looking puzzled.

'It's almost stopped', Baabra says, really disappointed.

'Ah, look back there!' cries Slye.

Behind them, the villagers are repairing the hydrant. The leak has stopped.

'Oh. Couldn't they wait until the race was over?' Baabra complains, with a smile. 'I don't know if you will all agree, but my boat was first when the water stopped. So I'm going to say I won!'

The friends look at her and then at each other. 'Yes Baabra, you win!' laughs Nolo, and they all clap for the winner.

Magnet Magic

Slye Snake is walking along the beach near Firefly Island harbour.

She spots a metal horseshoe half buried in the sand. 'Hmm', she thinks. 'That's strange. It's painted red, except for the ends'.

She takes it home and cleans it up in the garden shed. When she puts it on a shelf, a shiny nail starts sliding towards it! The nail sticks to one end of the horseshoe.

'It's magic!' she thinks.

She walks around, touching it against different things. In the kitchen, she touches the refrigerator and her horseshoe sticks to it!

'I think this is a magnet!' Slye thinks. She doesn't know much about them.

'I'll ask Mr. Horse', she decides, and she heads off to his house. He's at home.

'This is a horseshoe shape, Slye, but it's not a real shoe for a horse. It's a magnet, just as you guessed', says Mr. Horse. 'Watch', he goes on. He covers the magnet with a piece of paper and waves it over a little pile of paper clips on his desk.

'Hey presto!' he laughs. The paper clips jump up to the paper and stick to it!

'Wonderful!' cries Slye. 'I've found a real treasure! I want to play with it some more. Thank you, Mr. Horse!'

And she's off, touching things as she goes!

June

'The Best Daddy in the World', he says, reading the words printed on the shirt.

'Bouncer, did you draw this?' he asks, amazed. 'It's me! At the camping ground!'

'Yes!' cries Bouncer excitedly. 'And look at me and all my friends? I did it all myself!'

'Bouncer, this is wonderful. I'll wear it now and at work tomorrow', smiles Daddy.

'Then everybody will know you're the best Daddy in the world', laughs Bouncer.

'Thank you Bouncer, I love you', Daddy grins.

Cozy Wants to Fly

19 JUNE

Flap! Flappity flap! Flap-flap-flap!

The tiny chick, Cozy, is trying to learn how to fly. Her mummy, Hotta Toucan, is working in the café, so Cozy is in her playpen in the corner.

'Hello, Mr. Ptera!' calls Hotta as the general store owner comes in. 'Time for a nice, hot cup of coffee?' she asks.

'Oh yes please', he smiles. 'The store can take care of itself for ten minutes!'

Cozy has been flapping away all this time.

'Fly! Fly! Fly!' she cheeps.

'I see Cozy is getting ready to fly', chuckles Mr. Ptera. 'Shall I give her a lesson?'

'Of course! Give it a try!' laughs Hotta.

Mr. Ptera goes over to Cozy and flaps his leathery

Father's Day Surprise

18 JUNE

It's Father's Day at last, and Bouncer Brachio can't stand still. His present for Daddy came in the post yesterday. Mummy helped him to wrap it.

'Wake up, Daddy! It's Father's Day!' calls Bouncer as he and Mummy bring a special breakfast to Daddy in bed.

'Gosh, I feel really special', laughs Daddy.

'You are special!' cries Bouncer, giving his daddy a big hug.

'And I have a present for you too', adds Bouncer proudly. He hands Daddy a box.

Daddy unwraps it and takes out a t-shirt.

wings like mad. 'Do this, Cozy!' he calls. He flaps faster and faster.

Cozy flaps too, as fast as she can.

But Cozy stays stuck to the floor.

They flap and flap, staring hard at each other. Mr. Ptera lifts off the floor.

'Heee-heee-heee!' Hotta bursts out laughing. 'Mr. Ptera, you are teaching Cozy all the right things, but Cozy doesn't have her flying feathers yet! She can't fly!'

Mr. Ptera stops flapping, puffing a bit.

'You're right', he laughs. 'I forgot that you birds need feathers to fly. We pterosaurs have never needed them!'

I Doubt It!

20 JUNE

Nolo Giraffe, Bouncer Brachio and Hoopla Hippo are all playing a game of cards.

'One lemon!' announces Nolo, slapping a card on the table. Its picture side is down.

'I doubt it!' yells Hoopla. He gets to peek and see if Nolo was fibbing. 'Ha! It's a boat! Take it back', grins Hoopla. Nolo does.

'I'll never get rid of all these cards', thinks Nolo. 'If I don't, then I can't win'.

Bouncer puts down a card and says firmly, 'One chicken'. Nobody doubts him.

Hoopla puts down TWO cards, pretending they are one. 'One elephant!' he says.

Nolo looks hard at him but doesn't speak.

Now it's Nolo's turn. He puts down a card and cries, 'One boot!'

Bouncer shouts, 'I doubt it!' and he peeks. 'It's a duck! Take it back!'

'Two tomatoes!' Bouncer cries, looking guilty.

'I doubt it!' yell Nolo and Hoopla together. They get to peek. And it *is* two tomatoes!

'I won! I won! I don't have any more cards!' Bouncer cries.

'Oh dear! We were so busy doubting each other that Bouncer managed to get rid of all his cards!' cries Hoopla, and he starts laughing.

'HOOO, HO-HO-HO-HO!'

'HOOO, HO-HO-HO-HO!'

June

Midsummer's Night

21 JUNE

'Today is a special day. It's the longest day of the year', Mummy Zebra says as the family eats dinner this evening. 'It's called Midsummer's Night. Sunrise is the earliest it ever gets all year, and sunset is the latest it ever gets'.

'Is that why everybody is going to Firefly Meadow tonight?' Zig asks.

'Yes', says Daddy. 'There's a special treat for everyone after it gets dark!'

Zig can't wait to see what it will be.

Just after sunset, all the villagers meet at Firefly Meadow.

'Look over there', whispers Mummy Zebra as it gets darker.

'Ohhh!' cries Zag. 'There are little stars twinkling in the grass! See them?'

'The whole meadow is filled with tiny sparkling lights! What are they?' asks Zig.

'They're called fireflies – tiny insects that can light themselves up so they can find each other. This meadow and Firefly Island are named after them', explains Mummy.

'Super!' 'Wonderful!' 'Look over there!' whisper all the villagers.

The sparkling fireflies dance all around them.

'This is really magical', thinks Zag. 'I'm so glad we live here!'

A Double Party

22 JUNE

Baabra Sheep has called a secret meeting for the friends in the Hideout. But she hasn't told Zig and Zag about it, so they aren't there.

'Tomorrow is Zig and Zag Zebra's birthday', Baabra announces. 'What should we give them?'

'How about a pair of gloves or shoes?' asks Hoopla Hippo, with a naughty grin. 'That way they can have one each!'

Everybody laughs.

'No, I think we need to give each twin a present that's right for her', says Slye Snake. 'So what should we get for Zag?'

'She loves girly things', answers Baabra. 'How about a pink purse?'

Everybody thinks that's perfect.

'Zig is different from Zag, for certain', laughs Nolo Giraffe. 'She plays sports and loves nature'.

'Then how about a rucksack?' asks Hoopla. 'For all her sports things?'

The others nod. They have a plan!

Soon they are at Mrs. Brachio's gift shop.

'Look, this is perfect!' yells Baabra, holding up a shiny pink purse.

'And look at this!' Nolo says, trying on a nice rucksack.

'Just for fun, let's wrap the presents in the WRONG colour wrapping paper', laughs Hoopla. And that's what Mrs. Brachio does. Green for Zag, pink for Zig.

'I can't wait until tomorrow!' laughs Baabra.

Twice as Nice!

23 JUNE 'Here they come!' calls Zig excitedly as the friends arrive at the Zebras' house. Zag opens the door and they troop in.

'Happy Birthday, Zig! Happy Birthday, Zag!' they all shout.

Mummy Zebra joins them. 'I have a party game ready for you', she says mysteriously. 'Come out into the back garden'.

'It's called Stick the Tail on the Zebra!' she chuckles. 'Hoopla, you can go first'.

She hands Hoopla a bunch of string. 'This is a zebra tail. Your job is to stick it on that zebra over there', she says, pointing to a picture of a zebra with no tail, stuck onto a tree.

'That's easy!' hoots Hoopla. But then Mummy Zebra ties a scarf over Hoopla's eyes and spins him around and around.

'Ooh! I'm dizzy', he gasps, as he wobbles all over the place, feeling the air in front of him and searching for the tree.

He bumps into it and almost falls over.

'Aha!' he cries, and he sticks the zebra tail on the picture of the zebra - on its nose!

Everybody laughs and laughs as he takes off his scarf. Then they each have a go. Before long there are zebra tails all over the poor paper zebra.

'Now for some birthday treats', calls Mummy Zebra. The friends run inside.

'Gosh! Look at that!' exclaims Hoopla Hippo, licking his lips.

On the dining room table sit a beautiful birthday cake and a huge pie, with slices of green apples on the top.

'I know that Zig likes cake best, and Zag likes pie best, so I made both of their favourites. Now let's see how they taste!'

Of course, they are delicious. Double delicious!

June

Around the Island

24 JUNE

The whole village is at the dock today.

'Nolo, you did an excellent job naming our new ferry boat', says Mr. Horse, the mayor.

'You won a ferry boat ride all the way around Firefly Island today. Tonight you'll sleep at the camping ground and Captain Cow will bring you home tomorrow morning'.

'Yippee!' Nolo Giraffe yells, and he walks on board the *Tinker Bell*.

'Yippee!' cry Nolo's friends too. Why? Because they and their families can come as well!

Captain Cow rings the bell and they're off!

'Our first stop is the picnic ground, for a nice picnic lunch', Captain Cow says.

They eat sandwiches and go swimming. 'Next stop – the camping ground!' calls Captain Cow. And off they chug.

'I can see the camping ground!' yells Nolo soon. They set up their tents in the woods.

'Let's play hide and seek while our mummies and daddies cook dinner', Nolo says.

The friends have a great time playing in the woods.

'Dinner time!' calls out Nolo's mummy. The food cooked on the campfire tastes delicious.

'It's almost dark. Let's tell ghost stories around the campfire', Mr. Brachio says.

The stories are a bit scary, but fun.

'It was a wonderful day, but oh, I'm tired', yawns Nolo. He crawls into his tent and is fast asleep in seconds!

The Midnight Beast

25 JUNE

It is midnight in a dark tent. Bouncer Brachio is sleeping next to Hoopla Hippo, who is snoring.

On Bouncer's other side lies Nolo Giraffe.

Bouncer has just woken up.

He hears something outside the tent.

'What's that noise?' he thinks.

Bouncer holds his breath.

Silence. Then the noise again.

'What could it be?' he wonders.

The noise is coming closer. 'It's nothing, just the

wind', he whispers.

Another sound.

'Hoopla! Nolo! Wake up! There's something out there', Bouncer hisses.

They carry on sleeping.

Bouncer can't believe his friends can sleep while something scary is making noise just outside the tent. His heart is pounding and he's trembling. What can he do?

Bouncer grabs Hoopla's leg and gives it a shake. Hoopla snores away.

'Hoopla! Nolo! There's a monster out there!'

Bouncer whispers loudly. He shakes Hoopla's leg again.

Hoopla suddenly snorts and sits upright.

'Help! A monster!' he yells. 'It's got hold of me by the leg!'

'Hoopla!' cries Bouncer. 'That's me, you silly!'

A Real Sandwich Factory

It's Cooking Club day and the friends are going to make their own sandwiches. Mummy Hippo has set out all sorts of things to make them with.

'We've got cheese, sliced meat, peanut butter, lettuce and lots of different bread', she says.

'Yummy! I'm starving!' cries Hoopla Hippo.

'Just help yourselves', smiles Mummy.

'I'm going to make the tallest sandwich you have ever seen', says Hoopla.

'I'm going to make the skinniest, longest sandwich you have ever seen!' answers Slye Snake.

Hoopla starts piling things on his bread, and before long he has made a tower.

Slye takes one long, skinny loaf of bread and puts her things on it in a thin layer.

'Hoopla, can you eat all that?' Slye asks.

'Of course!' Hoopla replies, and he starts eating.

'Delicious!' he exclaims, chewing away.

A little while later, he's full, but he still has half of his sandwich left.

'Oooh, my tummy hurts!' he moans.

'Next time, make it half as high', says Slye smiling.

'That's a good idea!' sighs Hoopla. 'I wish I'd thought of that before'.

Mummy Hippo smiles and wraps the rest of his sandwich for tomorrow's lunch.

June

Firefly Tag

27 JUNE

Grandad Brachio and Bouncer are on the front porch of Grandad's cosy little farmhouse.

They are watching fireflies twinkle in Grandad's dark garden.

'Have I told you how to play Firefly Tag?' he asks. 'We used to play it when I was young'.

Bouncer shakes his head.

'You play it in the dark. One person is the firefly, and has a torch. The firefly hides and then silently counts to 30, then turns on the torch, just for a second. The firefly can move or stay still'.

'I understand', Bouncer nods. He is thinking fast. He has come up with a really good idea of how to win the game!

'The rest of the players stay in a group and count to 20. Then they split up and start looking for the firefly', Grandad says.

'When someone tags the firefly, they get to be the new firefly'.

'So let's get going!' says Grandad. He gives Bouncer a torch and starts counting.

Bouncer runs to his little garden and crawls inside his string bean teepee. Every time he counts to 30, he flashes the light of the torch on for a second, but Grandad can't find him!

'Bouncer, I give up! Come back!' he calls. And a proud Bouncer yells back, 'I won!'

Locked In!

28 JUNE

Slye Snake is at the library. She loves all the picture books.

'I'll borrow this one', she says, turning the pages of a book about a princess.

Suddenly Slye realises she needs to go to the bathroom. 'I've got to run!' she thinks.

She rushes to the bathroom and goes in, locking the door behind her.

'Phew! Just in time!' she giggles.

When she's finished she tries to unlock the door.

'It's stuck!' she exclaims. Her heart starts beating fast.

She shakes the door, but it won't open! 'Help! Help!' she shouts. But nobody comes. She looks around, thinking hard.

'Ah, wait a minute!' she suddenly says.

Slye bends right over and peeks through a narrow space under the door.

'I think I can squeeze out through here!'

And sure enough, she can fit through the space.

'I'm free! I'm free!' she cries. 'Gosh! I'm so glad that I'm skinny!'

Letters

It's almost bedtime.

Bouncer has had his bath, and now he's drawing a picture of his family.

'Mummy, can you write all the names for me?' he asks when he's finished.

Mummy tells him the name of each letter as she writes it, so Bouncer can learn them.

'When you know the letters, you'll almost be reading', Mummy smiles.

'And writing too', Bouncer sighs. 'That will be nice!' He yawns sleepily.

'You've made a really lovely picture, Bouncer, but now it's past your bedtime', Mummy says.

Bouncer's mummy tucks him into bed and gives him a goodnight kiss.

'Mummy, can you sing me a song?' Bouncer asks.

'Yes', says Mummy. 'A B C D E F G', she sings, starting the alphabet song.

But before the song has finished, Bouncer is asleep. He's dreaming of the day when he will be able to read and write.

Just like grown-ups do!

Lammie the Teaser

'Mummy!' cries Baabra Sheep angrily.

'Mummy!' echoes Lammie, her baby brother.

'Stop it!' yells Baabra.

'Stop it!' yells Lammie back.

'Mummy, please tell him to stop! Please!' cries Baabra.

'Mummy…', Lammie starts, but he can't say the rest. He's too little.

'Aha!' cheers Baabra. 'Got you!'

'Aha!' hoots Lammie back. 'Aha! Aha!'

'Mum-my!' wails Baabra.

'Mum-my!' laughs Lammie, having fun.

Mummy hears the noise and comes to see what is going on.

'He keeps saying everything I say!' yells Baabra.

'He…', starts Lammie.

'Oh, you sillies', laughs Mummy.

She tickles them until they can't stop laughing.

Finally, Lammie stops bothering his sister!

July

Bouncer's Made-Up Treat

1 JULY

Bouncer Brachio comes into the kitchen. He feels like cooking something new, so he looks in the cupboards.

'What's this?' He spots a packet of coconut flakes on the table. 'I have never seen those before. I wonder what they taste like?' he says to himself.

He opens the packet and tastes the flakes. They're crunchy, sweet – yummy!

He nibbles a few more.

'I wonder what Mummy makes with them?' he thinks. He eats another pinch of the coconut flakes and gets an idea.

Bouncer peels a banana and pours a little orange juice into a bowl. Then he dunks the banana in the juice and dips it into the coconut flakes. They stick to the banana.

He takes a bite.

'Oooh, delicious!' he smiles. He dips and dunks, dips and dunks. What a brilliant snack!

Just then Mummy comes in.

'Hello, Bouncer! I'm going to make – oh!' she exclaims. 'I suppose I'm not then!' she says.

'I was going to make you coconut cakes for dessert tonight, but I see you have made a really nice treat for us instead'.

Bouncer feels proud. 'I just tried making something new and different. And guess what?' he asks. 'It's really delicious!'

Just Like Mummy

2 JULY

Baabra Sheep loves doing girly things together with her mummy.

This morning, Baabra says, 'Mummy, can we have a 'Fancy Day' today?'

'Of course!' Mummy replies. 'What shall we do?'

'Oh... maybe put on some make-up, and do something fancy with my hair?' Baabra asks.

'That sounds like fun', Mummy smiles. 'Let's go upstairs and see what we can find'.

They both stand in front of a wide mirror.

'Here's some lipstick that will look good on you', Mummy says. She puts a little on Baabra's mouth. Baabra puckers up her lips.

'And this is for your eyelashes', Mummy adds, brushing them to make them prettier.

She squirts something on Baabra's neck.

'Oooh, that smells like flowers!' Baabra says.

Mummy ties a light blue bow in Baabra's curls and steps back to see how she looks.

'You look lovely!' Mummy smiles.

Then she quickly gets herself ready.

'Now let's go shopping', she cries.

Baabra claps and smiles. 'Oh yes! Thank you!'

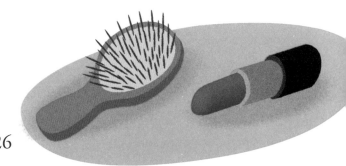

July

3 JULY — Scruffy Comes to Stay

Zig and Zag Zebra are at the dock, waiting for the *Tinker Bell* to arrive.

'I wonder what he's like', says Zig, peering at a photo she is holding of a young hyena.

'I really hope that he's nice', answers Zag. 'He'll be staying at our house all summer'.

They spot the *Tinker Bell*. Captain Cow toots the horn as the ferry docks.

'There he is!' cries Zag, pointing to a small furry figure looking at them. They clap and jump up and down. The figure does nothing.

'Hello, Scruffy! Welcome!' they shout, waving.

Scruffy just stares at them. Shortly, Captain Cow brings him over to Zig and Zag.

'Scruffy Hyena, this is Zig and that is Zag. Am I right?' she asks the twins. 'I hear that Scruffy is staying with your family this summer', adds Captain Cow. 'That will be lots of fun!'

'Maybe. Maybe not', says Scruffy.

Zig and Zag look at each other and blink.

'We hope you'll like it here, Scruffy', Zag says sweetly. 'Shall we go home now?'

'I suppose so', mutters Scruffy.

'It's this way, Scruffy', says Zag, and she leads the way towards their house.

Captain Cow shakes her head as she watches them leave. 'I really hope this works', she whispers to herself.

4 JULY — Lammie's Climb

Lammie Sheep is in his bedroom. He wants to look at some books.

'Books! Books!' he whispers, looking at a tall bookshelf filled with all his picture books.

There's a big book on the top shelf. It's far too high up for him to reach, but he wants to get it himself.

'Big book! Big book!' he squeals, and he starts to climb up the shelves to reach it.

'Uuunh! Uuunh!' he pants.

He reaches up.

'Help! Help!' he screams as the bookshelf starts to fall forwards. Books fall all over the place and the shelf lands on top of Lammie.

Mummy comes rushing into the room.

'Oh, no! Lammie, are you alright?' she cries.

Lammie has a cut on his nose and he's crying as if it's the end of the world.

'Oh, poor Lammie!' Mummy cries, wiping his nose. 'We'll have you sorted out in no time, but next time, please just ask me to get any of those big books down for you, will you?'

Lammie sniffs, nods, and says, 'Yes Mummy'.

5 JULY Finger Painting Without Fingers

Scruffy Hyena brought a present for Zig and Zag Zebra when he arrived.

'Here. For you', he says flatly. He hands it to them.

'Oooh!' squeal the twins at once.

'Lovely! Thank you!' they say together.

They open a box and find six jars of brightly coloured paints and a roll of shiny paper. They study these things carefully.

Then Zag asks, 'What is it?'

'Finger paint', Scruffy answers, without a smile. 'I know we don't have fingers, but we can still use it', he shrugs.

'Let's try it, Scruffy!' the twins say, and they take their gift to the kitchen table.

Soon they are covered in paint of all colours. Even Scruffy has joined in.

'Look! I can make my hoof prints!' cries Zig, clopping on her paper.

'Mine are big pads', says Scruffy, having fun now. He smears red and orange paint together, making a trail of brown prints.

Zag puts dots of different colours in a row and sweeps her leg in an arc, smearing them across the paper. 'Look! I've made a rainbow!' she cries.

Mummy Zebra comes into the kitchen and stares. 'My goodness! What a mess! But what fun! Scruffy, was this your present?'

Scruffy nods.

'It's wonderful!' Mummy cries, and she starts painting too.

'Whatever', Scruffy says.

Zig and Zag look at each other and shrug. They are both thinking that it is going to feel like a very long summer!

July

Slye Sleeps Over

6 JULY Slye Snake's mummy and daddy are going to a big dancing party on Big Island tonight.

They will be too late to catch the last ferry boat home, so they have asked Baabra Sheep's mummy if Slye could sleep at the Sheep's house.

'Of course!' says Mummy. 'We'd love that!'

Baabra is thrilled. 'Yippee! A slumber party!'

Slye arrives after dinner with a little suitcase. The friends play outside on the swings, eating popcorn that Mummy has made.

'Time for baths and bed', sings Mummy after sunset. The friends are soon tucked up in bed.

'Good night, Slye', whispers Baabra.

'Good night, Baabra, pleasant dreams', Slye replies. She falls fast asleep in a second.

Baabra is just starting to dream when something wakes her up.

Snnnrrr! Snnnrrr! Snnnrrr!

'Oh, my gosh!' whispers Baabra to herself. 'Slye is snoring! What can I do?'

She tries to sleep. She buries her head under her pillow, but then she can't breathe.

'I've got to make her stop!' she decides.

She gives Slye a little shake. 'Slye, please wake up. You're snoring', she whispers gently.

Slye turns over. Silence. Baabra yawns, but just as she starts to fall asleep, she hears S*nnnrrr. Snnnrrr. Snnnrrr* again.

Sighing, Baabra takes her pillow, goes down the hall, and climbs into her brother Lammie's crib with him.

'What a slumber party!' she giggles. Then she quickly falls asleep.

Yes You Were!

7 JULY 'Yes you were!'

'No I was not!'

Baabra Sheep and Slye Snake are eating breakfast the next morning. They are having a playful argument.

'You were going *Snnnrrr. Snnnrrr. Snnnrrr.* All night!' Baabra imitates Slye's snores, then giggles.

130

'No I was not!' Slye protests, laughing too. But Slye hates to think that she snores like Roota Rooster does sometimes, at the café.

Baabra's mummy tries to make the peace.

'I'm sure that if you were, Slye, it was very gentle snoring'. Slye rolls her eyes.

'In fact...' Mummy starts to say, but stops.

Slye's mummy and daddy have just arrived to pick Slye up. They are back from their dancing party on Big Island last night.

'Mummy! Daddy!' cries Slye, hugging her parents happily. 'Tell them I don't snore!'

Her mummy pats Slye's head and smiles. 'Well, Slye, I have to say that you do, sometimes. Very quietly. I think a lot of we snakes do. We have very tiny noses', she explains.

'Well, Slye, we're still best friends, you know!' Baabra says, trying to make Slye feel better.

'You should be best friends', adds Baabra's mummy, 'because I was just about to say that you snore too!'

Hoopla Gets Cool at Last

8 JULY

It's scorching hot today. That's a real problem for Hoopla Hippo.

'If I didn't have this thick hide and chubby body, I'd feel much cooler', he grumbles. 'Maybe there's a breeze outside', he thinks.

But the air is still in the back garden. Just then, a tiny, bright yellow bird flies past and lands in the bird bath nearby. It dips into the water and splashes a little spray of drops on itself.

Hoopla smiles as he watches. 'Lucky you, little thing. I'd love to be able to do that too, but I'm too big for the bird bath'.

Suddenly he has a brilliant idea.

'Mummy, can I make a hippo bath?' he calls. 'Of course!' she replies. 'I'll come out and watch!'

Hoopla peers into the garden shed.

'Hmmm', he says. He finds a watering can and a shovel. 'All I need to do is dig a hole and then add water!' he thinks.

He goes to a corner of the garden and digs a pile of earth out, making a nice hippo-shaped hole with high sides.

'I'd better check to make sure I fit', he says, settling into it. 'A perfect hippo bath!' he laughs.

Then he fills the watering can from the tap on the side of the house and pours it in. After a few trips, his hippo bath is full.

'Aaahhh!' he sighs, sliding into the water. He waves at the little yellow bird, who is still enjoying the bird bath. The little yellow bird chirps happily back at him.

July

Making Captain Cow Laugh

9 JULY

Nolo Giraffe has been collecting cow jokes to tell Captain Cow. He wants to give her a few laughs to thank her for the job visit he will soon be making to her.

'Hello, Captain Cow. Do you know what you call a dancing cow?' he asks.

'I have no idea Nolo', she smiles.

'A milk shake!' Nolo replies.

'That's funny!' she giggles.

'And what do cows do on the internet?' he asks.

'I don't know. Look for MOO-seums?' she asks.

'Not bad, eh?'

'Close', laughs Nolo. 'No. They send each other MOOsages!'

'Oh, Nolo, now you've really got to stop', the captain laughs.

'Just one more. What happens to a cow when it stands out in the rain?' Nolo asks very seriously.

Captain cow thinks and thinks. Finally, she has to give up. 'I'm afraid you're going to tell me', protests the captain.

'She gets wet!' crows Nolo.

Ivan's Contraption

10 JULY

'I am so excited!' exclaims Ivan Monkey.

He's been working very hard for days, building something in his back garden. Today it's finally finished. He is excited and proud.

'My very own catapult!' he breathes, looking at his strange wooden contraption.

It has a flat piece that holds something you want to throw, and a complicated collection of bits and pieces that do the throwing.

'Time to test it out', Ivan says to himself. 'I wonder if it will work! But what should I try throwing?' he asks.

He looks around his garden, and spots a long row

132

of tomatoes growing in the corner.

'Aha! Perfect!' He runs to get a basket and fills it with hard, green unripe tomatoes. 'I can't eat all these anyway', he thinks. 'So just a few unripe ones will do perfectly'.

'Here goes!' he says to himself as he puts a green tomato in the holder.

He pulls back the catapult's arm, and lets go.

The tomato flies out of sight, high over his roof.

'Amazing! It works!' he crows. 'Usually, nothing I make ever works!'

He sends green tomatoes flying out of sight into the sky. After the last of them has gone, he sits down to admire his machine.

'I wonder how far they went before they landed', he asks himself. He will soon find out!

11 JULY — It's Raining Tomatoes!

All over the village yesterday, hard green tomatoes fell out of the sky.

Some hit rooftops – *Splat!* – and slid down to the ground.

Some landed – *Plop!* – on pavements.

One hit – *Ping!* – the clock on the village hall.

Another bounced – *Boing! Boing! Boing!* – along the main street, scaring the villages who were out walking there.

And one – *Clunk!* – hit poor Mr. Horse on the head. There's no telling what damage it might have done to his hair!

'Are they coming from outer space?' asks Hotta Toucan, serving coffee in her café.

'What can we do?' asks Mrs. Trico when people come to pick up their post from the post office.

'How can this happen?' they all wonder.

Ivan Monkey slept late this morning. He is waking up slowly, tired but very happy with his latest experiment. He decides to go to the café for some morning coffee.

'What in the world is going on?' he wonders as he sees the villagers talking and waving their arms at the news board.

'Look at all this mess!' Mr. Ptera says, pointing to the remains of green tomatoes lying around. He spots Ivan coming up to the group.

'Hello Ivan. You're a scientist. Can you tell us what happened here yesterday?' he asks.

'I… er, I don't have the faintest idea', gulps Ivan. He rushes home, really embarrassed!

Firefly Meadow Rescue

12 JULY

Summer evenings are beautiful on Firefly Island. Villagers walk up to Firefly Meadow after dinner and watch the sunset.

The Zebra family has taken a picnic supper there this evening to show Scruffy the lovely place.

'Nice', he says, but mostly he is quiet.

'Can we stay until it's dark and show Scruffy the fireflies?' asks Zag.

'Yes, can we do that?' Zig chimes in.

Daddy laughs and says, 'What a good idea!'

The sun sets in a swirl of orange and red, and soon the fireflies start twinkling.

'Look, Scruffy, there they are! Let's go find a few', cries Zig. The zebra twins gallop towards a cloud of sparkling fireflies.

Scruffy follows them, but then he wanders off on his own. 'I wonder what the woods are like', he says to himself. He leaves the meadow and walks into the woods.

'It really is dark here. There are no fireflies either', he whispers. He's feeling rather sad and lonely.

'I had better get back to the Zebras', he thinks, but now he isn't sure where the meadow is. It's a bit scary in the dark woods, and he's alone.

Scruffy wanders this way and that, but he can't find the meadow. He's deep in the woods now.

'How can I find my way out?' he worries.

Suddenly he sees twinkling lights coming through the trees. He runs towards them.

'The fireflies! The meadow!' he cries, as he bursts out of the woods. The Zebra family is anxiously calling his name.

'I'm here!' he yells. 'The fireflies saved me!'

Teepee Time

13 JULY

Bouncer Brachio hasn't had time to visit his garden for quite a while.

'I wonder how it's coming along?' he asks as he grabs his big, floppy farmer's hat and cycles off to his grandparents' little farm.

'Hello, Farmer Bouncer!' Grandad Brachio calls. 'As you're wearing that hat, I suppose you want to see how your garden is growing!'

'Yes please', laughs Bouncer. 'Let's go and see!'

So they walk to the garden.

'Gosh!' Bouncer crows. 'Everything's so BIG!'

'You can start picking your lettuce and even some of the baby carrots', Grandad smiles.

They fill a basket with fresh vegetables.

'Look Grandad. Look over here!' Bouncer calls a moment later.

Bouncer's green bean teepee is now a tall, leafy tent. 'Look! The bean plants have climbed right up the poles we put in a few months ago! You can't even see the poles any more. It's all leaves!'

'When I was a boy I loved sitting in my own teepee, just like yours', remembers Grandad.

'Why don't you crawl in now Grandad?' Bouncer asks jokingly.

'I think I will!' Grandad replies. He gets down on his hands and knees and disappears inside.

Bouncer laughs – he can't believe his eyes.

'That's MY teepee', Bouncer giggles.

'That's what you think', answers Grandad. 'I think I'll just settle down for a little nap. See you in half an hour Bouncer', he adds.

'Ha! Alright!' laughs Bouncer, and off he goes.

Butterfly Hunter

14 JULY

Zag Zebra loves nature. She thinks exploring the outdoors is wonderful.

'I want to go butterfly hunting in Firefly Meadow', she thinks. She gets her butterfly net and things and cycles to the sunny meadow.

A breeze rustles the tall grass. 'It looks like water. I love that', she thinks.

Zag wanders around, hunting for butterflies.

'There's one!' she whispers. With a quick sweep of her net, she catches a beautiful yellow, orange and black butterfly.

'I'll put it in my collecting jar', she says. 'Then I can really look at it properly'.

The butterfly beats its wings inside the jar, and then settles down. Zag studies the beautiful butterfly for a long time. Then she walks further in the grass.

'Oh, look at that one!' she cries.

Sweep! goes her net.

'Got it!' she cries.

Soon a black and white butterfly is in a second jar.

'What a beauty', she thinks.

'I can't wait to show them to Zig and Mummy and Daddy and Scruffy', she says to herself.

Both butterflies start to flutter in their jars.

'Hmmm', she thinks. 'They don't seem very happy in there. I suppose I wouldn't be, either. Should I let them go?' she wonders.

'Why not? I can always catch others, look at them and let them go too', she decides.

She opens the two jars and the butterflies flutter out. 'Good bye for now!' she waves.

135

The Great Jumping Competition

15 JULY

Mr. Ptera, who runs the general store, is talking to Doctor Henny while she shops for groceries. 'Did you see the poster on the village news board?' she asks.

Mr. Ptera shakes his head.

'The Great Jumping Competition is going to be next week!' she says.

'Oh, that's wonderful!' he exclaims. 'Though that doesn't me give much time to plan what I'll do. Still, it's always such fun!'

'I can't wait. Roota Rooster and I are working on our plan already', smiles Dr. Henny. 'Bye bye!' she calls as she leaves.

'What is that all about?' asks Mr. Zebra, who is also out shopping for groceries. His family is new to Firefly Island, so he doesn't know what the Great Jumping Competition is.

Mr. Ptera explains. 'You try to think up the funniest way to jump off the dock and into the water', he says. 'You can do it on your own, or in a team. The winner gets a prize!'

'That sounds like a lot of fun!' laughs Mr. Zebra. 'I'll tell my family about it. Perhaps we'll enter'.

'Good luck if you do. Your family won the Leap Year Contest, so maybe you can win this one too!' laughs Mr. Ptera. 'Bye for now!'

'Good bye, and good luck to you too!' chuckles Mr. Zebra. But Mr. Ptera is already thinking hard about what he is going to do.

'Perhaps something to do with a kite?' he asks himself, a dreamy smile on his face.

Swimming Lessons

16 JULY

All the youngsters on Firefly Island learn to swim. They take lessons from Bouncer Brachio's daddy.

Scruffy Hyena has never learned to swim. 'Why would I? Where I live, it's dry most of the year', he explains to the friends, frowning. 'Anyway, I'm afraid of water', he adds.

'But it's so much fun!' laughs Hoopla Hippo.

The friends are cycling to the camping ground for today's lesson with Mr. Brachio.

'Hello, everybody!' he calls as they jump into the water. 'You must be Scruffy', he calls to the little hyena, who is standing nervously on the beach.

'Hello', Scruffy mumbles.

'Don't you like swimming?' asks Mr. Brachio.

'I don't know. I've never tried', mutters Scruffy.

'Well, let's start in the shallow water!' He helps Scruffy walk a little way into the water. The friends are splashing, diving, shouting and having lots of fun all around him.

'Just let yourself float, and then doggy-paddle… er, I mean, hyena-paddle… your paws', urges Mr. Brachio, holding Scruffy up in the water.

Scruffy is stiff with fear. But he slowly relaxes. His feet start paddling, all by themselves!

'Brilliant!' cries Mr. Brachio. 'You're swimming! Excellent Scruffy!' Scruffy swims off.

'Gosh, I really am swimming!' Scruffy shouts. Soon he's paddling around with the rest of the swimmers.

'I can't believe it!' he yips.

Nolo's Upside Down House

17 JULY

Nolo Giraffe has a sore throat – a very looong, sore throat.

Because of it, he has to stay in bed today.

'I've slept and I've read and I've done all my puzzles. So what can I do now?' he asks himself.

'Ah, I know. I'll play my upside down game!' he thinks happily.

Nolo likes to imagine his whole house has been turned upside down.

Then he pictures himself walking around in it, on the ceiling, which is now the floor!

He closes his eyes. 'I think I'll go to the kitchen for a glass of water', he decides.

'I need to step over the top of my bedroom door frame and walk down the hall on the ceiling. Then I step over the kitchen door frame'.

He thinks a minute.

'I have to reach up to the sink to turn on the water. I suppose the water will run upwards! It will be hard to catch it in a glass!' he chuckles.

He looks at pictures on the walls, and sees that they are all upside down too. 'What a strange, upside down world!' he murmurs.

But all this imagining is making him sleepy.

In his mind he drinks his glass of water and then goes back to bed.

But now, he is dreaming. Nolo is fast asleep!

July

Boat Building

18 JULY

The friends are making plans for the Great Jumping Competition. They want to enter it as a team.

'We could build something that we could all sit in, then roll it into the water', dreams Hoopla Hippo, 'but that sounds really difficult to do'.

'Yes', agrees Slye Snake. 'What about a big paper boat without a bottom? Like this'.

She draws a picture and shows it to the team. 'What do you think?' she asks.

'Yes!' 'Fabulous!' 'Super!' Everybody loves it.

'Right', says Slye, the planner. 'We need lots of coloured paper, some long, thin pieces of wood, glue and a captain's hat. Let's all look for those things and meet back here in an hour'.

The friends all cheer and run home. Soon they are making their boat.

'Slye, I had no idea this would be so easy!' laughs Zig.

'It's a good thing that it doesn't need to float, though', giggles Zag. 'And good thing we all can swim!' she adds, smiling at Scruffy. He doesn't answer, but she thinks that he looks rather proud!

'There! It's done!' exclaims Nolo Giraffe.

'Nolo, since you love boats, you should be the captain and sit at the front', Slye says. 'Let's see how well she sails!'

They climb into their paper boat with lots of laughing and practise stepping left-right-left-right

together until they can move fairly fast.

'This is going to be so much fun!' laughs Captain Nolo. 'Yo-ho-ho!' He waves his hat.

Umbrella Tunnel

19 JULY

All the friends are at the Hideout, moaning about the rain outside. Their umbrellas stand dripping in one corner.

'What can we do that's fun?' asks Baabra Sheep grumpily.

Everybody thinks. Suddenly Hoopla Hippo perks up. 'Let's make an umbrella tunnel!'

'A what?' blinks Baabra.

'Just watch', answers Hoopla.

'Right everybody, open your umbrellas and put

them in a row on the floor. Put them so one handle points to one side, then the next handle points to the other'.

They bustle around the Hideout. Soon they have a brightly coloured, slightly wet tunnel.

'Now let's crawl in and see what it feels like!' Hoopla exclaims, wriggling and squeezing his way between the umbrella handles.

Laughing and grunting, the friends cram themselves into their tunnel.

'Gosh! There isn't much room!' laughs Baabra.

'But it's really pretty, with all the different colours of our umbrellas', answers Slye Snake. They gaze around at their tunnel.

'Three cheers for Hoopla!' calls Baabra.

'Hip-hip-hooray! Hip-hip-hooray! Hip-hip-hooray!'

Hoopla laughs, 'Phew! Saved the day!'

Washing Day

20 JULY

'It's washing day!' Grandmother Brachio says to Grandad as they eat breakfast. 'Please make sure all your dirty clothes are in the basket'.

'Yes dear', smiles Grandad. 'Can I help?'

'Oh, no thanks', she laughs.

'Let me know if I can do anything', he says and he heads off, out to their garden.

Grandmother puts the dirty clothes in the washing machine and adds soap powder. She turns the machine on and it starts swishing.

Soon the clothes have all been washed.

'Now I'll hang them out to dry. It's breezy, so they should dry quickly', Grandmother thinks.

She carries a basket of clothes to the clothes line next to the garden and hangs them up.

'There. That's done! I'll make some soup for our lunch while they dry'.

She chops up some vegetables from their garden and makes a wonderful pot of soup.

'There's just enough time to bring the dry clothes in before we eat', she thinks.

She takes her basket out to the clothes line. But where are the clothes? They have all vanished!

'What in the world?' she cries. Grandad hears her and comes running.

'All our clothes have disappeared!' she exclaims.

'Oh, that explains it!' laughs Grandad.

He takes her hand and leads her to the far side of the garden. 'I think you forgot to use your clothes pegs, dear. The clothes all blew into our bushes!'

'Oh, silly me!' laughs Grandmother. 'But the good news is that they are all dry!'

July

21 JULY — Getting Ready to Jump

'Let's go and watch the villagers get ready for the Great Jumping Competition', Nolo Giraffe says to the friends.

They hurry to the dock.

Mr. Horse is setting up a tent.

'What's your tent for?' asks Slye Snake.

'I don't want anyone to see my outfit until the last second', smiles Mr. Horse. 'I really do hope I win. It would be my first time!'

Slye nods, knowing just how he feels.

Nearby on the dock, Ivan Monkey is setting up his catapult. It's much too big to hide.

Bouncer Brachio asks, 'What are you going to throw this time, Ivan? Not green tomatoes, I hope!'

'Shhh! That's my little secret!' he says sneakily, hammering away.

'Let's practise our walk again!' Nolo says.

All the friends line up in a row, with Nolo first. They are giggling and pushing each other around in fun. Nolo takes charge.

'Left! Right! Left! Right!' he cries, and they march forwards in step. Except for Hoopla Hippo, who uses the wrong foot every time. Then he trips and falls flat on his face.

'Oh no, Hoopla', groans Nolo, but Hoopla is laughing his head off.

'How can we ever win?' wonders Nolo. 'Still, it will be a lot of fun trying'.

22 JULY — The Competition

'Welcome to the Great Jumping Competition!' roars Mr. Horse through his megaphone. The whole village is by the shore, excited and wearing funny costumes. The friends go first. They stand inside their bottomless paper boat.

'Left! Right! Left! Right!' Nolo calls from the front. They march their boat right off the end of the dock, making a terrific splash.

'Hooray!' yells the crowd as they bob around.

'It's Ivan Monkey's turn!' honks Mr. Horse.

Ivan sits on his catapult. He pinches his nose and pulls on the string to fling himself into the water. *Craaack!* The catapult falls apart. 'Oh no!' exclaims Ivan. 'I'm much heavier than a tomato!'

Doctor Henny and Roota Rooster go next. 'We chickens hate getting wet, so we have these', she says, pointing to their diving suits and flippers. They flop down the dock and dive in.

'Watch out! Here I come!' yells Mr. Ptera, running with a red kite flying behind him. He doesn't watch where he's going, and he runs straight off the dock. *Neigh! Neigh! Neigh!* Mr. Horse thunders out of his tent on a skateboard! He is wearing a black mask and cape, and waving a wooden sword. At the very end he rears up, makes a Z in the air, yells 'Zorro!' and soars into the water. The villagers all cheer madly. He's the winner, everyone agrees!

'At last! I won!' he cries. A big day for him!

July

'Cozy, can you at least say please?' asks Hotta, not quite as patiently as before.

'Peas! Peas!' squeals Cozy.

She tilts her head and peeps, 'Feed me!'

'No, not peas, Cozy. Can you say please?' Hotta laughs, scooping up more seeds.

Cozy gets so excited that she starts flapping her tiny wings. One of them hits the spoon, and seeds fly all over the floor.

'Oh Cozy, what a mess!' Hotta sighs. She quickly sweeps up the seeds.

Cozy watches all of this quietly. As she opens her mouth to say something, Hotta quickly says, 'Feed me! Please! Feed me! Please!'

Cozy's mouth closes and she peers at Hotta for a moment. She makes up her little mind.

'Feed me! Please! Feed me! Please!'

'Oh Cozy, you did it!' croons Hotta.

'Feed me! Please! Feed me! Please!' chirps Cozy again. And Hotta does so, with a big smile.

Cozy Learns a New Word

23 JULY

'Feed me! Feed me!' cries the tiny chick, Cozy, every time she's hungry. Like now. Her mummy, Hotta Toucan, loves Cozy's chirps. But she would like Cozy to say other things too.

It's lunch time and Cozy is in her baby seat.

'Feed me! Feed me!' she cheeps.

'Can you say bird seed?' asks Hotta, waving a spoonful of seeds in front of Cozy.

'Feed me! Feed me!' calls Cozy even louder.

Hotta gives Cozy some seeds. Cozy is quiet while she grinds them up.

'Feed me! Feed me!' calls Cozy again, once her mouth is empty.

Scruffy Gets a Letter

24 JULY

Zig and Zag Zebra and Scruffy Hyena are picking up their post from the post office.

'I see you have a letter today Scruffy', smiles kindly Mrs. Trico, the postmistress.

'Really?' Scruffy yips, surprised.

'Here it is', Mrs. Trico says, handing it to him. It's

covered with stamps. 'I see it came from Africa. That's where your family lives, isn't it?'

'Yes', he mumbles. He shoves the letter into his pocket. Zig and Zag look at each other with big eyes, but say nothing.

Back at their house, they whisper to Mummy Zebra that Scruffy has a letter.

'Scruffy, would you like me to read your letter to you?' Mummy asks gently.

'I suppose so', mutters Scruffy.

'Dear Scruffy', she reads. 'We miss you so much and hope you are having fun with the Zebras. We are fine, but there is not much to eat and water is hard to find. Please ask the Zebras to help you to write back to us. Love from Mummy and Daddy and all the little Hyenas'.

Scruffy coughs and looks away.

'It must be hard to be so far from your family', Mummy whispers. Zig and Zag sigh.

'Yes', Scruffy answers. 'I'll write back soon'.

'That would really make your family happy', says Mummy. 'Tell me when you're ready'.

Zig and Zag want to show Scruffy they feel sorry for him, but how? 'Scruffy, let's play in the back garden', says Zig finally. He smiles. It worked!

The Name Game

Baabra Sheep is in her bedroom. 'What shall I do today?' she asks herself. Her eyes sweep over her dolls and toys. 'I know!' she exclaims. 'I'm going to give all my dolls and toys new names!'

She picks up a fluffy green dragon.

'You're Belcher, because you always blow smoke and fire out of your mouth and nose', she says.

Next she goes to a brown leather pony. 'You're Shoe-Shoe. You're made out of leather, like a shoe, and you need horseshoes. I mean, pony shoes!'

'You're Boo', she announces to a tiny, white ghost puppet. 'You scare everybody'.

'And you're Twinkletoes', she laughs, picking up a ballerina doll. She dances it across her pillow.

'Who are you?' she asks a woodpecker doll. 'Oh, of course. You must be Rat-a-Tat-Tat!'

Mummy Sheep has been listening to Baabra from out in the hall.

'And what about you, Baabra?' she asks. 'What would your name be if you got a new one?'

'Ah, that's not easy', Baabra is thinking hard.

'I think I know what I'd name you', Mummy answers. 'You'd be Curlylocks!'

'Curlylocks?' asks Baabra.

'Because you have such curly, soft fleece!' laughs Mummy, patting Baabra's head. 'Curlylocks it is', nods Baabra, and she fluffs up her fleece to make it even curlier. 'I like my new name!'

July

Measuring Tape

26 JULY

'My daddy got a wonderful thing for his birthday', Hoopla Hippo tells Nolo Giraffe today.

'Oh? What is it?' Nolo asks.

'A measuring tape'. Hoopla asks. 'Look'.

Hoopla shows Nolo a flat, shiny metal box. It has a sort of tongue sticking out of one edge.

'Look? You can pull the tape out', Hoopla explains, pulling on the metal tongue, 'and these marks tell you how long things are'.

Nolo and Hippo don't know their numbers yet, but that doesn't matter to them.

Hoopla pulls and pulls. The tape gets longer and longer. Nolo really wants to try it!

'Then when you've finished, you do this!' Hoopla says dramatically. He presses on a yellow button on the side of the tape measure.

Zzzippp! The tape slithers back into the box. But it still has a long piece sticking out.

'Oh no. I've broken it!' cries Hoopla.

'Here, let me try', says Nolo. He presses on the button and the rest of the tape slides in.

'That's lucky!' says Nolo. 'Can I try it?'

'Of course!' Hoopla says. Nolo walks around the garden, pulling the tape out to measure a chair.

'Eleven-teen. Eighty-teen. Two', he calls out, as if he knows his numbers.

Then he zips the tape back into its box. 'Gosh. I'm glad it worked this time!' he crows.

'I had better put it back now', Hoopla says. 'Daddy will be home soon'. Nolo grins.

Roota Rooster's Treasures

27 JULY

Roota Rooster is scratching away in the earth, having a wonderful time.

He has a new magnifying glass, which makes everything so much clearer!

'Treasures, treasures!' he clucks. Huge clouds of dust fill the air.

'Got you!' he cries suddenly, and jabs at something with his beak.

It's not a worm. It's a shiny silver button. 'A beauty!' he croons, flapping his wings, arching his neck and crowing.

Roota carefully carries the button to a tin can. He drops the button in and cocks his head so his little eyes can see inside. 'Aha!' he clucks.

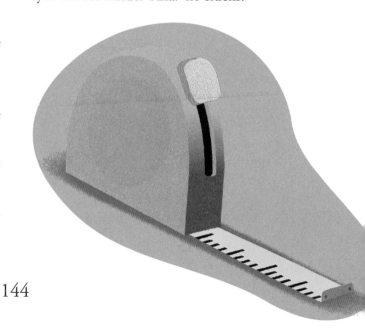

Dr. Henny, Roota's wife, comes home from work. 'Did you have a good day, dear?' she asks.

'Yes!' Roota spills all his twinkling things into the light. 'One silver spoon. Three shiny nails. A ball of tin foil. Two bright green bottle caps. A key chain with a gold key. A coin. A piece of blue glass and a paper clip. Just look at all my treasures!' he crows, pulling himself up tall and flapping again.

'My goodness Roota', Dr. Henny chuckles. 'You have been busy!'

Roota nods happily. 'And I can't wait for tomorrow!' he crows. 'More treasures!'

Dr. Henny smiles. 'Yes, dear!' She knows him very well. He's a born treasure hunter.

Nolo's Job Visit

Nolo Giraffe is really excited! He's wearing a bright orange life jacket for his job visit to Captain Cow on the *Tinker Bell.*

'Right, Nolo, blow the horn with one long blast and then three short ones', Captain Cow says. 'The long blast warns everyone we're leaving the dock. The three short ones say we're reversing'.

Nolo grabs the cord and pulls down hard.

Tooooooot! Then he pulls down three times, quickly.

Tooot-tooot-tooot!

'Excellent!' says Captain Cow. 'We're off!'

She looks all around to make sure nobody is in the way, then slides the ferry away from the dock. The motor churns up the water.

'Please collect our passengers' tickets now', Captain Cow says, and Nolo hurries off.

When he comes back, Captain Cow counts them and puts them in a little box.

Then she says, 'Would you like to steer for a little while?' Nolo's eyes get huge. 'Yes please!'

He gives the giant steering wheel a little turn. The ferry gently moves to the right.

'Oooh. I never thought I could steer a ferry!' he yells over the motor's low rumble.

Captain Cow laughs. 'Right, we're there. Sound one long blast so everyone knows we're docking, Nolo'.

Tooooooot!

'Today is definitely one of the best days of my life!' Nolo crows.

Paa-tueee!

29 JULY

The friends are sitting outside the Hideout. It's a hot afternoon, but they are having lots of fun.

Slye Snake has brought slices of cold watermelon to share with everyone.

'This tastes wonderful', hoots Hoopla Hippo after his first bite.

'Watermelon is my favourite fruit in the whole wide world', exclaims Baabra Sheep.

'I have never tried it before', says Scruffy Hyena. 'It's really good!'

'Watch this, Scruffy', says Bouncer Brachio. He takes a bite of watermelon, chews and swallows, and then puckers up his mouth.

Paa-tueee! He spits a watermelon seed out. It flies deep into the woods.

'Ha! I can do better than that!' cries Zag Zebra. *Paa-tueee!*

Everyone laughs, because Zag's seed really does go further than Bouncer's! Soon everybody is spitting seeds all over the place. It's a fun game that they have just invented.

Paa-tueee! Paa-tueee! Paa-tueee!

'I could never do this at home', gasps Slye.

'Nor me', giggles Zag. *Paa-tueee!*

They all stand in a row. Everyone gets one try to see who can spit a seed the furthest.

Zag wins.

'I told you so!' she crows. 'The World Champion!'

Two Jokers

30 JULY

The next day, Hoopla comes to Bouncer's house to play.

'Wasn't that fun yesterday, spitting the watermelon seeds?' he chuckles. 'My daddy had a good riddle for me when I told him about it last night'.

'What's the riddle?' asks Bouncer.

'When do you *go on red* and *stop on green*?' asks Hoopla.

'Hmmm', Bouncer says slowly, thinking hard. 'I have no idea. I give up!'

'When you're eating a watermelon! You *go* on eating the red fruit until you get to the green rind and then *stop*!'

Bouncer grins and gives Hoopla a friendly jab with his elbow. Hoopla laughs as only a hippo can do. 'HOOO, HO-HO-HO-HO!'

Now Bouncer remembers a joke about eating too. 'I've got one for you, Hoopla. Why didn't the teddy bear want to eat any more food?' he asks sweetly.

Hoopla shrugs. 'I have no idea, but I suppose you're going to tell me', he grins.

'The teddy didn't want any more food because he was already stuffed!' crows Bouncer.

'*Oh, nooo!*' hoots Hoopla, and he's off again.

'HOOO, HO-HO-HO-HO!'

'HOOO, HO-HO-HO-HO!'

The friends head off to the kitchen to see about a snack.

Bouncer is Amazed

31 JULY

Bouncer Brachio is sitting on the dock. Below him, in the water, tiny fish are swimming.

'Hello little fish', he whispers. He breaks a crust of bread into crumbs and sprinkles them on the water.

'You must be hungry!' he says, as they swarm up to the surface and start nibbling on the crumbs.

Suddenly, all the little fish stop eating. In a second, they swim away in a flashing dark cloud of tiny bodies.

'What on earth happened?' wonders Bouncer. 'Did I frighten them somehow?' Bouncer stares at the water.

Suddenly, a giant fish swims right under him and disappears under the dock.

'Gosh!' yells Bouncer. He's scared, even though the giant fish paid no attention to him.

The giant fish returns to where the little fish were. Bouncer pulls back from the edge of the dock in fear, but keeps watching. The fish swims up, sees the crumbs of bread floating in the water, and with a swish of its tail, splashes them away.

'My goodness!' cries Bouncer.

The giant fish swims close to Bouncer and suddenly does a backwards somersault in the water.

'Look!' cries Bouncer. 'It's as if you're giving a special show, just for me!'

The giant fish circles back to its spot under Bouncer. This time it rolls on its side, over and over.

'You certainly can do some fantastic things!' murmurs Bouncer. 'You're a star!'

Then, as suddenly as it came, the giant fish glides away to the darker, deeper water.

'What a huge fish!' he says, shaking his head.

August

Swapping Places

Mummy Zebra is staring at her twins, Zig and Zag.

Something is very strange this morning.

'You always eat cornflakes, Zig', she says.

'I would like muesli', Zig replies with a laugh.

'And you, Zag – you always eat muesli!' Mummy says, shaking her head.

'I would like corn flakes', says Zag firmly.

'What is going on today?' Mummy wonders.

She gets out two bowls and fills them with the different cereals.

'Can't you tell?' asks Zig sweetly.

Zig looks at Zag. They both burst out laughing.

'You two are up to no good somehow. I just know it', protests Mummy.

The twins can't stop giggling now.

Mummy looks at each of them very closely.

'Wait a minute…' she squints her eyes.

'Aha! I think I know!' she exclaims. Then Mummy Zebra laughs and shakes her head.

'You've swapped clothes, correct?'

The twins try to keep straight faces.

'Zag, you're wearing Zig's green-coloured shirt, aren't you?'

Zag nods.

'And Zig, you're wearing Zag's pink shirt, too. Correct?'

Zig nods.

'You rascals!' laughs Mummy Zebra!

The twins laugh and cheer.

'We almost fooled you, Mummy!' says Zag.

'But we really couldn't eat the cereals we don't like!' laughs Zig.

Ivan Repairs the Clock

'It's time we got our village clock working again', huffs Mrs. Brachio.

'It's been months since that snow storm broke it!' Ivan Monkey nods. 'I agree. I'll ask Mr. Horse if I can try to get it going again', and off he goes.

Later, Ivan climbs up a ladder into the clock tower in the centre of the village.

'Oooh, it's high up here!' he mutters. He can see the whole village below. Mrs. Brachio waves to him

and he waves back.

'Right. Let's get started', he says, and he begins taking the clock apart. Soon parts of it are all over the floor.

'Right. That piece goes here… and that one goes there, I think… no, perhaps not', he talks out loud to himself as he works.

A couple of hours later he finishes.

'There! That will do it!' He winds up the mechanism and starts the clock ticking.

'Yesss!' he cries as it ticks loudly. Down the ladder he goes, so happy that he has repaired it.

Bong! Bong! Bong!

'There go the clock's chimes!' Ivan smiles. He looks up at the clock. 'It's six o'clock'.

'Hmmm', he frowns. 'I heard three chimes'.

'So did I', says Mrs. Brachio, joining him. She's been watching the whole job. I wonder what went wrong?' puzzles Ivan.

'At least it's working and it shows the right time, even if the chimes are wrong!' he says, a little embarrassed. He heads off home to think.

Sixes and Nines

3 AUGUST

Slye Snake is playing at Baabra Sheep's house. She's learning numbers, so they are busy tracing numbers in a little colouring book.

'Numbers are everywhere!' Slye tells Baabra. 'Now

that I know some of them, I can see them!'

'Like where?' asks Baabra.

'There are lots on the TV remote', Slye says, clicking a make believe one. 'Sometimes I can pick the channels myself, so I know some of them. My favourite channel is four, with the children's shows'.

'Oh yes! Four is good fun', Baabra answers.

'And numbers are on telephones and computers and calculators too', Slye says importantly. 'I got a calculator for my birthday. I really like playing with it, even if I don't know all my numbers yet'.

'My mummy lets me call Grandmother on our telephone. Her number is sooo long!' Baabra rolls her eyes and laughs.

'Do you know what's strange? That six and nine are the same, just upside down', Slye grins.

'I don't know those yet', Baabra says. 'I just know one-two-three-four-five'.

'Look!' Slye takes charge. 'This is a six and here is a nine', she says, pointing in the colouring book. 'If you turn the book upside down, each one turns into the other!'

'Oh yes! That really is strange', Baabra agrees.

'You be a six, and I'll be a nine!' Slye cries. They bend and twist so their bodies look like the numbers. Slye does look like a nine. Baabra looks like… a little sheep trying to bend into a six. They both fall down laughing.

August

Water Bicycle

4 AUGUST

Bouncer Brachio's daddy is on the dock, waiting for the *Tinker Bell*.

'I have something really good for you!' calls Captain Cow after the ferry lands.

'I know!' he answers. 'It's a water bicycle for the camping ground! I can't wait!'

Captain Cow unties something floating behind the ferry. She pushes it towards Mr. Brachio.

'What a beauty!' he exclaims. 'Look at those huge water wheels! And the little pedals! I can't wait to try it. It really is fantastic!'

Mr. Brachio jumps onto the water bicycle and starts pedalling. The big wheels spin and the water bicycle moves away from the dock.

'Yahoo!' yells Mr. Brachio. He pedals faster and faster, and soon he's far from the dock.

'I think I could get to Big Island!' he says. Suddenly there's a loud *PING!* The water bicycle stops.

'Oh, no!' cries Mr. Brachio. 'I've broken the pedals by going too fast!'

The breeze is slowly pushing the water bicycle away from Firefly Island.

'Help! I can't get back!' cries Mr. Brachio.

Captain Cow chuckles and starts her huge ferry motor. 'Ahoy there, sailor!' she calls, her eyes twinkling. 'Need some help?'

The *Tinker Bell* glides near the water bicycle.

'Catch this!' she shouts, and she throws Mr. Brachio a long rope. 'Hold on tight!' she calls, and she heads back to the dock. The water bicycle bobs along as the ferry pulls it back to shore.

'Even Daddies can do silly things!' she laughs.

Ant Stamping?

5 AUGUST

Nolo Giraffe is wondering if he's done the right thing. He was feeling sorry for Scruffy Hyena. 'I am sure that I wouldn't like being away from my family for a whole summer', he had thought to himself.

So Nolo asked Scruffy to come over and play.

'Let's play builders', Nolo says.

'No, not builders', Scruffy says loudly. Then he asks, 'What's playing builders?'

'We put on some hooded sweatshirts and helmets and we make believe we are building a house or something else. I have lots of toy hammers, saws, drills and things', Nolo explains. 'It's fun!'

'No, that sounds silly', Scruffy declares.

'Well then, blocks?' asks Nolo.

'No. They're silly too', Scruffy declares.

'Cowboys?' asks Nolo hopefully.

'No'.

'Puzzles?' tries Nolo again, getting fed up.

'No'.

Nolo tries a different approach. 'Scruffy, what would you like to play?'

'Let's go outside and stamp on some ants', Scruffy says, watching Nolo's face.

'Stamp on ants? Do you really think that's fun?'

'Just joking', smirks Scruffy. 'I think I'll just go home', he says, and off he goes.

Nolo shakes his head in shock.

Stair Sledging

6 AUGUST

Bouncer Brachio and Hoopla Hippo are at Hoopla's house. They are ready to play a new game, called stair sledging. 'I discovered it by accident. A big accident!' Hoopla explains with a chuckle.

'I was walking down our stairs in my socks, and I slipped and fell. I slid all the way down the stairs on my bottom. But the carpet on our stairs is soft, so it really didn't hurt!'

Bouncer nods. 'That's lucky', he says. 'We have wooden stairs. They would definitely hurt!'

'You aren't joking', grins Hoopla. 'But here, it's fun. Come and try!'

The friends climb up the wide stairs.

'Just sit on the top step, lift your feet a little and lean back', he tells Bouncer.

'Wheee!' yells Bouncer as he slides down from step to step, all the way to the bottom.

'Here I come! Watch out beee-low!' bellows Hoopla, and down he bumps.

'Let's try a race now!' Hoopla cries. They scramble upstairs and sit on the top step.

'One, two, three, GO!' cries Hoopla, and they both slide down. Hoopla wins easily.

'I think I slide faster because I'm… bigger', he says, patting his tummy.

'You do have more… padding', laughs Bouncer, rubbing his bottom. 'It's fun, but I don't think I'll be able to sit down when I eat lunch!'

A Double Surprise Concert

7 AUGUST

It is almost sunset and the Zebra family is finishing a picnic at the beach. 'That was wonderful Mummy', says Zag.

'Tonight is Music Night', says Daddy Zebra. Zig and Zag have forgotten all about it!

'It's a pity. I hate to have to go home before the sun sets', sighs Zig. Zag nods.

'Can't we stay a bit longer?' Zag asks.

'I've got a surprise', grins Daddy. He reaches into their big picnic basket and brings out Zig's flute, Zag's trumpet, a toy piano for Mummy and a guitar for himself. 'We can play here!'

Mummy is giggling about her piano, but she really can play songs on it. 'This is wonderful!' she laughs. 'Let's play an easy song first'.

They start playing a tune.

All around the village, heads pop out of windows and doors. 'Who can be playing that lovely music?' the villagers wonder.

The Zebras go on playing, facing the water and the setting sun. They play until the sun sinks below the water. Then they stop.

Clap-clap-clap-clap-clap! Bravo! Bravo!

Waves of clapping and cheers rise from behind them on the beach. The whole village has come to hear the concert!

The Zebras are startled, but they laugh and bow.

'What a perfect way to end a summer's day', proclaims Mr. Horse, the mayor. 'Thank you!'

Scruffy Gets In

8 AUGUST

The friends are having an emergency meeting inside the Hideout.

'I know he's been a bit horrid, but I think we should be nice to him', Zig Zebra says.

'I don't understand why he's so unpleasant and grumpy', wonders Baabra Sheep.

'Shall we let him take the test?' asks Slye Snake.

'Maybe if he passes, he'll be happier and nicer', says Nolo Giraffe.

The friends think about it and then say yes.

Scruffy Hyena is sitting outside the Hideout.

'Scruffy, would you like to be able to come inside the Hideout with us?' asks Slye.

Scruffy looks around at them all. He looks away and then says, 'Yes'.

'You have to pass the test before you get the password', says Nolo sternly. 'Ready?'

'Alright', nods Scruffy, and Hoopla Hippo steps up beside him.

'You have to hold your breath longer than Hoopla', Nolo explains. 'Start when I say go. One, two, three, GO!'

Hoopla and Scruffy take deep breaths and hold them. The friends all hold theirs too.

Hoopla is turning pink, but Scruffy looks fine.

'Phew!' explodes Hoopla, and then Scruffy lets his breath go and smiles a little.

'You did brilliantly Scruffy!' Hoopla cries.

'I have strong lungs. I run a lot at home', Scruffy explains. 'So what's the password?' he asks.

'UNDERPANTS!' they all yell, and everybody falls down laughing. Even Scruffy. He looks a little happier now.

The Joke's on Who?

9 AUGUST Baabra Sheep is having a sleepover at her house.

'Nolo, Bouncer, Hoopla and Scruffy can sleep in the blue tent', Mummy Sheep says. 'The rest of you in the red tent'.

They play games until dark, have a snack, and then slide into their sleeping bags.

It's quiet now and Scruffy Hyena can't sleep.

'I've thought of something!' he whispers. 'Wake up!' The others in his tent sit up sleepily.

'Let's scare the others in the red tent', he says.

'No. That's stupid. I don't want to', says Bouncer firmly, and he goes back to sleep.

'Nor me', says Nolo, and Hoopla nods.

Soon Scruffy is the only one awake again.

He creeps out of the blue tent and sneaks over to the red one.

'Aaah-oooh! Aaah-oooh!' he howls softly.

Inside the red tent, Baabra, Slye, Zig and Zag sit straight up.

'What was that?' asks Baabra, terrified.

'I don't know, but I don't like it!' declares Slye. She slides out of the tent.

Suddenly, Scruffy yells, 'Help! Help!'

In the darkness, Slye has sneaked up on Scruffy and grabbed his foot.

'Now who's scaring who?' she hisses.

'It was a joke', Scruffy whines.

'Well, the joke is on you! Good night!' says Slye.

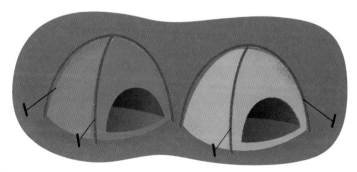

10 AUGUST — Building with Sand

This morning was not fun. Scruffy Hyena's joke during the sleepover has upset the friends.

'Let's just forget about it', says Nolo Giraffe finally, making peace. Everybody brightens up.

'Right. Let's go to the beach and build things in the sand', suggests Baabra Sheep.

'Brilliant idea!' 'Let's go!' they cry, and they all hop on their bicycles.

At the beach, each of them takes a bucket and spade from the chest of beach toys the villagers keep there.

They start digging, piling, patting and shaping the sand into all sorts of shapes.

'I'm going to make a fort', declares Scruffy.

'I'm making a lake with a palace for a princess in the middle', Baabra says dreamily.

Bouncer Brachio cries, 'Look at my dinosaur!'

Zig Zebra says, 'He'd better not wreck my village!'

Hoopla Hippo calls to Zig, 'I'll make a road to connect your village with my house!'

Slye Snake finishes an Egyptian pyramid.

'Gosh! Look what we have done!' says Baabra.

They walk around, admiring their work.

'It looks as though the bad feelings have gone', thinks Nolo. 'We *did* forget about them!'

11 AUGUST — Sorry!

'Oh no! Look at all this! What on earth has happened?'

Zig and Zag Zebra and Scruffy Hyena wanted to show Mummy and Daddy Zebra the wonderful things the friends had built at the beach.

But when they get there, they find that all the things they built have been ruined!

'Who would do this?' wails Zag.

'Somebody really nasty!' cries Zig.

'Hmmm. Look at this', calls Daddy Zebra. He points to some footprints in the sand.

'It looks as though someone has knocked things down and messed them up on purpose'.

Scruffy is feeling really uncomfortable.

'If you think that I did it, you're wrong', he cries.

'Nobody has suggested that, Scruffy', answers Daddy quietly.

'But nobody here likes me!' Scruffy yells. 'They'll all think that I did it!'

'That's not true!' replies Zig. Zag nods.

Just then the Sheep family comes along.

'We have a problem', says Daddy Sheep. 'Lammie went for a walk by himself. He just came home covered in sand. We wanted to know what he was doing on the beach'.

Daddy Zebra looks around. 'I think I know now. Lammie, did you do this?'

Lammie lowers his head and says, 'Sorry!'

August

Wishes Come True

12 AUGUST

It's the middle of the night. Nolo Giraffe's mummy and daddy tiptoe into his bedroom.

'Wake up darling!' Mummy whispers. 'Put on your slippers and come outside!'

Puzzled, Nolo rubs his eyes and stumbles outside.

'Look up!' whispers Daddy.

Zooom! Sparkle! Zooom! Sparkle! Zooom!

Up in the dark sky, falling stars leave a sparkling trail and then fade away.

'Gosh!' cries Nolo, wide awake now.

Every few seconds another star zooms across the sky, leaving a new trail of sparkles.

'Does this happen every night?' Nolo Giraffe wants to know.

'No, not every night. You can see some shooting or falling stars all through the year, but the middle of August is the best time to see a lot of them', Mummy Giraffe says, looking up at the sky.

'Oooh! There goes one – another – and another!' gasps Nolo.

'Should I make a wish?' Nolo asks.

'You certainly should', smiles Mummy. 'I don't know if it will work, but it can't hurt!'

'I wish I could stay and watch them until I fall asleep', Nolo says.

'That wish can come true!' Mummy smiles. She snuggles him up in a warm blanket and they all lie on the grass, watching the stars.

Ivan Repairs the Clock Again

13 AUGUST

'That clock is driving me mad! At three o'clock in the morning, it chimes ten times!' complains Mrs. Brachio. 'Ivan, please help!'

So Ivan Monkey is back in the clock tower.

'Let me see... This piece makes the bell ring', mutters Ivan. He takes it out, turns it upside down and puts it back in.

'Now I'll wait until four o'clock', he decides. He enjoys himself, looking out over the village, until it's four.

Bong! Bong! Bong! Bong!

'Yesss!' cries Ivan. He's so happy that he's repaired

the clock properly. Down the ladder he goes, straight to Mrs. Brachio's gift shop.

'I've repaired it! Our clock ticks and our bell works now!' he cries.

'Wonderful, Ivan', smiles Mrs. Brachio.

They look up at the beautiful face of the clock.

'Um… Ivan…' begins Mrs. Brachio. 'I thought I heard four chimes just now'.

'Yes', Ivan says proudly. 'Four o'clock!'

'But the clock says it's half past three now. Half an hour before four', Mrs. Brachio says.

'Oh no!' Ivan says, shocked. 'It's going backwards! I wonder how on earth that happened', he says. 'I'll have to think about this!' And he heads off home, wondering what to do.

'Ouch! Ouch! My ankle!' Daddy gasps. He grabs his ankle and rubs it.

'Daddy, what's wrong?' cries Bouncer, really scared.

'I think I've twisted my ankle badly', Daddy says, his face all scrunched up in pain. 'It really, really does hurt'.

'Oh, Daddy, I'm so sorry', cries Bouncer. 'I think some of my blocks were under my clothes on the floor. They made you fall', Bouncer says sadly.

'Really, Bouncer. We've told you to keep your room more tidy. Now you can see one reason why we tell you that', Daddy says.

'I promise I will be better', Bouncer replies.

He feels terrible as Daddy limps away.

Blocks Make Trouble

'Bouncer, it's time to go!' calls Daddy up the stairs to Bouncer in his bedroom.

'Yes Daddy, just a second!' Bouncer replies.

He's just finishing a tall tower of blocks.

A few minutes later, Daddy runs up the stairs and dashes into Bouncer's room.

'Bouncer, really, it's time… Argh!' Daddy cries.

Daddy slides on some clothes on Bouncer's bedroom floor, loses his balance and falls in a heap.

Bouncer's tower of blocks wobbles and crashes.

Now there are blocks and a daddy all over the floor.

157

Paying Daddy Back

15 AUGUST Just as he thought, Bouncer's Daddy has a badly sprained ankle. And it's all Bouncer's fault.

Daddy needs crutches to walk and his ankle is all bandaged up. He needs to sit with his foot up on pillows all day long.

'I'll take care of you, Daddy', says Bouncer. He's been crying a lot since Daddy fell over.

'Thank you, Bouncer', answers Daddy. 'Here, come and sit on my lap. Let's talk', he smiles.

Bouncer carefully snuggles onto Daddy's lap.

'Look, Bouncer. I know you feel terrible about my ankle. But that won't help anything now', Daddy says, rubbing Bouncer's back.

'I just wish I could make things different, so that your ankle didn't hurt. I know it's my fault', Bouncer sniffs, crying again.

'You can make things different', Daddy says gently.

'From now on, you can keep your room tidier so this will never happen again', he adds. 'Let's look to the future'.

'Don't you want to punish me, so I feel bad as well?' asks Bouncer, afraid of the answer.

'No, I think you've learned your lesson', smiles Daddy. 'But you *could* get me a glass of orange juice! Let's call that your punishment shall we?' He hugs Bouncer.

'Yes! And I'll get four biscuits too!' Bouncer laughs.

'Two for you and two for me!'

Bigger and Better

16 AUGUST 'Mummy, you should have been there!' gushes Zig Zebra.

The twins have rushed back from the dock, where the *Tinker Bell* has just arrived.

'A thousand children in green uniforms got off the ferry…' Zig begins.

'No, possibly fifty', corrects Zag, her twin.

'Well. Fifty. They had these gigantic packs on their backs…' Zig continues, moving her arms wide apart to show how big.

'Actually, about this big', smiles Zag, and she closes Zig's arms quite a lot.

'Yes, you're right', Zig nods.

'And two of them were carrying a canoe as big as the *Tinker Bell*…' Zig glances at Zag, who shakes

158

her head patiently.

'It couldn't be that big, because they came on the *Tinker Bell*!' laughs Zag.

'Well, anyway, it was huge!' Zig replies, opening her arms as wide as possible.

'And some of them had drums, and horns, and a piano, and…' Zig rushes on.

'I didn't see a piano', Zag says, shaking her head again. 'How could they carry a piano?'

'Well, maybe not a piano, but lots of musical instruments!' carries on Zig excitedly.

'Oh, they must be the junior band from Big Island! They are holding a music camp at our camping ground this week', explains Mummy. 'It must have been a sight, no matter what the truth is!'

Mystery Plant

17 AUGUST

Today, Bouncer Brachio is staying overnight at his Grandmother and Grandad's house.

'Would you like to look at our old photograph album?' Grandmother asks after dinner.

'Oh yes please!' Bouncer is curious.

Grandad gets the album down from a bookshelf and the three of them sit on the sofa.

'Here's one of Grandad when he was your age', Grandmother chuckles.

'He looks just like me!' exclaims Bouncer.

'You're right', laughs Grandad.

'And here we are when we got married', smiles Grandmother.

'Gosh, you were beautiful', exclaims Bouncer. 'I mean, you are now, but…' he adds.

'Thank you for that, Bouncer!' she hugs him.

'And look here!' cries Grandad, turning the page. 'This is the giant pumpkin I grew. It won first prize at the village fair!'

Bouncer sees a younger Grandad standing beside a pumpkin on a vine in his garden. It's enormous, almost half as tall as he is!

'Oh! It's gigantic!' cries Bouncer. Then suddenly Bouncer turns to Grandad.

'Isn't that vine in MY garden the same sort of plant as in this picture? Is my mystery plant a pumpkin?' he bursts out.

'You guessed it! That's why we wanted to show you the photographs tonight, Bouncer!' laughs Grandad. 'You are growing a giant pumpkin! And you didn't even realise it!'

Where Did It Go?

18 AUGUST

It is so hot today! Hoopla Hippo is really suffering.

'Mummy, please can I fill the pool?' he asks, wiping sweat from his forehead.

'Of course Hoopla. I'll read in the sun while you play in the pool', Mummy replies. 'I might even join you in the water!' she laughs.

Hoopla drags the garden hose to the plastic pool and puts the nozzle into the pool. He goes to the tap and turns the water on.

'I feel cooler just watching it fill up', he thinks.

In a little while the pool is full. Hoopla steps in.

'Oooh, it's cold!' he cries.

'That's because the sun hasn't warmed it up yet. And because you're so hot, it feels colder than it really is', laughs Mummy.

'Oh well, here goes!' yells Hoopla, and he gets in and rolls around in the water.

'Wonderful!' he cries. He has an idea.

'Watch this, Mummy!' he calls to her.

He gets out, trots across the yard and then dashes back and jumps into the pool. Huge waves crash over the sides.

'Yippee!' he yells. Then, puzzled, he asks, 'Where is all the water?'

Mummy can't stop laughing.

'You splashed it all out when you jumped in!' she giggles. 'You silly thing', laughs Mummy. And Hoopla laughs his hippo laugh.

'HOOO, HO-HO-HO-HO!'
'HOOO, HO-HO-HO-HO!'

Baabra's Postcard

19 AUGUST

The Sheep family has been on holiday to Big Island this week.

Today, Mrs. Trico, the postmistress, finds lots of colourful postcards in the postbag.

'How nice of her! Baabra Sheep has sent postcards to all of her friends', she thinks. She sorts them into the villagers' post office boxes.

Zig and Zag Zebra come prancing in to get their family's post a little later.

'I think there's something for you', Mrs. Trico says as they open their post office box.

'Goodie!' cries Zig. Zag claps and smiles.

'Oh, look, a postcard! Can you please read it to us, Mrs. Trico?' asks Zag.

'Of course!' She reads, "Dear Zig and Zag! We rode on the roller coaster and had hot dogs at the park. Love from, Baabra'. It looks as though her mummy wrote this card for her. She sent one to all your friends too', adds Mrs. Trico.

Zig and Zag look at each other.

'So, did our friends get each get a postcard?' asks Zig rather sharply.

Zag looks a little angry.

'Yes. Why. What's the matter?' asks Mrs. Trico.

'Well, we are two friends, not one', explains Zag.

'We don't like it when we get treated like one friend. We are two different zebras, even though we are twins'. Zig nods.

'I see', Mrs. Trico replies. 'Well. you do know that Baabra likes and misses you both. Still, two cards would have been nicer for you!'

'Yes!' the twins say together. 'Still, she likes us, and that's what matters!' Zig says.

'You're right Zig', adds Zag, and they nod.

Corn on the Cob

20 AUGUST

Bouncer Brachio's corn plants are huge now. They are even taller than his grandad!

'Let's find out if your corn is ready to eat', Grandad says to Bouncer.

He picks a plump ear of corn that has soft, dark threads coming out of the top.

'That's the silk. When the silk is dark like this, it means the corn could be ripe', Grandad says.

He pulls some of the green leaves back and squeezes a kernel of corn with his thumbnail.

'See that juice? It looks just like half way between water and milk, so that means your corn is ready to eat now'.

'Let's have a corn roast!' Bouncer cries. 'I've got enough to feed the whole village!'

'Good idea Bouncer!' declares Grandad.

'We can do it tomorrow night. Could we do it on the beach?' asks Bouncer.

'We certainly can!' exclaims Grandad.

'Why don't you hop on your bicycle and invite all the villagers. I'll pick the corn and get things ready', Grandad says.

'Lovely. I can't wait! I absolutely love corn on the cob!' crows Bouncer.

'And I think you'll love it even more because you grew it', chuckles Grandad. And Bouncer pedals off as fast as he can.

 ## The Big Corn Roast

21 AUGUST

Every villager is down at the beach this evening.

'I love fresh corn on the cob!' they all say.

Grandad Brachio has picked Bouncer's corn and has a huge basket full of it. He claps his hands to get everyone's attention.

'Welcome! It's good to see you all! Let's get started. Help yourselves!' he says.

The villagers pick out their ears of corn.

'We've never heard of this before', Zag explains.

'Peel back the long green leaves', Grandpa says.

'Done!' Zig says, and Zag nods.

Grandpa has made a huge bonfire in the sand. Everyone puts their ears of corn on sticks.

Hiss! Crackle! Hiss! goes the corn.

Hoopla sneaks up behind the fire and carefully pours some oil on the corn. 'HOO-HOO', he giggles. 'Wait and see! This will be a big surprise!' He quickly returns to his friends, hoping nobody will suspect it was him.

'Right. They're ready!' Grandad yells.

Suddenly, they hear a funny sound: *Pouf! Pouf!*

Kernels start popping, one after another. Popcorn flies everywhere.

'SURPRISE!' Hoopla yells, seeing all the amazed faces. The friends start laughing and soon everybody is enjoying fresh popcorn!

 ## Hoopla Escapes

22 AUGUST

Heeeeeeeee! Heeeeeeeee!

'Go away! Leave me alone!' grumbles Hoopla Hippo. It's late at night and still hot. There's no breeze, but his windows are open in case one comes.

Instead, lots mosquitoes have come! They are driving him mad!

Heeeeeeeee! Heeeeeeeee!

'My arms and legs are covered in bites!' he cries, scratching them all. It doesn't help.

He pulls the sheet up over his head so the mosquitoes can't get at him. That works.

'But now I can't breathe and it's even hotter under this sheet!' he mutters, so he pushes the sheet back down again.

'Got you! Ow!' he cries as he slaps the side of his head hard. He got the mosquito that was trying to bite him, but his slap hurt! 'I can't stand this any longer!' he cries, then he comes up with an idea.

He gets out of bed, taking his sheet and pillow with him and tiptoes to the bathroom.

'I'll sleep here in the bath. It feels much cooler in here and there are no insects – I hope', he says to himself. He climbs in, and before long, he is fast asleep.

In the morning Daddy finds him in the bath.

'That Hoopla is such a joker!' he thinks.

Ivan Finally Repairs the Clock

23 AUGUST

The villagers have laughed a lot at their clock, but Mrs. Brachio is fed up.

'What good is a clock that chimes the right number of times, but runs backwards?' she asks Ivan Monkey.

'Well, there aren't very many of them, so we are famous now', Ivan answers somewhat weakly.

'But a clock should tell the correct time, and its bell really ought to chime the right number of times', Mrs. Brachio points out.

So Ivan gets his ladder and climbs up into the clock tower yet again.

'I really had better get it right this time', he worries.

He takes several pieces out of the clock, polishes them and puts them back in. 'Now I'll wind the clock up and start it. Oh, I really hope I've repaired it properly this time!' he sighs.

He climbs down his ladder and sits on a bench where he can see the clock.

'I've been awake really late for so many nights, worrying about this clock', he thinks.

His eyes slowly shut. Soon he's fast asleep. Above him, the clock ticks away.

Bong! Bong! Bong! Bong! Bong!

Ivan jumps to his feet. 'What time is it? What time is it?' he cries to Mrs. Brachio.

'It's five o'clock, Ivan!' she smiles.

'I think you really did repair it this time! It's going forwards and chiming the right number of times! You did it!' and she gives Ivan a hug.

'Phew!' murmurs Ivan as he walks home with his ladder. 'What a relief!'

Tick-Tock Talk

Baabra Sheep is getting better and better with her numbers. At least, the ones up to ten.

'Baabra, would you like to learn a little about telling the time?' Mummy Sheep asks today.

'Oh yes!' answers Baabra.

They sit at the kitchen table together. Mummy shows Baabra a clock.

'This clock is different from the one Ivan's been fixing in the tower', Mummy says.

'I can see that. This one doesn't have a round face and hands, just numbers!'

'Yes! So this is how it works. The first numbers, the ones in front of the little dots, tell you the hour. Do you understand?' asks Mummy.

'Yes. So that's an eight. Is it eight o'clock?' Baabra asks, getting the idea.

'Yes, a little bit after eight. You can tell that, because the other numbers, the ones after the dots, tell you how many minutes it is past the hour'.

'A zero, then a five', Baabra says.

'Yes. That means it's five minutes past eight right now', Mummy says.

'Ooops! Now it's six minutes past eight!' laughs Baabra, as the number changes.

'Even if you don't know the numbers bigger than ten yet, we can still use this clock. Let's decide that we are going to go shopping when the hour side shows a nine and the minute side shows two zeroes.

That will be nine o'clock, when Mr. Ptera's store opens', Mummy explains.

'Lovely! I'll sit here and colour for a while. When it says nine o'clock I'll come and get you!' says Baabra, feeling very important and grown up. 'You had better get ready!' she adds.

What Smells?

'Phew! It smells like a dead fish in here!' cries Bouncer's mummy when she comes into his bedroom this morning.

'Hmmm?' mumbles Bouncer, waking up.

Bouncer's mummy opens the windows wide.

She waves her arms around to try and push the air outside.

'What is making that smell?' she asks.

'I can't smell anything', Bouncer answers.

'That's probably because you've been sleeping in here all night and you're used to it', Mummy says, looking around the room.

'It's lovely that you are keeping the floor clear ever since Daddy twisted his ankle, Bouncer', she adds. 'But something really smells in here!'

She gets down on the floor and spots a pile of clothes under Bouncer's bed.

'What's all this?' she asks sharply.

'Oh. That's clothes', Bouncer says weakly. 'It's there so my floor isn't messy', he adds.

Mummy pulls clothes out from the pile.

'Found it!' she exclaims. 'Oh dear!'

She unfolds his swimming trunks.

'Bouncer, these have been sitting here for three days, wet!' she says, a little crossly.

'Yes, Mummy', Bouncer murmurs. 'But at least my floor is clear!' he says.

'Oh, Bouncer, you are a rascal!' Mummy grins.

The Litterbug

26 AUGUST

Mr. Brachio, the camping ground manager, is walking to work. His ankle is better now.

He spots a sweet wrapper on the path.

'Someone wasn't thinking, I suppose', he sighs, and picks it up. A little further on, he sees another.

'Hmmm. This is not good', he says to himself.

Before long he finds more sweet wrappers.

'This really is very bad. Somebody just doesn't care about keeping our island looking clean and nice', he says out loud.

He starts trotting ahead. 'I'll find this litterbug and make sure they stop doing this!' he says.

He comes around a bend in the path and sees Scruffy Hyena, with a bag of sweets. Scruffy is just about to drop a wrapper on the path.

'Stop!' orders Mr. Brachio.

Scruffy jumps in surprise and whirls around.

'Scruffy, look what I've found along the path', says Mr. Brachio seriously, showing Scruffy all the sweet wrappers.

Scruffy looks guilty and swallows a sweet.

'I… I've always done this', he stammers.

'I know you are far from home, but even so, I don't see why you'd want to drop litter anywhere. It's not nice for others to see. And who is supposed to clean up your mess?' Mr. Brachio asks.

'I see what you mean', Scruffy says weakly. 'I'm sorry. I won't do it again'.

'I could do with some help cleaning up the camping ground today…' Mr. Brachio says.

'I'll help!' replies Scruffy eagerly. 'I've learned my lesson!'

August

Baabra Comes Back

27 AUGUST

Baabra Sheep knocks at the door of the Zebra family's house. She's got a bag of biscuits with her.

'Baabra! You're back!' cries Zig Zebra.

'Look Zag', she calls, 'Baabra's here!'

Zag appears and says, 'Welcome home! You must have had a lovely holiday on Big Island!'

'Oh yes!' Baabra says, excitedly. 'We went to the park, and we went to a funfair, and we went to the cinema, and...'

Baabra chatters away, then notices the zebra twins aren't looking that happy.

'You told us about the park, in your postcard', Zig says carefully.

'Thank you for sending it', Zag adds, but her voice is a little strange.

'Is something wrong?' Baabra asks.

'Well, not really wrong', Zig begins.

'It's just that…' Zag tries to go on.

'It's just that we liked it that you sent us a card, but…' Zig starts again.

'…but it's hard for us when we don't get treated like two different zebras', Zag finishes.

'Oh, my gosh!' Baabra is really embarrassed.

'I really didn't mean to hurt your feelings!' she cries. 'Oh, I'm so sorry!'

'Baabra, we know you like us. Like us both. We like you lots and lots. So we just wanted to tell you', Zig says. And all three friends hug and start laughing.

'Let's have some biscuits and milk!' Zag says, and they all head off to the kitchen, happy now.

Roota's Secret

28 AUGUST

Roota Rooster is so excited!

He has a surprise for his wife, Dr. Henny. He found it while treasure hunting.

'She'll be so happy!' he thinks to himself.

He carefully turns over a smooth, white object in a little nest of straw that he has built.

He settles down on it and fluffs out his feathers.

'I'm doing a good job of keeping it warm', he says proudly to himself.

'I should tell her soon', he thinks. 'In fact, today!'

He can't keep his secret much longer.

Dr. Henny comes home from the clinic later.

'Henny, dear, come and see what I have!' Roota says. He leads her to his nest.

'What in the world!' says Henny in surprise when she sees it.

'It's an egg! We're going to have a chick! Just like Cozy!' he exclaims.

'Oh, Roota, what a nice idea! But I'm sorry, darling. That's not an egg. It's a table tennis ball!'

'What?' cries Roota. He can't believe it.

'It is lovely though, Roota', soothes Dr. Henny.

'It was a wonderful idea. Thank you so much!' And she gives him a big hug.

A Giant Sundae

29 AUGUST

Hotta Toucan and Chilly Penguin have invited the whole village to a big, end-of-summer party.

On a long, long table, Hotta and Chilly have placed a long, long ice cream dish.

'Welcome, dear friends!' cries Hotta. 'We want to make the world's biggest ice cream sundae. But we'll need your help!'

'Can you please divide yourselves up into four teams?'

The villagers laugh, wondering what's next.

'You're the ice cream team', Hotta says, handing the first group tubs of ice cream and scoops.

'You're the topping team', she laughs, handing out jars of chocolate sauce and spoons.

'You're the nuts team', Hotta says.

'You mean, the nutty team!' hoots Hoopla Hippo. Hotta gives them bags of nuts and spoons.

'And you're the whipped cream team', says Hotta, giving them bowls of fluffy cream and spoons.

'What about cherries on top?' asks Slye Snake.

'Yes. You can be the cherry team!' Hotta laughs.

The ice cream team scoops lots ice cream into the long dish.

'Make way for the topping team!' Bouncer Brachio cries. The sauce is spooned out.

'Nuts to you! And you! And you!' laughs Hoopla as his team gets to work.

'And now, whipped cream!' giggles Mrs. Brachio as the whipped cream team starts.

'And now, the finishing touch. Ta-daaa!' giggles Slye, putting a line of big red cherries on top of the giant dessert.

'And now, friends, enjoy your sundae!' cries Chilly. Everybody picks up a spoon and starts eating. What a wonderful party!

August

 **30 AUGUST**

Digging to China

The friends are on the beach with their buckets and spades.

'Let's dig a deep, deep hole!' says Nolo Giraffe.

'That sounds like fun', answers Slye Snake, and the others agree.

After a while, they have managed to dig a hole that is so deep they can stand in it and not be seen. Even Nolo, with his long neck!

'It's getting difficult to dig out the sand', Nolo says after a while.

'What if we fill buckets with sand and pass them out to the others?' Slye suggests.

That works well and the digging goes on.

By now, there is water at the bottom of the hole.

Mr. Ptera, the general store owner, comes strolling by. He peers into the hole.

'You know, if you keep on digging like that, you'll go all the way to China!' he says, chuckling. 'Can you speak Chinese?'

The friends stop working.

'I can't speak it', answers Slye, frowning. 'Are you serious?' she asks.

'I certainly am!' answers Mr. Ptera. 'And what if some children in China are digging right now as well?' Slye asks.

'Then we might have some visitors for a while!' answers Mr. Ptera, and he strolls away.

Was he being serious? The friends aren't sure.

'We'd better learn some Chinese!' laughs Slye.

 31 AUGUST

Candle Boats

'Today is the last day of August', Mr. Horse announces from his soapbox this evening.

'We send our wishing boats out into the water on this day every year. Let's get started'.

All up and down the dock, villagers have gathered, holding tiny wooden boats that carry candles on top.

'I'll light our candle', says Daddy Brachio and then hands the boat and candle to Bouncer.

'Now make a wish and set our boat off', Daddy tells Bouncer.

'Hmmm. What should I wish?' Bouncer asks himself. 'Do I tell what I wish for, or keep it secret?' he asks his daddy.

'Usually you don't tell people what you wish, but when we send out our wishing boats, we do'. Daddy replies.

'Right. Then I wish that we will have another summer next year that is as good as this one has been', Bouncer announces.

He puts the little boat in the water. It bobs and turns, but floats perfectly. The candle burns brightly.

'It really is pretty, isn't it?' Bouncer asks, feeling a little sad. Summer is almost over.

All along the shore the tiny boats are taking off. They float away from Firefly Island to the deep water, carrying their wishes.

September

1
SEPTEMBER

Pen Friends

Mr. Horse is trotting up and down impatiently in front of the post office, waiting for Mrs. Trico to open it. He keeps looking at the village clock.

'I hope I have a letter!' he keeps thinking.

Mrs. Trico finally opens the post office door.

'Is there any post for me today?' Mr. Horse asks hopefully.

'Why, yes there is!' Mrs. Trico says. 'I saw a very pretty postcard from Big Island'.

Mr. Horse hurries to his post office box, turns the dial with his secret code and opens the box.

'Oh! That really is a pretty card!' he says.

He turns the card over and reads it, smiling more and more.

'She's coming for a visit!' he chuckles.

Mrs. Trico smiles. 'I'm very happy for you and I hope she has a good time here. Who is she?'

'She's my pen friend. We've been writing back and forth for a year now and soon she is coming for a visit. I haven't met her in person yet. I do hope she likes me', Mr. Horse says in a rush, a little nervously.

'I'm sure that she will', smiles Mrs. Trico.

Mr. Horse says goodbye and leaves the post office. When he gets outside, he gives a little whinny and does three prancing jumps.

'She's coming! She's coming!' he laughs. 'Miss Pinto Pony is coming to visit!'

Village Fair Meeting

2
SEPTEMBER

The villagers are having a meeting with Mr. Horse tonight.

'What's on your minds this month?' asks Mr. Horse, starting the meeting off.

'Isn't it time to organise our village fair?' asks Mrs. Brachio.

'Yes!' cheers Dr. Henny.

'Let's hold it on 18 September', suggests Mr. Horse. 'I'll put up a big tent'.

'And I'll arrange the prizes', Mr. Brachio says.

'What are the prize categories this year?' asks Grandad Brachio, who already has a secret plan.

'Best Desserts!' 'Sweetest Fruits!' 'Most Beautiful Art!' 'Finest Woodwork!' The villagers are as excited as the youngsters about the categories.

'That all sounds perfect', agrees Mr. Horse.

'What about a new one?' asks Grandad Brachio, with that same odd look. 'Biggest!' he continues.

'That would be fun!' someone says.

'Right. We all agree', says Mr. Horse. 'Any villager of any age could win that prize'.

Grandad Brachio stops off at Bouncer's house on the way home from the meeting.

'Bouncer, the village fair has a new category for prizes: Biggest', he says, raising one eyebrow.

Bouncer understands straight away what Grandad means.

'I think I could win that one', he answers. He pictures his giant pumpkin, which is getting bigger and bigger every day.

'In fact, I know I can win!' Bouncer laughs, and Grandad nods.

'You've got about two weeks for it to grow bigger', Grandad smiles. 'Let's hope for good pumpkin-growing weather!'

Scruffy's Job Visit

'Hello, Scruffy! Come in!' Mr. Ptera calls to the young hyena. It's time for Scruffy's job visit at Mr. Ptera's general store.

'Thank you. But I don't know what you do', mutters Scruffy. He doesn't look very interested.

'Well, how about stocking the shelves? The shop opens soon', says Mr. Ptera.

They put new things on the shelves. Food, paint, books, games, clothes – even sweets.

'General stores have a little of everything', chuckles Mr. Ptera. 'I try to stock all the things the villagers might want or need'.

'Baabra Sheep said you were scared of the basement', Scruffy says, watching Mr. Ptera.

'Oh, that', Mr. Ptera laughs. 'I was wrong about those ghosts. They were pigeons!'

They put the last things on the shelves.

'Look at this! It's brilliant!' Scruffy says excited. He holds up a cap with 'I Visited Firefly Island', written on it.

'Do you like it?' asks Mr. Ptera.

'Yes', answers Scruffy shyly.

'Then I'd like to give it to you', smiles Mr. Ptera. 'Think of us when you wear it!'

'I certainly will', smiles Scruffy, for the first time today. 'Thank you! What else can I do?' he asks.

'Time to open the shop now, Scruffy', says Mr. Ptera. 'And here come the villagers!'

September

Stair Racing

4 SEPTEMBER

'Look at this amazing stopwatch', says Nolo Giraffe to the friends in the playground this morning.

'What do you do with it?' asks Hoopla Hippo.

'You can see how much time something takes', explains Nolo.

He clicks the watch and the numbers start turning. When he clicks it again, they stop.

'That was five seconds', he says, looking at it. 'These are the minutes and here are the seconds. Seconds are short and minutes are a lot longer', he explains. 'Come over here!'

Nolo leads them to the long set of steps that go up to the clock tower on the village hall.

'Let's see who can run up and down the steps the fastest', he suggests.

'Yes!' cry the friends. They love the idea!

'I'll go first – I'm sure to win!' laughs Slye Snake. Sure enough, she slithers up and down the steps in a flash.

'One minute and four seconds!' cries Nolo.

The friends go up and down, one by one.

'Now watch me!' cries Hoopla.

Hoopla rumbles up the stairs slowly. But he comes down fast, sliding on his bottom.

'One minute and two seconds!' Nolo cries.

'HOOO, HO-HO-HO-HO!'

'HOOO, HO-HO-HO-HO!'

Hoopla's laugh fills the air. 'That hurt a little, but I won!' he chuckles.

Pumpkins All Over!

5 SEPTEMBER

Mrs. Trico smiles at Bouncer Brachio as he comes into the post office to get his family's post.

'Hello!' she calls out. 'How's your garden doing?'

'Good! Yummy thank you!' Bouncer laughs.

'Someone told me that you're growing something really big', Mrs. Trico says.

'Um… yes. But it's a secret', Bouncer says, picturing his giant pumpkin.

'Is it a pumpkin?' Mrs. Trico asks.

'Um… as I said, it's a secret', repeats Bouncer, his face turning a little red.

'I just asked, because I've seen a lot of giant pumpkins in the gardens round the village this summer. I hope yours wins the prize for biggest at the fair', Mrs. Trico smiles.

Bouncer nods and gets the post from the box. He says goodbye and leaves.

'Who else is growing giant pumpkins?' he wonders. 'I'm going to have a look around'.

Bouncer wanders all over the village, peering over fences and around bushes.

'Pumpkins are hidden everywhere!' he exclaims. He races to Grandad Brachio's farm.

'The village is full of giant pumpkins!' he cries.

Grandad laughs. 'I was afraid of that! I'm sure yours will be the biggest. Just you wait and see. I know what I'm talking about!'

'I hope so, but I think I'll give mine a little extra water today to be sure!' says Bouncer.

6

SEPTEMBER

Super-Duper Bubbles

Baabra and Lammie Sheep's grandmother has come to visit.

'Look what I brought you two', she exclaims, pulling out a big, flat package.

'Oh', says Baabra. 'What is it, Grandmother?'

'It's a super-duper bubble maker!' Grandmother says. 'Let's go outside and try it!'

'Pour this soapy stuff into this container', she tells Baabra. 'Lammie, you can get the bubble maker out of the box'. Soon they're ready.

'Dip the bubble maker into the soapy stuff. Now hold it up to the wind', Grandmother says.

'Gosh! Look at that!' the youngsters yell. A gigantic bubble, as big as a Lammie, slowly comes out of the bubble maker!

'Me try!' cries Lammie.

'Yes Lammie', answers Grandmother. 'But you are so little that you need to be up higher to make a really big bubble. Stand on that bench over there!' Grandmother holds the soapy water. Lammie dips the bubble maker in, then holds it up. A huge bubble, bigger than the first one, comes out!

'Now watch this!' Grandmother exclaims. She climbs up on the picnic table, dips the bubble maker in the soapy liquid, and holds it up to the wind. A bubble bigger than a car comes out!

'That's amazing! Thank you!' laughs Baabra. 'What a wonderful present!'

Lammie claps and crows, 'Thank you! Thank you!'

173

Scruffy strikes a match and looks at the flame as it quickly burns down to his finger.

'Ouch!' he cries, and he throws it away.

The burning match lands on a piece of paper in the corner of the Hideout. Suddenly the paper bursts into flames!

'Quick! Get out of here!' yells Nolo, and the friends rush to the door.

But Hoopla stays behind. He stamps on the burning paper and puts the fire out. Then he comes outside. He is furious. Scruffy is looking at the ground.

'That was really stupid!' cries Hoopla. 'I hope that's the last of your wonderful ideas!'

'Hoopla, I'm really sorry', says Scruffy. 'I won't ever do that again'. He walks home, ashamed.

Playing with Matches

7
SEPTEMBER

The friends are at the Hideout. Scruffy Hyena has something to show the friends.

'Matches!' they cry, alarmed.

'We can't play with them', says Zig Zebra, firmly. Her twin, Zag, shakes her head and frowns.

'Scruffy, what were you thinking?' asks Nolo Giraffe. 'They're dangerous!'

'Are you really afraid of these little things?' teases Scruffy.

'No. Not as long as they aren't burning', says Hoopla Hippo.

'Well, I'm going to light a few', announces Scruffy. Zig and Zag leave the Hideout.

Scruffy's Punishment

8
SEPTEMBER

'I just thought it would be fun', Scruffy Hyena tells Daddy Zebra the next day.

'Fun? What is fun about almost burning down the Hideout? What would have happened if Hoopla Hippo hadn't put that fire out?' Daddy asks, very angry.

'And what if someone had got hurt?' Daddy continues. 'I wasn't thinking', Scruffy says. 'I'm really sorry. I won't ever do that again'.

'Scruffy, you are not my son, but I have to punish

you just as if you were. That was a terrible thing to do', Daddy says.

Scruffy nods, feeling dreadful now.

'Please go and talk to Mr. Horse, our mayor. Tell him that you will wash the fire engine all by yourself. While you do that, think about how dangerous matches are'.

Scruffy nods and leaves to find Mr. Horse.

Three hours later, a very tired Scruffy comes back. He's soaking wet and looks very sad.

'I did as you told me to', he tells Daddy Zebra. 'I'll never play with matches again', he says.

'I'm glad you've learned your lesson', Daddy says. He smiles and adds, 'Anyway Scruffy, let's put this behind us and have dinner',

'Yes please', whispers Scruffy, and he joins the Zebra family at the dinner table.

Miss Pinto Pony

9 SEPTEMBER Mr. Horse is at the ferry dock, nervously pacing up and down. He holds a bouquet of flowers for his pen friend, who is coming to visit.

'I think I can see the *Tinker Bell* now!' he cries.

A pretty black and white spotted pony watches from the railings. Mr. Horse waves his flowers to her. 'Miss Pinto Pony! Welcome to Firefly Island!' he calls out.

Soon the little pony is standing beside him. For once, Mr. Horse can't speak.

'Did you have a good journey?' he finally gulps.

Miss Pony looks up at him with her big, black eyes and smiles sweetly. 'Yes, I did, thank you'.

'Would you like to go for a walk around the island?' Mr. Horse asks.

'That would be lovely', Miss Pony nods.

They stop at the news board to look at the map of Firefly Island before they start off.

'I'd like to see the waterfall', Miss Pony says.

'Good idea!' Mr. Horse exclaims. They trot down the path towards the lake. Mr. Horse and Miss Pinto Pony soon get to the waterfall.

'It's beautiful!' Miss Pinto Pony cries.

'I'm so glad you like it', answers Mr. Horse.

'It must be wonderful to live on Firefly Island', Miss Pinto Pony sighs.

'Maybe one day you could... you could live here too', whispers Mr. Horse. Miss Pinto Pony blushes.

'That would be a dream come true', she answers, giving Mr. Horse a little nudge and a smile.

Now it's Mr. Horse's turn to blush. It looks as if they are falling in love!

September

A Long Ride

10
SEPTEMBER

Grandmother Brachio loves her exercise bicycle. Every afternoon, she gets on and pedals fast.

'Time for my ride', she says this morning.

She gets on, sets the timer on the bicycle, and starts pedalling.

Grandmother enjoys looking through a magazine while she pedals.

'That's a nice recipe', she says, turning the pages.

'And I like that hat', she adds.

The pedals go round and round as she reads. She finishes reading one magazine and opens another.

'I must be tired today. It's not going as fast as usual', she thinks, turning more pages.

After a while she has finished reading the second magazine. She is getting really tired now!

'I think I'll have a nap this afternoon', she says, puffing hard. The sweat is pouring down her cheeks and her back.

'How much longer do I have to pedal before the timer goes off?' she wonders.

She looks at the timer. It hasn't started!

'Oh, my! I forgot to start the timer! How long have I been cycling?' she asks herself.

She looks outside. 'Gosh! The sun is setting! I have been pedalling all afternoon. Oh, silly me! No wonder I am so tired!'

A Fishy Dream?

11
SEPTEMBER

Ivan Monkey, Zig and Zag Zebra, and Bouncer Brachio are sitting on the dock this evening, watching the sunset.

'I love the way the sun turns golden, then orange, then red, as it goes down', says Zig.

'It makes me think of that giant golden fish we saw when we were on the ferry last spring', Zag sighs. 'Remember, Zig?'

'Wait a minute – did you see a big golden fish?' asks Ivan excitedly. 'I almost caught it!'

'I saw a huge golden fish once, right under this dock too!' Bouncer adds, pointing down to the water below them.

They stare at each other, then into the water.

176

'Do you think it's the same fish?' Bouncer asks.

'I bet it is', Ivan replies thoughtfully.

They fall silent, watching the water. Suddenly, far out from shore, a huge golden fish leaps out of the water and splashes down like a dolphin.

'OH! DID YOU SEE THAT?' yells Ivan.

'That was our fish! Our fish!' cries Zig.

'My gosh! It was!' echoes Zag.

'It's as if the fish heard us talking about him – or her – and wanted to say hello or something', exclaims Bouncer.

They see a shape coming toward them, just below the surface of the water. It swirls around in the water under their feet. Then the golden fish leaps out of the water right next to them!

SPLAAASH! A huge wave of water soaks them. The fish swims slowly away.

'This is like a dream!' cries Ivan. 'That fish is listening to us and answering!'

'It's no dream, Ivan', laughs Bouncer. 'We are definitely all wide awake and WET now!'

Sock Puppets

The friends are at Hoopla Hippo's house. Mummy Hippo is helping them to make sock puppets.

She gives each youngster an old sock, a piece of cloth and some thin cardboard to make the puppet's eyes and mouth.

Now they can put their hands in their new puppets and make them talk.

Yak-yak-yak! Mooo! Aaah-wuuuh! Cock-a-doodle-doo! Woof-woof! say the puppets.

'Hello! I'm Ivan Monkey!' giggles Hoopla Hippo, making his monkey puppet talk.

Hey! Hee-haw! brays Nolo Giraffe's donkey puppet.

'I have an idea!' *Hee-haw!* 'Let's put on a play!'

'I'll be the hero who slays the dragon!' yells Hoopla.

'No, I will!' cries Nolo.

'No, I will', agues Hoopla, 'because I'm the strongest'.

'And I'm the tallest', Nolo replies.

Then Bouncer Brachio intervenes. 'You should both be heroes? You can be the Invincible Two!'

'Yes!' the arguing heroes cheer.

'And I will be your best friend, who is with the Invincible Two on all your adventures!' Brachio says proudly.

They cheer and start playing straight away.

13 SEPTEMBER

Teaching Cozy to Whistle

Mr. Ptera is having his morning cup of coffee at the café. Cozy, the fuzzy chick, is in her playpen in the corner.

'Cozy, can you whistle?' Mr. Ptera asks.

'Whistle! Whistle!' she cheeps. She has no idea what she's saying.

'No, I mean, can you do this?' Mr. Ptera puckers up his lips and blows through them. A beautiful song fills the air.

'Pttt! Pttt! Pttt! Pttt!' goes Cozy, trying to sound just like Mr. Ptera.

'Not so hard, Cozy. Blow gently, like this', Mr. Ptera says, and again he trills and warbles.

'Phew! Phew! Phew! Phew!' breathes Cozy.

'That's a little better', Mr. Ptera says. 'Just keep on trying, and before long you'll manage it'.

Chilly Penguin, Cozy's daddy, joins them. 'I'm glad you are teaching Cozy to whistle', he says. 'We penguins can't sing pretty songs like some other birds. I hope Cozy can at least whistle songs when she gets bigger'.

'Twooot! Twooot! Twooot!' honks Cozy.

Mr. Ptera winces a little at the ugly sound, but he quickly says, 'Keep trying, Cozy! You can do it!' He winks at Chilly and whistles a fine tune.

Cozy claps and laughs. Maybe one day she will!

14 SEPTEMBER

Scruffy Writes a Letter

Mummy Zebra and Scruffy Hyena are sitting in the garden after dinner.

'Scruffy', Mummy says, 'Would you like to send a letter to your family? I know how happy you were when you got theirs. I'm sure they would love to know how you are getting on'.

Scruffy thinks for a second, then nods. 'Could you write it for me please?' he asks.

'I'd love to', Mummy Zebra replies. She gets a pen and some paper.

'Dear Family', begins Scruffy. 'Thank you for your lovely letter. It made me really happy. I miss you a lot and think of you every day'.

'I'm having fun with the Zebra family. Most of the time I can tell which twin is which. Zig and Zag have nice friends and they make me feel almost as though I belong here'.

'But Firefly Island is not like home. I miss you, and our home and just everything. I can't wait to get back'.

Scruffy stops and looks at Mummy Zebra.

'I don't mean that you aren't being nice to me', he says quietly. She pats his shoulder.

'Scruffy, we know how hard it must be for you. We really like you. So don't worry. Did you know you're more than halfway through your stay with us?' smiles Mummy Zebra.

'Really?' Scruffy perks up. Then he gives her a hug. 'I suppose soon I'll be missing you instead!'

15 SEPTEMBER Water Balloon Surprise

Splash! Pop! Splosh!

There is a battle going on at the Hideout!

The friends have split into two teams. They stand in two lines, facing each other.

'Got you!' 'Yes!' 'Ha-ha!' fills the air.

Brightly-coloured shapes sail back and forth.

'Take that!' cries Hoopla Hippo, hurling a yellow water balloon at the other team. It lands right in front of Baabra Sheep and bursts open, soaking her to the skin.

'Oh, you're going to be sorry, Hoopla!' she yells. She throws a blue water balloon at him, and it explodes on the ground, splashing him.

Hoopla has an idea. 'Keep on throwing. I'm going to sneak up behind them', he whispers to Nolo Giraffe. Nolo nods.

Hoopla creeps along the edge of the tall grass until he gets to a spot right behind the other team. They have made a huge pile of water balloons, all ready to throw at his team.

'Ha!' he yells, and he jumps up and down, bursting all their balloons. 'We won!'

Baabra's team is speechless. And very wet!

'Our hero!' Hoopla's team cries. 'Hooray for Hoopla!' Then both teams fall about laughing.

September

Oops!

16 SEPTEMBER

Slye Snake is on the sofa, watching the television. It's her favourite programme and she is soon giggling at the cartoons.

'I'm thirsty', she thinks. 'Mummy is in the garden, but I can get a drink by myself'.

Slye goes to the refrigerator and takes out some chocolate milk. She pours it into a glass *very* carefully. Slye goes back to the sofa and watches more cartoons. She sips her cold chocolate milk. A clown suddenly makes her laugh out loud.

'Oops!' cries Slye.

She's tipped her glass over while laughing and chocolate milk has gone all over the sofa!

'Oh, no!' Slye gasps. She runs to the kitchen.

'Quick! A cloth!' she exclaims. Slye grabs one and starts dabbing at the sofa.

Mummy hears all the noise and comes in.

'Oh, Slye! Our sofa!' Mummy exclaims.

'I'm sorry, Mummy!' cries Slye, still mopping.

'You know you aren't allowed to have drinks on the sofa', Mummy says crossly, starting to mop the chocolate milk up too. 'No you can see why. We'll have to wash the sofa cover now'.

'I'll help you do it', says Slye quietly. 'And I won't drink *anything* on the sofa again', she adds.

'I'm sure you won't', Mummy says, smiling a little. 'I know you won't forget doing this'.

Slye hugs Mummy and they start taking the sofa cover off so they can wash it.

'It *was* yummy chocolate milk though', Slye thinks!

Ivan's Vacuum Robot

17 SEPTEMBER

Ivan Monkey is very excited! He ordered a special machine last week and it has just arrived.

'I *really* don't like vacuuming', he mutters as he opens the box. 'It seems so silly. I hope this takes care of the problem'.

He takes the machine out and puts it on the floor. 'I had better read the instructions first', he says to himself wisely.

He reads about half the book and throws it on the floor. 'It's really simple', he thinks.

He turns the machine on and it whirs and spins

around for a second. Then it starts to move. When it bumps into a table leg, it goes back, turns a little and then goes forward until it hits something else.

'It works! A real robot that vacuums! It will do all the work for me!' crows Ivan.

The little robot vacuum hums away and wanders around the room, sucking up the dust. Suddenly it gobbles up one of Ivan's dirty socks.

'Stop! Stop! That's my sock!' Ivan yells.

The robot moves on a little way, then gobbles up the other one!

'Give that back! It's mine!' Ivan shouts.

He wants to turn the robot off, but he didn't read that part of the instruction book.

The robot rolls on, eating up the instruction book, Ivan's glasses and a coin. And the dust!

'I can't turn you off!' Ivan wails. 'I'm going to have to wait until your battery goes flat!'

Ivan opens his back door and sends the robot out into his vegetable garden.

'Help yourself. I hope you like salad!' he calls, shaking his head.

The Village Fair

18 SEPTEMBER

All the villagers are at Firefly Meadow today. 'At last! The Village Fair!' Bouncer Brachio thinks, impatiently.

There are tables loaded with wonderful pies, wood carvings, artwork and toys. Shelves of fresh fruit

and vegetables shine in the sun. The villagers walk from place to place, admiring everything. Mr. Horse has already given out prizes for the best tomatoes, the sweetest fruit and lots of other things.

'And so my fellow villagers, we come to the 'Biggest' prize. Can we see the entries please?'

The villagers all clap as Bouncer Brachio and several others go inside a tent and come out pulling carts that hold gigantic vegetables.

Bouncer's giant pumpkin is bigger than he is!

'Hmmm', Mr. Horse says, looking them over. He's the judge of this category.

'Bouncer's pumpkin is the biggest bay far! I declare Bouncer Brachio the winner!' Mr. Horse exclaims.

Bouncer can't believe his ears. 'I won! My mystery plant – my pumpkin – won!' he yells. He gives Grandad Brachio a big hug.

Grandad whispers, 'Remember that picture of my own giant pumpkin in our photo album? I won too, back then. So I knew you would'.

'Thanks to you, Grandad!' beams Bouncer.

September

Pumpkin Boats

19 SEPTEMBER

'I asked the villagers who grew the other giant pumpkins if we could use them for a special race', Grandad Brachio tells Bouncer today.

'A race? Are you serious?' Bouncer asks.

'I certainly am! Get on your bicycle and ask all the villagers to meet us at the ferry dock at noon!' says Grandad mysteriously.

When everybody is gathered, Grandad announces, 'Welcome to the Great Pumpkin Boat Race! Please help scoop out these giant pumpkins. Then let the race begin!'

Soon, the pumpkins are bobbing in the water. Each of the youngsters climbs in and grabs a paddle. They look at the finish line, far away.

'One, two, three, GO!' yells Grandad, and the youngsters paddle like mad.

Hoopla Hippo can only make his pumpkin go round in circles. He's bellowing his hippo laugh. Zig Zebra falls out of hers and climbs back in.

'Go on, Zag!' she calls to her twin, who's really moving fast! Nolo Giraffe is sinking.

Bouncer crosses the finish line first. 'Hurray! I won! In my own pumpkin!' he cries. The villagers all cheer. 'What a fun race!' Bouncer yells.

Homesick Scruffy

20 SEPTEMBER

Scruffy Hyena is doing puzzles with Nolo Giraffe today. Nolo can see how grumpy Scruffy is.

'I hate this puzzle', grumbles Scruffy.

Nolo stares. 'Are you alright?' he asks.

Scruffy stares back. 'I'm fine', he says, but without much feeling.

'I was just wondering, since you seem so… so sad. Do you miss your mummy and daddy?' Nolo asks. He knows that *he* would.

'Yes', Scruffy replies. 'But they say it's better for me to stay here this summer. There isn't much food or water at home now'.

'Really?' Nolo can't imagine that.

'I didn't get to choose if I came here or not. So I'm sort of cross', Scruffy says very quietly.

'But you have plenty of food here, and we like you', Nolo points out.

'I suppose so', answers Scruffy, not sounding certain.

'Anyway, thank you for asking', he adds.

'Scruffy, I'm your friend', Nolo replies.

'Poor Scruffy. No wonder he's grumpy!' Nolo thinks.

They smile at each other and carry on playing.

September

Poor Scruffy

Mummy Zebra is giving Zig and Zag their bath before bedtime.

'Mummy, what's wrong with Scruffy?' asks Zag. 'He seems cross or sad all the time'.

Mummy sighs. 'Your daddy and I have known Scruffy's family for ages', she says. 'When we told them that we were moving to Firefly Island, they asked if we would let Scruffy visit us this summer'.

'He doesn't like it here', declares Zig.

'I'm not sure about that, but he certainly misses his family', Mummy answers.

She washes Zig's back. 'They think it's good for him to be with us. They have to work so hard to find food and water. Here we have plenty. But we aren't his family, even though we like him'.

'So that's why he's sad or cross?' asks Zag.

'I think he's a little cross that they just sent him here. He didn't get to choose whether to come or stay at home', Mummy says, washing Zag's back. 'Right. Out of the bath!' Mummy smiles.

'Zig, let's try to make Scruffy feel better about being here', says Zag.

Zig nods. 'I was just going to say the same thing. Imagine if it was us, far away from Mummy and Daddy!' she shivers.

Mummy gives Scruffy his bath while the twins get ready for bed. They hear two voices and water swishing in the bathroom.

'I'm glad I'm at home', says Zig, and Zag nods.

Cozy Can Whistle!

Hotta Toucan is busy laying the tables this morning at her café. Her chick, Cozy, is in her playpen in the corner.

Hotta hears a bird singing a beautiful song.

'Listen, Cozy! Isn't that lovely?' she says, busy with the silverware.

The birdsong goes on.

'I wonder what sort of bird that is', Hotta murmurs, going on to lay the next table. 'I've never heard anything like it'.

Now the song changes and gets louder.

'Isn't that beautiful, Cozy?'

Hotta turns to see if Cozy likes the song too.

She blinks twice and runs to her chick.

'Cozy! Is that you? Are you the bird I can hear?'

Cozy is standing in her playpen, whistling away. Her beak is high in the air, and beautiful silver notes are pouring out of it.

'Oh, Cozy, you can sing!'

'Whistle!' Cozy chirps.

'Oh, this is singing, not whistling, Cozy. Who

would have guessed that a toucan and a penguin could have a beautiful singing daughter?'

Hotta is so happy!

'We have to tell Mr. Ptera what you can do', Hotta says. 'He will be thrilled!'

Cozy goes back to singing, or whistling as she calls it. Hotta goes back to work, smiling.

Just Bad Luck!

23 SEPTEMBER Mummy Snake and Slye are in their back garden. They are playing a game of catch with a plastic frisbee.

Slye loves playing catch with her mummy!

'You're getting good at this!' Mummy says.

She spins the red frisbee through the air.

'I love the way it floats and zooms', Slye laughs, catching it.

Slye throws it back to Mummy.

Mummy catches it and calls out, 'Right Slye. Get ready for a long one!'

Slye goes back quite a long way and her mummy throws the frisbee really hard.

Slye runs further and further back.

The wind suddenly comes up. It catches the frisbee and blows it off to the side, straight towards Slye's bedroom window.

'Oh dear!' cries Slye.

CRASH! The window breaks into pieces.

'Oh no!' cries Mummy.

They run to Slye's room.

'Slye, you'd better stay outside in the hall', Mummy cautions. Mummy gets a dustpan and brush and starts sweeping up the broken glass.

'I feel a bit silly, breaking this window', Mummy says, shaking her head.

'It's alright, Mummy', Slye says. 'Accidents can happen'.

Mummy grins. 'That's true, but I am sure you are glad that it was *my* accident, and not yours!' she laughs.

She finishes her sweeping. 'Daddy can fix it tonight. So that's that. Let's play a bit more', she says, and they go back outside.

Just Like Flying!

24 SEPTEMBER

Baabra Sheep and her grandmother are going roller skating.

'You'll love it', Grandmother smiles. 'It's just like flying!'

Baabra nods. 'I love ice skating, so I'm sure I'll love roller skating too', she replies.

Grandmother puts a pair of beautiful new roller skates on Baabra. Then puts on her own.

'First, let's make certain that you know how to stop. That's important!' laughs Grandmother. 'Here is what you do'.

She skates a little way, then puts her toe bumper down, and stops.

'Right. Your turn!' she calls.

Baabra does the same. It works!

'I'm roller skating! Whoopee!' yells Baabra.

Baabra's a bit wobbly, but she's quickly getting better and better. She skates up and down, faster and faster. Suddenly Baabra's skate hits a crack and she falls over.

'Ouch!' she cries, rubbing her knee.

'Poor you!' exclaims Grandmother, skating over to Baabra. 'Are you alright?'

'Yes, it hurts a little, but I'm fine', Baabra says, getting up.

'I know what! Let's skate to the café and get an ice cream', Grandmother says.

'I don't think my knee hurts anymore', Baabra smiles. 'Let's go for some ice cream!'

Understanding Scruffy

25 SEPTEMBER

The Hideout is buzzing with talk about Scruffy Hyena. He's not there yet.

The friends finally understand what has made Scruffy so difficult to get along with.

'You mean he just suddenly got sent here to stay with the Zebra family?' Hoopla Hippo says, shaking his head.

'Well, his parents were trying to do their best for him. To let him spend the summer somewhere where he'd have lots of food', says Nolo Giraffe, remembering what it feels like to be hungry.

'I would miss my family so much', Baabra Sheep says. 'I couldn't bear to be so far away. No wonder he's had some bad days'.

'He's done some strange things, but he's a nice person', Bouncer Brachio says. 'Why don't we give him a leaving party?'

'Yes!' they all agree. They start planning.

When Scruffy arrives later with Zig and Zag Zebra, everyone suddenly stops talking.

'Um… Scruffy, what's your favourite kind of ice cream?' asks Baabra.

'Me?' Scruffy asks, surprised. 'Chocolate!'

'Me too!' 'Me too!' 'Me too!' lots of them say.

'Why did you ask?' Scruffy turns to Baabra.

'I was just curious', says Baabra sweetly, with a wink to the friends.

'Let's play hide and seek!' Nolo cries, winking back. 'Scruffy, you get to be IT first'.

'One! Two! Three! Four!' Scruffy starts counting and everybody scrambles out of the Hideout to find a good hiding place in the woods.

'Ready or not, HERE I COME!' yells Scruffy, and he starts looking for his friends.

Everybody Wins

Nolo Giraffe, Bouncer Brachio, Hoopla Hippo and Scruffy Hyena are playing a board game.

'You try to win as many bananas as you can', explains Nolo to Scruffy.

He deals out some cards and they choose their markers. There's a pile of small yellow plastic bananas in the centre of the board.

Laughing away, they march their markers around the board when they guess what's on the cards.

'I'm winning!' crows Bouncer early in the game.

But then Hoopla starts moving ahead. 'I'll beat you!' he laughs at Bouncer.

Now Nolo is ahead. He thumps on his chest.

It's Scruffy's turn. He guesses right about the card and reaches for a banana.

'Oh no', cries Hoopla.

'What's wrong?' asks Nolo.

'I'm going to sneeze!' Hoopla gasps, a funny look on his face. The others stare at him.

'Ah-ah-ah-ah-ah-CHOO!' explodes Hoopla. As he sneezes, he tips the board over. Cards, markers and bananas fly through the air, all around the room.

'Oh! I'm really sorry!' Hoopla begins, but it's so funny, he can't stop himself.

'HOOO, HO-HO-HO-HO!'

'HOOO, HO-HO-HO-HO!'

'I suppose we can say now that we'll never know who won', laughs Nolo. 'Let's decide we all did!'

September

Roota's discovery

27 SEPTEMBER

Roota Rooster is excited. He's worked out how to become taller!

'I've always wanted to be tall', he says to himself. 'So I hope this will work'.

Roota has found two wooden blocks in his garden. He attaches one underneath each of his claws with a strap.

'Right!' he cackles. 'My stilts are ready!'

'That's it!' he clucks happily. Roota puts one foot after the other. *Stamp! Stamp! Stamp! Stamp!*

Marching through his garden with his neck stretched high, he can see what is happening on the other side of the garden wall.

'I can see *everything*!' he crows proudly.

Staring over the wall, he suddenly sees Mr. Horse kissing Miss Pinto Pony. Then she laughs shyly and he giggles too. They don't notice Roota.

'I have to tell my wife this! She is in the clinic looking after her patients', Roota says.

Dr. Henny is talking to Hotta Toucan as Roota rushes in.

'I just saw our mayor, Mr. Horse, kiss Miss Pinto Pony'. he says excitedly. 'Can you believe it?'

'Really? Are you serious, Roota?' Hotta says. 'I have to tell Chilly Penguin and the guests at our café about this!' And she rushes off home.

At that moment, Mr. Horse enters the café and the guests start cheering. 'Congratulations! Mr. Mayor and your new girlfriend!'

Mr. Horse turns red. 'How did you know about that?' he stammers, a little embarrassed.

'Well, good news travels fast', Hotta laughs.

'Well, it is good news indeed!' beams Mr. Horse.

Zag's Job Day

28 SEPTEMBER

Mr. Brachio is at the camping ground, on the path that comes from Firefly Village.

'Ah, here she comes!' he says, waving as Zag Zebra cycles through the fallen leaves.

'Hello, Mr. Brachio', she calls.

'Welcome! Let's get to work. We have a very important job to do today', he replies.

He leads Zag into the woods.

'We need to put this sign up next to some mushrooms that are poisonous', he says, showing Zag a stick with a little sign on it.

'Poisonous?' blinks Zag. Do you mean like in the Snow White story when the wicked step-mother poisons an apple?'

'Exactly like that', Mr. Brachio answers. 'These really can make you very, very ill. So we want to make sure nobody touches or tastes them at all', he says.

Soon they come to a patch of mushrooms. They have reddish heads and white spots.

'They look pretty. Like little umbrellas', says Zag. 'Who would guess they are poisonous?'

'Exactly', says Mr. Brachio. 'Youngsters should never touch or taste mushrooms without a grown-up who knows all about them. The good types can taste lovely. But some types, like this one, are dangerous – and that's no joke!'

He hands Zag the sign. She sticks it in the ground next to the patch of mushrooms. 'I'm saving somebody's life!' she exclaims.

'You really could be doing that', Mr. Brachio says, smiling.

September

29
SEPTEMBER

Skipping

It's a beautiful evening. Families are enjoying themselves on the harbour before the sun sets.

Baabra Sheep and Zig and Zag Zebra are skipping, using a long rope on the dock.

Baabra and Zig are turning the rope and Zag is jumping in the middle. She's really good!

The Brachio family walks by.

'Can I try?' Bouncer asks. He loves it.

'Of course! With a name like Bouncer you must be good!' laughs Baabra.

Bouncer runs into the centre, where the rope hits the dock. He jumps, then dashes out.

'Brilliant, Bouncer!' calls Zag.

'Can we try?' asks Daddy Brachio, grabbing Mummy's hand. She laughs.

The youngsters stare at the grown-ups.

'Why… why yes!' exclaims Zig, astonished.

Holding hands, Bouncer's mummy and daddy run into the centre. They jump around as if they're at a dancing party, kicking and waving their arms. Then they dash out.

'That was amazing!' cries Baabra.

'Can we try too?' asks Mummy Hippo, who's walking by with Hoopla and Daddy Hippo. The three hippos run in, jump like mad, and run out.

'Who would think our parents could jump like that!' cries Bouncer, as everybody claps.

'We were young once, too you know!' laughs Daddy Hippo.

 ## Scruffy Goes Home

30 SEPTEMBER Today Scruffy Hyena is leaving Firefly Island to go back home. The friends are at Hotta Toucan and Chilly Penguin's café.

The Zebra family is walking towards the ferry dock. Zig and Zag look as if they could burst!

'Scruffy! Come over here for a second', Baabra Sheep calls. Scruffy walks over.

The friends crowd around Scruffy as he comes to Baabra's table. She whips a cloth off something and they all yell, 'Surprise!'

Scruffy jumps. He sees a beautiful chocolate ice cream cake. It has his name on it!

'Gosh!' he cries. 'What's this for?'

Hotta comes over. 'It says 'Come Back Soon, Scruffy!' We all wanted to give you a going away party, and we know you like chocolate ice cream cake the best!'

'Oh!' is all that Scruffy can say. He looks around at everyone and grins.

'You have all been really kind to me. I'm sorry I wasn't that nice all the time. But I really loved Firefly Island… and you all. I will miss you', he adds softly.

'Three cheers for Scruffy!' cries Nolo Giraffe.

'Hip-hip-hooray! Hip-hip-hooray! Hip-hip-hooray!' they shout, and Hotta serves the cake.

Tooooot! goes the *Tinker Bell* as she lands.

They finish the cake and walk with Scruffy to the ferry. Captain Cow waves at him.

Scruffy hugs everyone. He takes a deep breath. 'Thank you everyone! Maybe I can come back next summer!' he says, and he runs onto the ferry. 'Goodbye!' he yells, waving to all the new friends he has made.

October

face too. Baabra laughs again.

'What is going on, Baabra? This isn't like you. You're so good almost all of the time', Mummy says, puzzled now.

Lammie pulls his mouth into a funny shape with his fingers.

Baabra points to him, laughing again.

Mummy turns round, sees Lammie, and bursts out laughing too.

'You little rascal!' she cries, giving Lammie a hug. She turns back to Baabra.

'I see now, Baabra! You two are so silly!'

'I'm sorry, Lammie', Baabra chuckles, and they all laugh together!

Making Faces

1 OCTOBER

Baabra is in trouble. She has eaten a biscuit that her mummy gave to Lammie and her mummy is cross.

'Baabra, you had your own biscuit. It wasn't right to eat Lammie's too', Mommy scolds, shaking a finger at Baabra.

Lammie is standing behind Mummy. He's making an angry face and shaking a finger at Baabra, just like Mummy is. Mummy can't see him, but Baabra can.

Baabra laughs. That makes Mummy more cross.

'It's not funny, Baabra! Please tell Lammie you are sorry', Mummy says sternly, shaking her finger.

Lammie shakes his finger again, making a funny

Beach Treasures

2 OCTOBER

Zig and Zag Zebra love walking along the beach by the harbour, looking for treasure.

'Look at this!' cries Zig, picking up a pretty stone.

'Maybe it's a diamond!' she exclaims.

'Oh! That's beautiful!' breathes Zag.

'What's that?' asks Zag, pouncing on something else. 'An emerald from a crown?'

'Let's ask Mr. Ptera!' says Zig, and Zag nods. He is walking towards them along the sand.

They show their treasures to him.

'I think your stone is an agate, Zig. You are Zig, aren't you?' he smiles.

'Yes', she answers. 'So it's not a diamond?'

'No, but it's still a beautiful stone', Mr. Ptera says, turning it over and over in his hand.

'What about mine? Isn't it pretty?' asks Zag.

Mr. Ptera laughs. 'Well, yours is actually a piece of glass from a green bottle! It's been rolling around in the sand and water for so long that it's got smooth and polished'. He hands it back.

'So it's really a piece of rubbish?' Zag looks sad.

'Well, it might be, but it's really pretty. Pretty enough for a crown!' answers Zig.

Hoopla the Climber

Hoopla Hippo has a wonderful tree in his back garden. It is a perfect tree for climbing in.

Daddy Hippo always helps Hoopla to get up to the first branch. But Daddy is working.

'I'll push that chair up to the tree and stand on it. Then I can reach that branch', Hoopla thinks.

He pushes a garden chair next to the tree.

'Ummmph! Ummmph!' he grunts.

'Yes! I can reach that branch now!' he cries.

He stretches high and just barely grabs it.

'Ummmph! Ummmph!' he grunts, slowly pulling himself up. He settles in a fork of the tree's branches and looks around the garden.

'I'm really high up now! And I did it all by myself!' he says happily.

Birds come and perch in the tree above him.

Hoopla decides to climb a little higher.

'Ummmph! Ummmph! This is hard!' he mutters, standing up on the branches to reach up higher.

Suddenly Hoopla slips and falls backwards!

His foot gets caught in the fork of the branches as he falls. How he is completely stuck there!

Hoopla is now hanging by one foot, upside down.

'Ouch! That hurts!' he cries. 'But I'm really lucky', he thinks. 'I could have fallen all the way to the ground. That would have hurt a lot more!'

'Help! Help!' he shouts, over and over again.

Just then Bouncer Brachio comes around the corner of the house. He stops and stares.

'Hoopla! What happened?' he shouts.

Hoopla waves his arms and one leg and yells, 'I'll tell you after you get me down!'

Bouncer runs to get Mummy Hippo. She helps Hoopla to untangle his foot and get down. Hoopla hugs Bouncer.

'Thank you! You saved my life!' Hoopla pants.

October

Caveman Nolo

4
OCTOBER

Nolo Giraffe is looking at his favourite book these days. It is about cavemen.

'They had a wonderful life, living in caves and shooting mammoths for food', he thinks.

'I'll make a bow and arrow!' he decides.

He goes outside and finds a curved stick.

'Now I need some stretchy string', he murmurs. 'Maybe Mummy has some'.

Mummy does, but before she gives it to Nolo, she says, 'I want you to promise me that you will never point your arrows at anything that's alive or that could break. Do you promise?'

'Yes', answers Nolo very seriously.

Nolo ties the string to the ends of his stick.

TWANGGG!! it goes when he plucks it.

Now he needs some arrows. He goes back to Mummy.

'I can give you three wooden skewers, but I want to hear you promise again that you will not shoot at anything that's alive or breakable'.

'I promise, Mummy', Nolo says.

Now he's ready to be a caveman. He puts his toy elephant on a box.

'You're going to be a mammoth today!' he whispers to it. He puts an arrow against the string of his bow.

'Now I just pull the string and arrow back, point at the mammoth, and let go', he thinks.

TWANGGG! The arrow flies at the mammoth and hits it!

'I did it! I could be a caveman!' he cries. 'Mammoth steaks for dinner tonight!'

Birds of a Feather

5
OCTOBER

Cozy, the chick, is growing fast. She whistles beautifully now!

Dr. Henny hears her when she comes into Hotta Toucan's and Chilly Penguin's café.

'My goodness, Cozy, you sound wonderful!' cries Dr. Henny, clapping the chick.

'Maybe we could learn to do a song together one day', she adds. 'You know, I'm taking singing lessons now. I started out sounding really awful,

but I'm getting better!' Dr. Henny explains. Cozy doesn't understand a thing, but that doesn't matter. She goes on whistling beautiful tunes.

'La-la-la-LA-la-la-la', sings Dr. Henny, warming up her voice.

A glass next to her explodes into pieces.

'Oh, my goodness!' she cries. 'I'd better sing more softly, I think!' Hotta cleans up the mess.

'Twee-twee-twee-TWEE-twee-twee-twee', answers Cozy, flapping her wings.

They start singing and whistling together. Dr. Henny sounds much better when she sings softly.

'They actually sound rather good!' smiles Hotta as she serves the customers coffee and cakes.

'Maybe if you two practise together, you could put on a show for the village', says Chilly.

'That would be lots of fun!' exclaims Dr. Henny.

'Would you like that, Cozy?' Hotta asks.

'Like that! Like that!' Cozy echoes, with no idea what she's saying. Still, she loves whistling so much, she will definitely love to give a concert with Dr. Henny. What fun she'll have!

Grandmother Brachio's Spaghetti Sauce

6 OCTOBER

Grandmother Brachio is really proud of her spaghetti sauce.

'Grandad's tomatoes are so delicious', she always says. 'How could I possibly make a bad sauce?'

Today she's making a big batch to save for the winter. The kitchen smells wonderful.

'Let's have some of that sauce tonight please', begs Grandad when he comes through the kitchen.

'Yes dear', laughs Grandmother. She adds a pinch of salt and stirs the sauce.

Grandmother lays the table. She adds a pinch of salt to the sauce and stirs it again.

Now she starts cooking the spaghetti. She adds a pinch of salt to the spaghetti sauce.

The spaghetti's ready! Grandad puts some spaghetti and sauce on his plate and adds some cheese.

'I can't wait!' he says, and takes a big mouthful. Then he freezes.

'What's wrong dear?' asks Grandmother.

'Salt!' croaks Grandad, grabbing a glass of water and drinking the whole lot in one go.

'Salt? What do you mean?' asks Grandmother. 'I just added one pinch, like I always do…. Oh no. Maybe I added a pinch, and then a pinch, and then a pinch. That's far too much salt!'

She tastes it and grabs her water glass too.

'I did add too much! Sorry, dear – I'll make some new sauce tomorrow. I really am silly!'

195

A Sharp Pain

7 OCTOBER

Roota Rooster is having a cup of coffee this morning at Hotta Toucan's café.

'Ouch!' he cries out suddenly, putting his cup of coffee down on the table.

Hotta comes over, worried about him.

'What's the matter, Roota?' she asks.

'I don't know', Roota answers, rubbing his eye and shaking his head.

'Every time I take a sip of my coffee, I get a sharp pain in my right eye'.

'Really?' Hotta exclaims. 'You'd better go and see your wife, Dr. Henny, straight away!'

'Well, maybe I should', agrees Roota. 'But your coffee tastes so good, I want to finish this cup before I go to the clinic'.

'That's nice to hear, Roota. But don't take too long. Something's wrong!' Hotta says.

'Yes', Roota says, nodding. He lifts his cup up to take another sip of coffee.

'Ouch!' he cries again.

Hotta bursts out laughing.

'I don't think you need to go and see Dr. Henny after all, Roota. I already know how to cure your pain', she chuckles.

'Really?' blinks Roota.

'Yes. Try taking the spoon out of your cup!'

Roota slowly takes the spoon out. 'Ahem… thank you', he says rather sheepishly!

Fairy Tale Game

8 OCTOBER

'Let's play fairy tales', says Slye Snake this afternoon.

She's playing at her house with Nolo Giraffe and Bouncer Brachio.

'What do we do?' asks Bouncer.

'Well, we act out a fairy tale', explains Slye. 'I'll be the princess. One of you is the evil prince and the other is the good prince. Who is who?'

'I'll be the evil one', Nolo laughs.

'Then I'll be the good one!' says Bouncer.

'So you've captured me, Prince Nolo, and taken me to your evil castle. Prince Bouncer, you have to rescue me', says Princess Slye.

She climbs up on a table and waves to Bouncer. 'I'm trapped in the tower! Oh, help me!' she cries in a squeaky little voice.

'You are my prisoner!' growls Nolo.

'I'll save you, Princess!' answers Bouncer. He pretends to stab Nolo in the tummy.

'Take that!' he cries. 'And that! And that!'

'Oh no. You got me!' yells Nolo, and he falls.

Bouncer bows to Princess Slye, who gets off the table.

'My hero!' she cries.

Prince Nolo sits up. 'That was fun!'

'Not as much fun as cops and robbers, though!' laughs Bouncer.

October

Spots and Stripes

9 OCTOBER

Miss Pinto Pony has come to visit Mr. Horse again. They are very happy to see each other! As they walk along the harbour, Zig and Zag Zebra pass by.

'Hello Mr. Horse', Zig says.

'Hello, Zig and Zag', Mr. Horse answers. 'This is my friend, Miss Pinto Pony', he says, and everybody smiles.

'Mr. Horse tells me that you moved to Firefly Island this year', Miss Pony says. 'Do you like it?'

'Oh, yes', smiles Zig.

'We love playing with our friends here', Zag adds. 'We have learned how to play hide and seek!'

'I imagine you're very good at that, with all your stripes', Miss Pony smiles. 'I notice things like that, because I have spots'.

'What do you mean?' Mr. Horse asks.

'We'll show you. Close your eyes', Miss Pony tells Mr. Horse, and she winks at the twins. They tiptoe into the shadowy bushes.

'Okay, now see if you can find us!' calls Miss Pony. Mr. Horse looks around.

He peers this way and that, but he can't see them anywhere at all!

'Here we are!' calls Miss Pony, and the three come out back into the sunlight.

'You really were invisible in the shade!' Mr. Horse exclaims. 'I wish I had spots or stripes!'

'Sorry, it's too late now. Anyway, you have such a beautiful long mane instead', laughs Miss Pony. 'It's lovely to meet you Zig, and Zag', she smiles. The couple stroll away. Zig turns to Zag. 'I think they're in love', she grins.

A Useful Long Neck

10 OCTOBER

Nolo Giraffe is on his way to Hoopla Hippo's house.

But before he gets there, he passes where Ivan Monkey lives.

'Did I hear something?' he asks himself, stopping to listen hard.

'There it is again!'

'Help! Help! I'm stuck! Oh, help!' he hears.

The cries are coming from inside Ivan's house.

Nolo goes to Ivan's door.

'Ivan, are you in trouble?' he calls.

'Yes! Please come in! I'm stuck!' yells Ivan.

Nolo goes inside and sees Ivan in a corner of the living room. He's got a paintbrush and a can of floor paint next to him.

The whole floor has been painted, except for the place where Ivan is standing.

'Ivan, what in the world?' laughs Nolo.

'I started painting my floor, but I didn't think which direction to work in. So I painted myself into this corner. I'll be stuck here until tomorrow morning, when the paint is dry and I can walk on it!' Ivan cries.

'Perhaps I can help', Nolo smiles.

He stays where he is, just outside the living room. Slowly he leans his long, long neck forwards across the wet paint.

'Jump onto my neck and I'll lift you out', he says.

Ivan hugs Nolo's neck and Nolo slowly carries him over the wet paint. He's free!

'Hurray! You're a genius!' cries Ivan. 'I'm glad it was you and not Hoopla who came. Hoopla doesn't have much of a neck, and he's got the biggest feet on the island!'

The Toy Library

'Mummy, what's recycling?' asks Bouncer Brachio. He has heard grown-ups talking about it.

'It's finding new ways to use things that we used to just throw away as rubbish', Mummy says.

Bouncer thinks about his toys. He hasn't played with some of them for ages.

'You mean if I throw away a toy I don't want any more?'

'Exactly', answers Mummy. 'It's a shame'.

'I wonder how we could recycle toys', he thinks. His face lights up.

'What if we had a place for toys we get tired of? Maybe somebody else would see them and then they could carry on playing with them'.

'What a good idea!' answers Mummy. 'See what your friends think. If you want, you can use a corner of my gift shop to recycle old toys'.

'Perhaps we can say that if you bring a toy to recycle, you can pick out a different one to take home!' says Bouncer.

'Excellent!' Mummy says. 'Those toys will love it if children keep on playing with them!'

Later, at the Hideout, Bouncer tells the friends about his idea.

They think it's brilliant.

Slye Snake says, 'It's like a library. You take a book home, have fun with it and bring it back. This is the same, but with toys!'

'So let's call it our toy library!' laughs Bouncer. 'We just need to go through our toys and bring some to the gift shop. Let's each bring five old toys tomorrow!'

October

The Toy Library Opens

12 OCTOBER

The gift shop is full of excited youngsters and old toys.

'Bouncer, this was your idea, so you can start', Mummy Brachio says.

'My mummy has given us this bit of her shop to use for our toy library', Bouncer explains, pointing to a corner with empty shelves.

'Let's put our old toys over there. Then we can take other ones home!' he laughs.

The friends line up their toys on the shelves.

It looks just like a toy shop!

'Right, now it's time to pick out a toy you want to take home', Bouncer says.

The corner is a beehive of busy youngsters, all giggling as they decide. Finally, everybody is happy with their 'new' toys.

'Let's say that from now on, each time you bring an old toy in, you can take a different one home', Slye Snake says. 'We'll always have lots of different toys to choose from'.

Everybody nods. This is a dream come true!

Mummy Brachio speaks up. 'I think it's wonderful that you have started recycling, all by yourselves. So I made a cake to celebrate'.

She brings out a big cake. It's covered with tiny little toys. The youngsters cheer.

'It says toy library day!' Mummy explains as she cuts the cake. 'It's a perfect start of new lives for these old toys!'

Slye's Job Visit

13 OCTOBER

Mr. Horse is frantically cleaning his office. Dust is flying everywhere.

Sly Snake is coming to work with him on her job visit today. He wants everything to be perfect.

'I'll just put these papers here', he thinks, 'so everything is tidy'. He shoves a pile of papers under his desk.

'Hello, Mr. Horse', calls Slye as she comes in.

'Hello Slye, nice to see you!' he exclaims.

'What is it like, being a mayor?' Slye asks.

'You have a great many things to do!' laughs Mr. Horse. 'You have to make sure all the villagers' problems get sorted, such as our clock that was broken in the winter storm'.

'Yes!' laughs Slye. 'Ivan Monkey did that'.

'And you make speeches and give awards', he adds, pointing to his megaphone and soapbox.

'And then there's all the paperwork', he sighs.

'Well, how can I help you?' asks Slye.

'I was thinking that perhaps you could make a welcome speech at the little concert that Cozy and Dr. Henny are giving tomorrow. Would you like

to do that?' he asks hopefully.

'Oh yes! I'd love to!' Slye smiles. 'I'll need some tips on what to say. But first, we could file all those papers stuffed under your desk?'

Mr. Horse stares at Slye, then looks down.

'Um, that would be really, really good Slye!'

They pull out the pile and start filing, talking about tomorrow's speech as they work.

Musical Tea Party

14 OCTOBER The café is packed with villagers of all ages today.

Hotta Toucan and Chilly Penguin have invited them for a tea party. There will be music performed by Dr. Henny and their chick, Cozy.

'My fellow villagers, welcome!' exclaims Slye Snake, standing on Mr. Horse's soapbox. 'I am Slye, and I am Mr. Horse's assistant today'.

Everybody chuckles and claps.

'We are lucky to be able hear two new musicians this afternoon. Dr. Henny has been taking singing lessons and she has become really good at it, and Mr. Ptera has taught Cozy to whistle. So let's welcome them!' Slye exclaims. She bows and steps down.

Dr. Henny winks at Cozy and they begin a song. The villagers are amazed.

'Wonderful!' 'Terrific!' 'So beautiful!' think the villagers as they listen.

When the songs are over, the villagers clap and clap. Nobody expected the concert to be so good!

'And now, please help yourselves to treats', Hotta smiles. Slye makes a dive for some chocolate cake.

Mr. Horse comes over to Slye. 'You did a really good job', he beams. 'Your speech was short, friendly and to the point'.

'Thank you, Mr. Horse', Slye says. 'And thank you for letting me try to be a mayor!' she smiles.

She thinks, 'The speech was easy. I just did what I've been telling Mr. Horse to do all year!'

15 OCTOBER — Heave-Ho!

Grandad Brachio is riding a small tractor, cutting the grass. The ground is muddy because it has been raining a lot. 'I have almost finished', he thinks. Just then one of the tractor's wheels hits a patch of mud. Then another one does.

The tractor stops moving – it's stuck!

'Oh no!' he exclaims. He hops off and tries to push the tractor forward, but it won't move.

Bouncer Brachio rides up on his bicycle.

'Let me help!' he calls.

They push and push, but it doesn't help.

'I'll get my friends to help', Bouncer tells Grandad. 'You'd better get your long rope!'

A short while later all the friends come pedalling up. Bouncer takes charge.

'Let's tie this rope to the front', he says.

'Hoopla, grab the rope. Pull when I shout HO', he explains. 'The rest of you push from behind'.

'Heave-HO! Heave-HO! Heave-HO!' he yells.

With each 'HO!' Hoopla pulls and the others push. The tractor starts rocking backwards and forwards. Then it slowly rolls out of the mud.

'Hooray! We did it!' the friends cry.

'Hoopla, you were brilliant!' exclaims Grandad.

'I loved it', Hoopla laughs. 'The mud was what was really good!' And he starts his big hippo laugh.

'HOOO, HO-HO-HO-HO!'

'HOOO, HO-HO-HO-HO!'

16 OCTOBER — Miss Pinto Pony Writes

Miss Pinto Pony has been working at her home on Big Island today. She writes story books for children.

But at the moment, she is writing a postcard.

'Dear Mr. Horse', she writes. 'Good news. I have just finished the book that I've been writing!'

She smiles, thinking about Mr. Horse.

'It has really been fun getting to know you. I think about you, Firefly Island, and the villagers a lot. The youngsters are wonderful!'

She draws a smiley face.

'I hope we I can see you again really soon. Love from Pinto'.

She sticks a stamp on the card and writes Mr.

Horse's address on it. Then she wraps up the pages of the story book she just finished writing and trots off to the Big Island post office.

She sends her postcard and package off and on the way home, she goes to the ferry dock.

'Here comes the *Tinker Bell* from Firefly Island', she thinks. Suddenly she jumps with surprise. Mr. Horse is on the ferry!

'Mr. Horse! Hello!' she shouts, waving to him. He waves back. As soon as the ferry docks, he trots over to her and gives her a kiss.

'I have been thinking about you all morning, so I just got on the ferry to come and say hello', he says, looking a little pink.

'I have been thinking about you as well!' Miss Pinto Pony answers, pink too. 'In fact, I have just sent you a postcard. It says that I hoped we could meet again soon. And here you are!' she laughs.

'Let's have some tea and a chat', he says, and off they go. What a lovely surprise!

Hoopla Meets the Fish

17 OCTOBER

Hoopla Hippo is strolling out along the dock today.

'Here, fishy-fishy-fishy-fishy', he calls, throwing some pieces of bread into the water. Hoopla has heard about the golden fish that some of the villagers have seen. He wants to meet it too.

He peers into the water. Then he walks to a different spot on the dock and looks down again.

'I think they are playing a joke. No golden fish', he sighs.

Suddenly he realises that there's a huge shape deep in the water, right under him.

'Is that it? The fish?' he wonders.

The shape rises slowly. Two golden eyes fix Hoopla's own eyes with a direct stare.

Hoopla is almost afraid for a second. Then he pushes his lips out so he looks a little like a fish and says, 'Whooo… arrre… youuu?'

The fish shakes its head from side to side.

'You won't tell me?' Hoopla shrugs.

'Arrre yooou a boooy or girrrl?' he asks.

The fish shakes its head again.

'I suppose I'm not going to get any answers', laughs Hoopla. 'But it certainly is amazing to be talking to a giant golden fish!'

A Second Secret

18 OCTOBER

Grandmother Brachio and Bouncer are making a huge pot of vegetable soup with things from Bouncer's garden.

'When it's ready Bouncer, we'll put it in the freezer. That way we can enjoy the summer in the middle of winter!' smiles Grandmother.

'I'll never forget my secret plant – my giant pumpkin. Or the giant pumpkin boat race afterwards', laughs Bouncer.

'Did you enjoy the second secret that Grandad planted in your garden?' asks Grandmother.

'What secret? Is there another one?' asks Bouncer curiously. 'I'm sure there isn't anything growing in my garden that I don't know about by now'.

'Oh! Silly me! I forgot I wasn't supposed to say anything yet!' exclaims Grandmother. 'Please don't tell Grandad I said that'.

Bouncer looks closely at Grandmother. 'Can't you tell me now?' he asks sweetly.

'My goodness, no!' Grandmother says. 'You must just pretend that I haven't said anything!'

'Please, sweetest Grandmother, please tell me the big secret!' Bouncer begs.

'Heavens, no!' Grandmother exclaims. 'Your grandad would be very disappointed with me'.

Bouncer smiles. 'Alright. I promise not to say anything!' He keeps wondering what else could be in his garden.

'That grandad of mine loves a joke!' he thinks.

Being Greedy

19 OCTOBER

Zig and Zag Zebra are playing in their room.

'I'm bored with our toys', sighs Zig. She finishes a puzzle and puts it on the shelf.

'Then let's go to the toy library and swap them for some new ones', suggests Zag.

'Good idea!' Zig perks up. 'We have to bring in an old toy to swap for another, yes?'

'That's how it works', laughs Zag.

Zig picks a puzzle, and Zag takes a beach ball. They jump on their bicycles and cycle off.

'Hello, Zig! Hello, Zag!' calls Mrs. Brachio when they arrive at her gift shop. 'I see you're here to visit the toy library!'

'Hello! Mrs. Brachio. Yes!' they say together, and they run to the shelves full of toys.

'Look, there's my old rubber duck!' says Zig.

'Nobody wants you, little duck?' she croons.

They walk up and down along the shelves.

'I want this crown', decides Zag.

'I want this book and this toy horse', Zig says.

'Wait a moment, Zig', Mrs. Brachio says, frowning a little and coming over to them.

'You can only swap one for one. Not one for two',

'But I want both', Zig says firmly.

'I can see why. They're both lovely. But you don't want to be greedy, do you?' asks Mrs. Brachio gently.

'No… I suppose not', says Zig.

She puts the horse back on the shelf. Then she thinks for a second and brightens up.

'Of course! I can come back next week and swap this book for the horse! I'll still get to play with both, just not at the same time!'

Slye's Little Brother

20
OCTOBER

'Hello Wiggler!' whispers Slye Snake, playing in her room.

'Would you like to play with blocks?' she asks sweetly. 'Yes? Then let's do that'.

Slye would really like a baby brother, but she doesn't have one.

So she has a make believe one. He is two years old and his name is Wiggler.

'We put the big block down first', she explains to Wiggler. 'Then we can put smaller ones on top. Why don't you try it?' she asks.

Slye pretends to be Wiggler. She puts a smaller block on the big one. 'Good boy!' she nods.

'And then a pointed one on the top', she says. Wiggler picks it up and puts it on the tower. The tower wobbles and falls down.

'That doesn't matter Wiggler', Slye says gently.

'Now how about a story book?' Slye asks.

She imagines Wiggler nodding.

Slye picks out one of her baby books and sits on her bed. She shows Wiggler the pictures and tells the story.

'Oh, I can see you're getting sleepy. Time for your nap', Slye says.

She pretends to put Wiggler into her cradle. After she rocks the cradle for a little while she tiptoes out of her room.

'Gosh! It's hard work being a big sister. Now I want to go and play with my friends!'

Slye jumps on her bicycle and cycles off to visit Baabra Sheep!

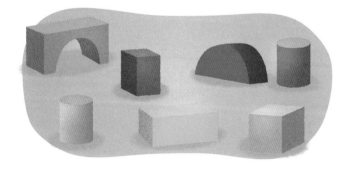

21 OCTOBER — Baabra's Little Brother

'I am so cross with Lammie!' says Baabra when Slye walks in to her bedroom.

'What do you mean?' asks Slye, surprised, thinking of Wiggler.

'Look! He broke my CD player!' she points.

'He plays with my things and breaks them. He wakes up in the middle of the night and I can't sleep. He teases me. Mummy spends more time taking care of him than me. He doesn't have to eat everything I do. And he doesn't get punished. Aaagh!' Baabra cries.

'But I thought you loved him', Slye says slowly.

'I do!' Baabra says. 'But sometimes I just wish he wasn't here'.

She takes a deep breath and calms down.

'The rest of the time he's lovely, and he's funny, and I really do love him', she grins.

'Well, I wish I had a little brother', Slye says. 'Even if they can be horrible sometimes, they are still lots of fun, aren't they?' she asks.

'Yes. You're right. Anyway, what shall we play?' asks Baabra, glad to change the subject. 'Puzzles? Watch cartoons? Something outside?'

'Anything but playing house!' laughs Slye. 'It sounds as if you've had enough of that for today!'

So the friends take Baabra's racquets and some balls and they go out to play happily in the back garden.

22 OCTOBER — Nolo's Biscuit Competition

'Listen. I have an idea for a new competition!' Nolo Giraffe says to his friends in the Hideout. They turn to him, curious about what he could be thinking now.

'I'll win! I know I will!' yells Hoopla Hippo.

'You don't even know what it's about yet!' giggles Baabra Sheep.

'It's simple. The first one who can eat six salty biscuits and all their crumbs in less than one minute wins', explains Nolo. He hands a paper plate and six square biscuits to each friend.

Then he gets out his stopwatch.

'Are you joking? That's much too easy!' says Baabra.

'Just you wait and see. It's harder than you think.

One! Two! Three! Go!' Nolo yells.

The friends start chewing.

The first two biscuits go down easily. But by now their mouths are really dry.

'I can't chew!' mumbles Baabra, her mouth full.

'I can't swallow!' laughs Hoopla, surprised.

The friends all thought this would be far too easy, but strangely, it's almost impossible!

Only two of them have managed to eat five biscuits and the seconds are ticking past.

'Time is almost up! Go-go-go!' cries Nolo.

Hoopla stuffs his sixth biscuit into his huge mouth and works hard to chew and swallow. His eyes bulge and blink with the effort.

'Time's up!' Nolo cries. Hoopla takes a bow.

'I won! I won! I told you that I would!' crows Hoopla. 'But I don't want to see or eat another dry biscuit ever again in my life!'

Riddle Time

23 OCTOBER Baabra's grandmother loves telling riddles and jokes. Tonight she's putting Baabra to bed with a few that she knows. 'Tell me. Which animals can fly higher than a house?' Grandmother asks.

Baabra knows. 'Birds and bats', she says.

'Actually, all animals can fly higher than houses, because houses can't fly!' laughs Grandmother.

'What's big, black and eats rocks?' she asks, challenging Baabra.

'Hoopla!' chuckles Baabra. 'Well, he's big and black. But mostly, he eats biscuits!'

'The answer is, a big, black rock-eater', giggles Grandmother. 'Now. What gets wetter the more it dries?' Baabra is completely stumped.

'A bath towel!' says Grandmother. 'Get it? And what weighs the same no matter how big it gets?' Baabra thinks hard but it doesn't make sense.

'A hole!' exclaims her grandmother.

'I've got one for you', says Baabra. 'What does a one ton canary say?'

Grandmother frowns. 'I don't really know'.

'TWEEEEEEEEEEEEEEEEET!' yells Baabra.

Grandmother and Baabra laugh and laugh.

'It looks as though loving jokes and riddles runs in our family, Baabra. That was a good one! I can't wait to tell it to somebody!' Grandmother says.

Then Grandmother hugs Baabra and gives her a goodnight kiss. She tucks her in and turns off the light.

October

Sock Puppet Theatre

24 OCTOBER

Tonight, the puppet theatre is set up in the village hall.

Everyone is eager to see the play the youngsters have made up and are going to perform.

The friends are ready with their new sock puppets on their hands.

'Help! I'm stuck in the mud!' says Nolo Giraffe, playing the part of Grandad Brachio.

'I'll go and get my friends to help you!' cries Bouncer.

All the puppets come running and puppet Grandad ties a little rope to the toy tractor. The other puppets grab the rope and pull.

'Heave-HO! Heave-HO! Heave-HO!' they yell. The tractor rocks back and forth. Then it slowly slides out of the mud.

'Hooray! We did it!' cry the youngsters.

'Thank you all so much!' exclaims Grandad Brachio in Nolo's voice.

'You're welcome!' answers Bouncer.

'THE END', he exclaims.

All the puppets take a bow. But this makes the puppet theatre tip forwards. It falls with a crash, leaving the youngsters staring at the audience.

It's silent for a moment. Then the audience starts laughing and clapping.

'What a wonderful play!' Mr. Horse says.

He holds medals on red ribbons, just like the ones in the Olympics.

'For strength, fine acting and giving us a laugh!' he reads. Then he hangs a medal around the neck of each of the friends. The villagers clap and cheer like mad!

Spooky Eyes

25 OCTOBER

Hoopla Hippo is in bed. It's pitch black in his room, except for a thin crack of light that shines in from under the curtain.

Hoopla is a little bit scared of the dark.

'What's that?' he freezes and listens.

'Oh. Just a breeze, moving the tree branches outside. It really sounded like a monster'.

He looks around his room.

'What's THAT?' he whispers. Two huge eyes are

staring at him from across his room!

Hoopla doesn't know whether to turn on his bedside light or dive under his blanket.

His heart is pounding so fast, he can hardly hear anything else. His mouth is dry.

'Who… who… are you?' he squeaks.

Silence.

'I must be brave', he tells himself, but he can't move.

'Come on, Hoopla! Be a hero!' he urges himself.

He reaches out and switches on the light.

'Oh gosh!' he breathes. 'It's just my teddy! The light was making his eyes glow!'

Hoopla is so relieved, he starts laughing!

'HOOO, HO-HO-HO-HO!'

'HOOO, HO-HO-HO-HO!'

26
OCTOBER

Football Anyone?

'I wish we had more friends here on the island', says Zag a little sadly.

'We have plenty!' answers Zig, her twin, really surprised at what Zag has said.

'I don't mean it that way. I was just wishing we could play a game of football. Our friends here are wonderful, but it's not like back home where we had enough people for two teams. You need eleven players for a team, you know'.

'Hmmm', says Zig, thinking fast. 'What if we asked the grown-ups to play too?'

'Yes! That would be fun!' Zag says, and she runs to tell their parents. They love the idea.

Zig and Zag cycle to their friends' houses and ask if everybody wants to have a game.

They all think it's an excellent idea. They agree to meet at the playground.

Zag makes up the team lists.

'I'll be captain of the red team and Slye Snake will be captain of the blue team', she announces.

Then she reads out the names for each team.

'I want to be on the red team!' cries Baabra Sheep. 'I want to play with Zag'.

Zag looks uncomfortable. 'Well, does anyone on the red team want to be on the blue team?'

Nobody answers. They all want to be on the red team because they look as though they will be the better team. All except for Bouncer Brachio. He doesn't care about winning.

'I'll swap teams. I just want to play!' Bouncer says with a smile.

The red team is relieved.

'Right, teams. Our game will be in two days, so good luck, reds and blues!'

October

Leaf Watchers

27 OCTOBER

'Autumn really is my favourite season', sighs Baabra Sheep, sitting with some friends in her back garden.

'Just look at those beautiful leaves!'

Slye Snake and Zig and Zag Zebra look up, and sigh too.

Red and gold leaves fill the air.

'And it SMELLS so lovely!' continues Baabra.

'This would be a perfect time to visit Mr. Trico in his tower!' says Slye suddenly.

'Yes! Let's go right now!' the friends say.

They jump on their bicycles and race through the woods.

Mr. Trico spots them with his binoculars, waves and shouts, 'Come on up!'

They start counting the steps as they climb. Slye can count all the way up to 100. When they reach step 100, she starts all over again. Finally they get to the second 100th step. They keep on climbing, puffing and laughing as they go.

'Phew! We made it!' they finally cry. And then in one voice, they all yell 'WOW!'

'Isn't it amazing?' asks Mr. Trico. The forest below is a carpet of red, yellow, gold and brown, with a few green spots here and there.

'I could stay here forever', sighs Baabra.

'Well, these apples won't last forever, but I'll share them with you today!' laughs Mr. Trico. They munch away, high above the autumn colours.

The Football Game

28 OCTOBER

'Welcome to the first Firefly Island Football Championship!' says Mr. Ptera. He is referee today. Mr. Horse, the mayor, is the goalkeeper for the red team.

'Right, team', says the red team captain, Zag Zebra, 'let's give it our best try!'

'Right, team', says the blue team captain, Slye Snake, 'we can do it!' The game begins.

'The grown-ups are fast, but the youngsters play better', thinks Mr. Horse in his goal. Suddenly Slye kicks the ball at the red goal.

'GOOOAAALLL! The blues have one point!' cries Mr. Ptera into the megaphone.

Ivan Monkey is nervous as the blue goalkeeper. 'I hope they don't shoot at my goal!' he thinks.

But here comes the red team, thundering towards him. Zag takes a kick – it's a goal!

'The reds have one point!' cries Mr. Ptera. 'It's a tie!'

The game is almost over. 'Come on, reds, let's get one more goal!' cries Captain Zag.

ZING! Zag scores again!

Ivan is flat on the ground. He has almost fainted from the excitement! Slowly he gets up.

'I'm glad it's over', he says. 'At least I played my best'.

'The reds have two points!' cries Mr. Ptera.

'And time is up! Game over! The reds win!'

'Yippee!' cry all the reds. Zag is so happy!

October

The Second Surprise

29 OCTOBER

Grandad Brachio and Bouncer are walking in the garden.

'It's time to pull up the plants that have given us our food', he says.

They yank out the pumpkin vine and take down Bouncer's bean teepee. That leaves the corn stalks.

'Look at this Bouncer', says Grandad, with a funny look on his face. 'You've still got some ears of corn left here'.

'Oh, good! I love corn on the cob!' Bouncer exclaims.

'But guess what', Grandad grins. 'This isn't ordinary corn. Can you guess what it is?'

'No. Corn is corn, isn't it?' Bouncer asks.

'Yes and no. This is popping corn!' Grandad laughs.

'Popping corn? You mean, for making popcorn?' Bouncer asks, astonished. 'Do you mean you can really grow popcorn?'

'You certainly can! Let's pick all the ears, and then I'll show you what to do', Grandad says.

'So this is your second secret, the one Grandmother almost told me about!' chuckles Bouncer as they pick the ears of popcorn.

Back in the kitchen, Grandad shows Bouncer what to do.

'Pull off the husks and silk. Now use your thumb to push against the kernels so they pop off the cobs', he says.

The kernels soon fill a huge glass jar.

'There you have it! Your own supply of popcorn to pop on those long winter nights!' Grandad says, patting Bouncer's back.

'I just hope that you'll remember to share some with your good old grandad!'

Nolo's Costume

30 OCTOBER

'Look! Guess what tomorrow is!' Nolo Giraffe exclaims at breakfast this morning.

'Halloween!' answers Mummy. 'There's a costume competition at the village hall tonight', she adds. 'Let's make yours right now!'

Nolo eats fast, thinking hard. The ferry *Tinker Bell* blows her horn in the harbour.

Suddenly he knows what he'll be, and he tells Mummy excitedly.

'That's brilliant, Nolo!' she exclaims. 'I think I know how we can make it'.

They collect a bell, a whistle, a lifebelt swimming ring, some rope and all kinds of other things. Then they get to work. Soon his costume is ready.

Nolo looks in the mirror. 'It's amazing Mummy!'

he laughs. 'Thank you very much!'

That night Nolo lines up with his friends in front of the costume competition judges. They look at each one and whisper back and forth.

Soon, Mr. Horse climbs on his soapbox.

'Congratulations on all your wonderful costumes. We have picked a winner. And the winner is… *Tinker Bell!* Nolo, here's your prize!'

Nolo, dressed up as a ferry boat, is thrilled. He waves to Captain Cow.

'*Tooot-tooot-tooot*' he bellows. 'I won!'

Halloween Scare

31 OCTOBER

It's a dark and stormy Halloween night. But every youngster is walking from house to house, wearing a costume and playing trick or treat.

Bouncer Brachio and Hoopla Hippo are out together. The wind whips their costumes as they get to Ivan Monkey's door.

'Do you think he'll have sweets or apples?' whispers Bouncer. 'Last year it was sweets'.

'I hope it is again!' murmurs Hoopla.

They spot a rope hanging by Ivan's door. A sign on it shows a short red word that they can't read, and a black arrow pointing down.

'Hmmm', says Bouncer. 'Is that Ivan's doorbell? Should we pull the rope?'

'It must be', says Hoopla importantly. He grabs the rope and pulls, calling, 'Trick or treat!'

Suddenly there's a crashing thunder of clanging, banging metal. A pile of pots and pans flies off a shelf above Ivan's door and they all bounce noisily on the ground.

'Ayeee! Ayeee! Ayeee!' scream the two friends, running away into the darkness.

Ivan opens his door and looks at the pile of pots and pans. He peers outside.

'Hmmm. Someone must have come to play trick or treat. I wonder why they didn't stay to get some sweets?' he mutters.

'At least my new door bell works!' he smiles.

November

All Gone?

Zag Zebra is smiling, standing all alone in the sunshine in the middle of Firefly Meadow. She is waiting for some butterflies to fly past her.

'Hmmm', she says, after a long wait. 'Not a single one! Something's really wrong here!'

She walks around the meadow.

Now she's worried. She starts to cry. 'Poor things! Where can they be?' she sobs.

'I've got to tell Mr. Brachio. Something's wrong!' she decides. She gallops through the woods. Mr. Brachio, the park ranger, knows everything about nature.

'Mr. Brachio!' she cries as she spots him. 'Something awful has happened. The butterflies in the meadow have all disappeared!'

Mr. Brachio gives Zag a little hug. 'Poor you! Don't be sad, Zag. You're right, they have gone, but that's normal', he says gently.

Zag calms down and wipes her tears away.

'The butterflies can't live through our cold winters here on the island. So they fly to a place far away that stays warm all winter. They will fly back next spring, when our weather is warm again'.

'Really?' Zag asks, amazed. 'You mean those tiny, beautiful things can really do that?'

'They certainly can!' Mr. Brachio laughs. 'Don't worry, Zag, they'll be back. I promise'.

'Then I'll be here to welcome them when they return', laughs Zag. 'What a relief!

Baabra's Job Visit

'Hi-ho, hi-ho, it's off to work I go!' sings Baabra Sheep as she skips towards the post office.

'Good morning!' Mrs. Trico calls out.

'Hello Mrs. Trico', answers Baabra. 'It's my job visit. What can I do to help?'

'We can start by sorting this morning's post. Do you know your numbers?' Mrs. Trico asks.

'Yes!' answers Baabra proudly.

'Good. I'll tell you what post office box number you need to put each letter in. This one goes in box number four', starts Mrs. Trico.

'This is like a game', laughs Baabra as she puts the

letters into the correct post office boxes.

'Next we'll sort the post that's going out. A pile for the post that stays on Firefly Island and one for post that will go out on the afternoon ferry', says Mrs. Trico.

'Island. Ferry. Island. Ferry', chants Baabra.

'And now you can stamp all those letters with today's date', Mrs. Trico says, handing Baabra a rubber stamp and ink pad.

Stamp! Stamp! Stamp! goes Baabra. 'I love this – it's just like a craft project!' she giggles.

Ting-a-ling! sounds the bell over the door. It's Mr. Horse. 'Any post for me? In box four?' he asks.

Mrs. Trico points to Baabra. 'There is!' Baabra says. 'I put a letter in box four just a moment ago!'

Mr. Horse turns the lock on his box and opens the little door. 'Hooray!' he cries. 'My friend, Miss Pinto Pony, has written to me! Thank you, Baabra!' And off he goes, reading his letter and smiling!

Scary Haircut

Hoopla Hippo hates to have his hair cut. He is worried that his little ears will get cut instead!

He is sitting in the barber's chair in front of the mirror in the barber's shop on Big Island.

'Now Hoopla, just sit very still and it will be fine', Daddy Hippo says gently.

But Hoopla's ears are twitching right and left. He is feeling more and more nervous! The barber starts cutting.

Clip! Clip! Clip! go the scissors, right by his ears. Little clumps of hair fall onto the floor.

'Halfway there!' sings out the barber soon. But poor Hoopla can't keep his ears still.

Snip! Snip! Snip! The barber's scissors are right next to Hippo's ear now. He jumps.

'Ouch! That hurt!' bellows the barber. He sucks the tip of his little finger.

'I'm sorry!' Hoopla gulps. 'I just got scared'.

The barber looks at his finger. 'It's just a tiny nip. Not even bleeding', he smiles.

But that's enough for Hoopla. He springs out of his chair, holding his ears.

'I'll never ever get another haircut!' he howls.

Daddy gives him a big hug. 'It was just an accident, Hoopla. It won't happen again'.

'It certainly won't!' cries Hoopla. 'I'm never coming back!' And he runs out of the door!

November

One Cold Hand

The weather has turned very cold. Bouncer Brachio is cycling home from the Hideout.

After riding a short way, he stops.

'My hands are really cold!' he mutters. He fishes a mitten out of a pocket and puts it on.

'Where's my other mitten? I must have lost it', he thinks, digging around in the other empty pocket. He starts pedalling again.

The icy wind blows hard on his bare hand. Before long his fingers are frozen and numb.

'I can't let go!' he thinks. Finally he arrives home. He stops his bicycle and gets ready to jump off. He can't open his hand at all!

Bouncer rolls his bicycle to the front door and rings the bell with his mittened hand.

Mummy opens the door. 'Mummy! Help! My hand is frozen!' he sobs.

Mummy rushes to him. 'Oh, poor you! Bring your bicycle inside and stand close to the fire in our fireplace, while I get some warm water', Mummy says, running to the kitchen.

In a moment Mummy is back. She starts sponging Bouncer's hand. Slowly he begins to wiggle his fingers. Finally he can let go of the bicycle.

'I'll never lose a mitten again', sniffs Bouncer. His mummy smiles. 'Let's have some hot chocolate to really warm you up', she whispers, giving Bouncer a big hug.

Roota Saves the Day

The village is going mad. Mr. Horse has lost the key to the safe in the village hall!

'I don't know what happened', explains an embarrassed Mr. Horse to the villagers at an emergency meeting. 'It's always on my key ring. I still have the ring and all the other keys. But the one for the safe has gone'. He shrugs.

'Let's blow the safe up!' suggests Ivan Monkey. 'Then we can get inside it'.

'No', chuckles Mr. Horse. 'That's not a good idea'.

Roota Rooster is listening, cocking his head from side to side. Suddenly he leaps to his feet, yelling, 'Just wait here! I have an idea!'

He flaps out of the village hall, leaving everyone

buzzing and wondering what's going on.

A few minutes later Roota comes puffing back, proudly carrying his can of precious things. He dumps them on Mr. Horse's table.

'Is there anything there that could open the safe?' he asks. Mr. Horse looks over the pile.

'Hmmm. This might work', Mr. Horse says, pulling out an old key. He walks to the safe and tries it. It fits! The safe door opens.

'It's not the key I lost, but it doesn't matter. It works! Three cheers for Roota!' cries Mr. Horse. The villagers cheer and clap.

'It's nothing', protests Roota. But he's thrilled!

Mr. Ptera's Gramophone

6 NOVEMBER

The youngsters are buying sweets at Mr. Ptera's general store.

Baabra Sheep smiles and asks, 'Have you seen any ghosts in your cellar lately?'

Mr. Ptera laughs and says, 'No, thankfully!'

Slye Snake wants to know what that's all about.

'Let's go and see', Mr. Ptera says. They all creep down to the cellar behind Mr. Ptera.

'No ghosts down here', complains Slye. 'But what's that thing?' She points to a box in a corner. It has a huge golden horn on top.

Mr. Ptera says, 'That's an old, old thing – it's called a gramophone. It plays music without using electricity. It was my mother's. Listen'.

He pulls a flat, black record out of a paper cover and puts it on a round silver plate on top of the box. Then he turns a handle round and round, as if he's starting an old-fashioned car. Then he lifts a metal arm up and puts it on the record and music flows out the horn!

'Gosh! That's incredible!' cries Slye. 'It sounds strange, but it's super!'

The singer's voice is high and scratchy and the orchestra sounds a bit like a musical box, but it's still a really catchy tune.

'Here's how my mother danced to this song in the good old days', Mr. Ptera says. He starts dancing, waving his arms around. Then he puts his hands on his knees and makes them seem to wobble on their own.

'It's called the Charleston. Try it!' he cries.

The youngsters have a fun time jumping around, flapping their arms, and trying that knee thing. Suddenly the music slows down and stops.

'I've got to wind it up again!' puffs Mr. Ptera. He turns the handle, and off they go. What fun!

November

Window Flowers

7
NOVEMBER

Baabra and Lammie Sheep have woken up early today. Their mummy and daddy are still asleep.

'Lammie, come and look!' Baabra whispers.

She pulls the bedroom curtains open.

'Oooh!' gasps Lammie. 'Pretty! Pretty!'

The window is nearly covered with what look like beautiful white leaves and flowers.

'It's called frost – they're made of ice', explains Baabra. 'Touch it, Lammie'.

Lammie gently touches the icy glass.

'Cold!' he giggles.

'Watch this, Lammie', Baabra whispers. She blows on a clear spot on the window. It turns frosty white. Lammie starts puffing away on the glass. Soon it's completely fogged over.

'Look', Baabra says. She sticks a finger in her mouth and then draws a dark, wet line.

'Me too!' crows Lammie. Before long they've painted the whole window. It's a work of art.

'That's wonderful!' calls Mummy, who has slipped into the bedroom. 'Let's send a photo to your grandad. He used to do the same thing with me when I was young'.

Baabra and Lammie pose in front of their beautiful window. Mummy takes a picture.

'Cold! Pretty!' cries Lammie, going back to work on the window. Suddenly he stops.

'Cold finger!' he adds, and everyone laughs.

Time Traveller

8
NOVEMBER

Ivan Monkey has read a book about a time traveller. The traveller went forwards and backwards in time and Ivan wants to do that too.

'First I need to build a box', he says. He saws and hammers away until he's built a big box with a little window.

'Now for a lock to keep the door closed', he thinks. He gets his bicycle lock and key.

'All I need to do is step in, lock the lock and say some magic words', he mutters.

He does that, throwing the key out the window.

'I want to visit the future', he announces.

'Future-kootshure, mega-zim-zam!' he says. He closes his eyes and waits for the magic to happen. Nothing does.

'Hmmm. Maybe I said the wrong thing', he sighs. 'Future-lootcher-dootcher!' he cries.

Nothing happens.

'Maybe I should read the book again', he thinks. He tries to open the door, but it is locked.

'Oh, no!' he wails. 'I'm stuck in here, forever! That's what my future will be! Help!'

Ivan pounds on the box and yells as loudly as he can.

'What's that noise?' wonders Hoopla Hippo, who lives next door. He runs to Ivan's house.

'Ivan, is that you?' Hoopla asks.

'Yes, I'm locked in!' cries Ivan. 'The key is on the floor!' Hoopla picks it up and lets Ivan out.

'I wanted to see the future, but I'm stuck in the NOW', Ivan says sadly.

'Cheer up Ivan. At least you're not stuck in that box', laughs Hoopla. And Ivan grins!

String Mittens

9
NOVEMBER

'It's lovely and warm in here!' Bouncer Brachio says, coming into Grandmother's kitchen in a cloud of cold air. She gives Bouncer a big hug.

'I heard you lost one mitten the other day', Grandmother says. 'So I knitted you a new pair'. She hands Bouncer a pair of blue mittens.

'Thank you! I really need them!' cries Bouncer, giving Grandmother a kiss.

'But what's this for?' he asks, puzzled. A long string of wool ties the two mittens together.

'Let me have your jacket, and I'll show you', laughs Grandmother. She slides a mitten down one sleeve of Bouncer's jacket, and the other down the other sleeve.

'You can never lose string mittens', chuckles Grandmother. 'Give them a try!'

Bouncer puts on his jacket. His new mittens hang on the string, right where his hands are. He puts them on. They fit perfectly.

'This is brilliant! No more lost mittens and no more frozen hands! Thank you!'

'And now, would you like to help me bake some biscuits?' Grandmother asks. 'I've got the dough all made'.

'Wonderful!' laughs Bouncer. But then he looks at his grandmother thoughtfully.

'Please can I eat some of the dough before we bake it?' he asks, trying to sound just like a little angel.

Grandmother chuckles. 'Yes. Youngsters love biscuit dough as much as they love biscuits!'

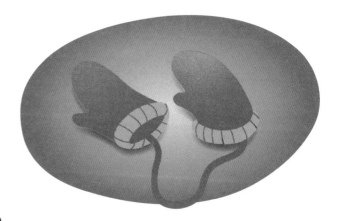

November

Zipwire

10 NOVEMBER

The daddies are making something special for their youngsters.

'First, we'll build a tower on top of the Hideout roof', says Daddy Brachio, drawing a picture in the earth.

'What in the world?' the youngsters wonder.

Before long, there's a sturdy tower on top of the Hideout. A ladder leads up to it.

'Let's build a little fence up here so nobody can fall off', laughs Daddy Zebra. Soon that's finished.

'Now we'll tie one end of our cable rope to the tower and the other end to that tall tree'.

'What next?' asks Nolo Giraffe, puzzled.

'We attach this handle to the cable, like this', answers Daddy Hippo. 'Do you want to go first?' he asks Nolo. Nolo gulps and nods.

'Stand here, grab the handle, hold on tight and JUMP!' says Daddy Hippo.

In a moment, Nolo is zooming down through the air, whooping with joy.

'I'm flying! I'm flying!' he yells. Towards the end of the cable, he slows down, stops and drops to the ground. 'It's fantastic!' he pants, waving to the friends.

One by one they try the zipwire. Hoopla Hippo is last. He jumps and starts zooming.

'HOOO, HO-HO-HO-HO!'

'HOOO, HO-HO-HO-HO!'

Hoopla is heavier than the rest, so he goes farther.

His round body bumps into the friends, and they all fall down. What a laughing heap!

The friends untangle themselves.

'Thank you Daddy!' they all exclaim. And the daddies are just as happy as the youngsters with the wonderful new plaything.

Putting the Garden to Bed

11 NOVEMBER

Bouncer and Grandad Brachio are putting Bouncer's garden to bed.

That's what Grandad calls it.

'We'll clean the garden up and feed it so it can sleep through the winter', explains Grandad. 'When we've finished, there's a sweet garden treat for us'.

Bouncer smacks his lips. 'What do we do?'

'Let's pull up the old plants and put them in this wheelbarrow', Grandad says.

'We'll store your teepee poles in my shed', Grandad adds. Bouncer puts them away.

'Now you can throw compost over the whole garden, to feed it ready for next year'.

Bouncer has fun throwing compost everywhere.

'Let's leave the wheelbarrow by our compost pile. Then it's treat time!' Grandad laughs.

'What could a "sweet garden treat" be?' wonders Bouncer as they finish their work.

Coming into the cosy kitchen, Bouncer smells something wonderful, buttery and sweet. It reminds

him of being at the cinema.

'Caramel popcorn, made from your own corn, Bouncer', chuckles Grandmother. 'You're just in time to stir it'.

Bouncer stirs a big bowl of popcorn to mix it with warm caramel. He tries some. 'It's delicious! Thank you!'

'Thank YOU for the popcorn, Bouncer!' smiles Grandmother. Grandad takes a handful and laughs, 'Here's to next year's garden!'

Car Painting

12 NOVEMBER

It's raining today, so Hoopla Hippo, Bouncer Brachio and Nolo Giraffe are playing with cars and trucks at Nolo's house.

Vroom! Vroom! Vroom! growls Hoopla, pushing a big truck across the floor.

Beep-beep! honks Nolo, with a red car.

'Putta-putta-putta!' purrs Bouncer, pushing a heavy tractor beside the sofa.

'My goodness, what a lot of traffic!' exclaims Mummy Giraffe. 'Would you like to do some car painting? Yes? Right, go and get some of Nolo's tiny cars and bring them to the kitchen'.

The friends have no idea what's going on, but it sounds like fun.

Mummy shows them how to put layers of different colours of poster paint on big sheets of paper on the kitchen table.

'When you drive your tiny cars through the paint, you'll see all sorts of colours coming through. You can use your brushes to mix the colours up as well, if you like. Start your engines!'

Vroom! Vroom! Vroom! growls Hoopla, pushing a tiny blue truck across the paint.

Beep-beep! honks Nolo, turning corners with his little yellow car.

Putta-putta-putta! purrs Bouncer, pushing along a funny little green tractor.

'This is fantastic! Our tyres make tracks in all kinds of colours Mummy!' cries Nolo.

When they have finished, they help Mummy wash the paint off the cars. What a fun idea!

November

'Oh yes!' both twins exclaim.

At the village hall, Dr. Henny is giving the injections. Each villager rolls up one sleeve. Dr. Henny puts a shiny machine on their arm and pushes a button. There's a quick popping sound. That's it!

Soon it's Zig's turn. She's scared, but she holds out her arm.

Dr. Henny smiles and says, 'Hello, Zig! I really like your hair ribbon!'

'Oh, thank you!' Zig replies. 'I got it – ouch – was that it? That hardly hurt at all!'

'I know', answers Dr. Henny. She quickly gives Zag and Mummy their injections, and it's all done. 'Time for our treat!' the twins say. They gallop over to the café. Mummy follows, smiling.

Flu Vaccinations

13 NOVEMBER

On Firefly Island it's time to get a flu vaccination. All the villagers get theirs on the same day, at the village hall.

'I don't want to go', declares Zig Zebra.

'I don't either', echoes Zag.

'Nobody likes getting an injection', answers Mummy. 'But they help us to stay well'.

'But it hurts!' cries Zig.

'Yes!' pouts Zag.

'I have heard that Dr. Henny is using a new machine this year. It hardly hurts at all', Mummy says.

'Anyway, it's time to go, so let's get it done and then have a treat at the café. Does that sound better?' asks Mummy.

Pretty Leaves Forever

14 NOVEMBER

Baabra Sheep and Slye Snake are back at Baabra's house after going for a walk in the woods.

'Look, Mummy!' Baabra cries as they come inside. 'We found lots of beautiful leaves!'

'Oh, they really are pretty! Red, gold, brown, yellow, and even some green', says Mummy.

'Can we save them somehow?' Baabra asks.

Mummy thinks for a second. 'When I was your age, we used to put leaves between the pages of big books. Give it a try'.

Baabra and Slye are off in a flash to the living room, where there is a shelf, full of big, fat books.

'I'll take this one', says Slye, tugging at a massive brown book.

'And I'll take this one', answers Baabra, sliding a thick blue one onto the floor.

They are quiet while they put their beautiful leaves between the pages of the books.

'There. All done!' says Baabra at last.

They head off to the kitchen for a snack.

Later that night, Daddy Sheep needs to check something in one of his books. He lifts it off the shelf and opens it on the table. A shower of brightly coloured leaves flies around the room!

'What in the world?' he cries, startled.

Baabra comes running in. 'Oh Daddy! It's just our leaf collection! You can read as much as you want, but please put them back when you've finished'.

Daddy laughs. 'You're so funny sometimes!'

15 NOVEMBER — Wood Heats you Many Times

Daddy Brachio is putting on heavy gloves. He's standing next to a big pile of logs.

'It's time to chop these logs into smaller pieces so we can burn them in our fireplace this winter', Daddy Brachio says.

'Can I do that?' Bouncer wants to know.

'No, that's hard and dangerous work with a sharp axe. But thank you for asking. You can help stack the pieces on our wood pile though'.

'Oh yes!' agrees Bouncer. He's proud to help.

After Daddy splits each big log, Bouncer picks up the pieces and takes them to the wood pile. He carefully lays each piece on the pile so that it won't tip or roll off.

'Wood is much heavier than I thought', he tells Daddy after his tenth trip. He's really getting hot!

'They say that wood heats you twice. Once when you cut it and once when you burn it', Daddy says, wiping sweat from his face.

'Wait a minute', Bouncer says. 'Our wood heated the villagers when they cut this tree down last winter. Now it's heating you, as you chop it. Then it heats me as I carry it to the pile. And then, finally, it will heat us when we burn it. That's four times, not two!' Bouncer laughs.

'It's a shame the tree fell down, but it's giving us all lots of heat now!' Daddy chuckles.

November

Camping Ground Closing

16 NOVEMBER

Mr. Brachio is already at the camping ground, early this sunny autumn morning.

Today is the big closing day party at the camping ground.

The villagers are already starting to arrive.

'Can we help?' they ask.

Mr. Brachio gives them jobs. Some put the signs in the shed. Others carry the canoes to the boat house next to the lake.

Soon it's lunch time.

'Okay!' calls Mr. Brachio at last. 'Soup's ready!'

The villagers line up. Mr. Brachio scoops delicious soup into their bowls. It goes fast.

'Now that our work's done and we've had lunch, let's have a sack race!' he calls.

He hands out cloth sacks to half of the villagers.

'Pick a partner. Each of you must put one leg in your sack. Then go to the starting line!'

'Hey, this is really difficult!' hoots Hoopla Hippo, trying to work out how to walk with Nolo Giraffe as they learn to share a sack.

Falling and laughing, everybody gets ready at the starting line.

'One, two, three – GO!' shouts Mr. Brachio.

The racers stumble and tumble to the finish.

'We won!' yell Zig and Zag. Everybody claps.

A Wonderful Surprise

17 NOVEMBER

Mr. Horse is visiting Miss Pinto Pony on Big Island today. He has planned a big surprise for her.

'Please put this on', he says, handing her a blindfold. She puts it on. He leads her down the street. They walk carefully for some time.

'Now we're going to climb inside a big basket', Mr. Horse explains, and Miss Pinto Pony nods. Soon they are both inside.

Whoosh! There's a blast of warm air. The basket rocks a little and then rises up into the air.

'Now you can take the blindfold off', Mr. Horse says. Miss Pinto Pony does, and she gasps. 'Oh my goodness! We're flying!'

They are in a hot-air balloon, floating up over Big Island! Soon they are sailing over the trees and farms, heading for Firefly Island.

Mr. Horse looks into Miss Pinto Pony's eyes.

'I love you', he says. 'Will you marry me?'

Miss Pinto Pony smiles and nods. 'I love you too and yes, I would be very happy to marry you!'

Mr. Horse rubs his nose against hers and says, 'I'm so pleased!' They smile and smile.

The balloon is drifting towards Firefly Meadow. The happy couple wave to the villagers as they fly over. Slowly the balloon lands in the meadow. There's going to be a wedding!

🗓 18 NOVEMBER — A Touch of Magic

Hoopla Hippo has a new magic trick. He's been practising hard in front of his bathroom mirror. Today he's ready to try it out on his friends.

'I can push a coin right through my head!' he tells the friends at the Hideout.

Hoopla picks up a coin in one hand and passes it to the other. Then he seems to push the coin into one ear. He reaches up his first hand, and pulls the coin out of his other ear! Everyone is so surprised!

'Tell us how you do that please! I bet it's not real magic. It's a trick!' yells Slye Snake.

'Well… I'm not supposed to do this, but I'll tell you how the trick works', grins Hoopla.

'Pick up the coin. You make it look as if you pass it from one hand to the other, like this, but you really keep the coin in the first hand, and pretend it's gone. Make a fist with the second hand and pretend to hold the coin'. He shows them how.

'Make sure you look at your empty hand as though it's got the coin in, then pretend to push the coin into your ear'. He does that slowly.

'Then just put your first hand, the one that really has coin, up to your other ear. Slide your fingers back from the coin, and pretend to pull it out of your ear. Hey presto! Magic!'

🗓 19 NOVEMBER — Diggers and Stampers

There's a big hole in the road leading to the dock on Firefly Island. A team of workers has come to repair it.

The whole village has come out to watch.

'Look at that digger!' cries Ivan Monkey. He wishes he could be operating it.

'That dumper truck is amazing!' exclaims Nolo Giraffe. It tips its container up and dumps a load of earth and stones into the hole.

'I can't believe how much noise these things make', yells Grandmother Brachio over the sound of the machines.

The hole has been filled in now and the workers drag a machine off their trailer to stamp the earth tightly into the hole.

Bup-bup-bup-bup-bup! it goes, stamping the loose earth into the hole. Nolo loves it.

'Hello there! Do you want to try this?' calls the worker running the machine.

'Who, me?' shouts Nolo. He can't believe it.

'Yes! Give it a try', laughs the worker.

Nolo grabs the handles of the machine and presses the button. Off it goes, pounding the earth to make it hard. Nolo's whole body jumps and shakes!

'O-o-o-o-h-h-h!' he tries to say, through teeth that are chattering away.

Everybody laughs. Nolo is bouncing as much as the machine is. But he's doing a very good job. Finally Nolo stops. 'My body is still vibrating!' he laughs. 'That was lots of fun!'

Grandmother Sheep's Ankle

Grandmother Sheep is cross at herself! She twisted her ankle yesterday, on her very first ride on the zipwire at the Hideout.

'I should have been more careful! Now I have to stay in bed for two weeks!' she moans.

Grandmother really does not like sitting around. Baabra knocks on the bedroom door.

'May we come in?' she asks.

'Yesss! I'm going mad in here!' cries Grandmother.

The door opens and all the friends exclaim, 'Surprise!'

They troop into the room, pretending to be a marching band and playing imaginary instruments. Grandmother is speechless.

'We're so sorry you landed so hard!' says Nolo Giraffe, handing her a picture he has drawn.

'We want you to get better soon!' adds Bouncer Brachio, giving her a carton of juice.

'We hope these cheer you up', says Zig Zebra, giving her a box of biscuits.

'We made them ourselves', adds Zag.

'We love it that you play with us', Baabra says, giving her a bunch of colourful leaves.

'An apple a day keeps the doctor away', laughs Hoopla Hippo, giving Grandmother a red one.

'So get well soon!' says Slye Snake, tying a yellow balloon to the bed.

'Oh, my friends, you are just wonderful', cries Grandmother, wiping a happy tear away.

'Thank you so much! Here – let's taste these wonderful biscuits!'

She hands them out to all the youngsters. And they all chew away in happy silence.

Apple Juice Bicycle

21 NOVEMBER

Bouncer Brachio loves apple juice time. Grandad grows more apples than he can eat or give away. So he makes juice with the ones that are left.

'It smells SO good here!' laughs Bouncer, finding Grandad already working in the garden.

'That's part of the fun of making juice, I think', smiles Grandad. 'Do you want to pedal again this year?' he asks.

'Oh yes!' says Bouncer. He jumps on a special bicycle that powers the apple crushing machine.

'Go!' calls Grandad, and Bouncer pedals like mad. The crusher squeezes and mashes the apples Grandad pours in, and apple pulp pours out into big buckets. Bouncer jumps off the bicycle, exhausted.

Grandad lifts the buckets and pours the pulp into the juice press.

'Look at that, Bouncer! There's our juice!' he exclaims, as it pours out of the other end of the press, filling other buckets.

'May I have the first cup?' he asks.

Grandad grins. 'Why am I not surprised?'

He pours Bouncer a glass of the honey-coloured juice, then pours one for himself.

'Oh! I'd forgotten how good it tastes!' cries Bouncer, smacking his lips.

'There really is nothing like freshly-pressed apple juice', agrees Grandad.

Cozy Loves Leaves

22 NOVEMBER

Cozy, Hotta Toucan and Chilly Penguin's chick, has loved watching the colourful autumn leaves float by the window near her playpen.

Now the trees outside the café are bare.

There are no more falling leaves and Cozy feels sad. Hotta tries to cheer her up.

'Cozy, here's a mirror. Can you see yourself in it?' asks Hotta.

Cozy peers at the mirror and pecks it. She thinks it's another chick. The other chick stares back.

'Peep-peep!' she cheeps. But the other chick says nothing.

Cozy sulks.

'How about this bell?' asks Hotta, showing Cozy how to peck at it and make it ring.

Cozy pecks a couple of times and then sulks.

'Cozy, listen. The leaves will come back next year. Then you can watch them fall again', Hotta explains. But she knows Cozy doesn't understand. Then Hotta has an idea.

'Cozy, watch this!' she says. She gets some coloured paper and scissors, and starts cutting. Soon she has a pile of colourful paper leaves.

'Look, Cozy!' Hotta says, and she showers Cozy with the paper leaves in her playpen.

Cozy watches. She brightens up. She crows!

Hotta picks up the paper leaves and showers Cozy again. Cozy is happy now.

And so is Hotta.

23 NOVEMBER The Memory Matching Game

Nolo Giraffe is teaching Slye Snake a new card game. It tests your memory.

'You win if you find the biggest number of matching pairs of pictures', Nolo explains. He puts the cards in rows with their pictures facing downwards.

Slye turns over a card with a cat, then another with a tree. 'No match', she says, turning both pictures down again.

It's Nolo's turn. He turns over a different card. A house. Then a tree. 'No match either', he says.

'But I can make one!' Slye says, and she turns over the two trees.

Nolo frowns. He is already losing. Suddenly Nolo points out the window. 'Look at that!'

Slye goes to the window and looks. 'I can't see anything', she says, coming back.

'I thought I saw a funny bird', Nolo says, turning over a bicycle card. And another one!

'Aha! A match!' he cries.

Slye can't make a match on her turn. But Nolo does. He's winning on each go now.

Slye squints her eyes and stares at Nolo.

'Did you peek at the cards when I was looking out the window?' she asks. 'You're suddenly winning all the time. You cheated!'

Nolo turns red. 'I just couldn't stand it that you were beating me in your first ever game!'

'Oh, Nolo', laughs Slye. 'I've been playing this game for ages. I was going to let you win!'

229

November

Ivan's Leaking Boat

24 NOVEMBER

Ivan Monkey loves his little fishing boat. But it has a hole in it. It leaks.

His boat, now nearly full of water, is in the shallow water by the beach.

'I really need to repair that hole', he thinks.

He wades into the cold water, squashes up a piece of paper, and sticks it in the hole. 'Hmmm. That didn't work. It's still full'.

Ivan thinks for a while, then puts a piece of chewing gum into his mouth. He chews it, shivering in the cold water.

He pulls the wet paper out of the hole and sticks the chewing gum in, then waits.

'No luck. My boat's still full!' he mutters.

Mr. Horse walks by. 'Going fishing?' he asks.

'No, I'm trying to fix the leak in my boat', explains Ivan. 'Nothing works. I've tried paper and chewing gum, but my boat is still full of water!'

'Ah, I see', says Mr. Horse seriously. 'You know, repairing the hole won't empty your boat. Maybe if you scoop the water out first, you could glue a wooden patch over the hole. That will keep your boat dry'. He walks off.

'Hmmm', says Ivan. He grabs his hat and starts scooping water out of the boat. More water comes into the hole with every scoop.

'I'll have to think about this overnight', Ivan mutters. He goes home to warm up. Silly Ivan!

Ivan to the Rescue

25 NOVEMBER

Mrs. Trico has a wood-burning stove in her post office. It keeps the shop warm all through the winter.

'I need to light the stove this morning', she tells herself when she opens the office. So she builds a small pile of firewood and paper in the stove and lights the paper with a match.

A sudden gust of wind blows down the chimney. The paper flies out of the stove and lands on the carpet, still burning.

'Oh, no!' cries Mrs. Trico. The carpet has caught fire and it is starting to burn fast.

She runs to the door of the office and yells, 'Fire! Fire! Help!'

Ivan Monkey is walking by, thinking about his leaking boat problem. He hears Mrs. Trico's cries and runs straight to his boat, yelling 'I'll save you!' He pulls his heavy, water-filled boat out of the water and pushes it across the road to the office. Then he takes off his hat, scoops water from the boat and throws the water onto the flames.

Mrs. Trico grabs an empty teapot and does the same thing. Back and forth they go, throwing water on the fire.

'I think it's almost out!' she pants.

'Yes! If we can just get a little more water on it, that fire will die', cheers Ivan.

He's enjoying being a hero.

At last the fire is nothing but a puff of smoke.

'Good thing, too! We're out of water! And my boat's empty too! Hooray!' cries Ivan.

'My hero!' cries Mrs. Trico.

Ivan blushes!

Too Much of a Good Thing

26 NOVEMBER

Hoopla Hippo can't believe his eyes when opens his curtains today. 'Snow!' he cries. Everything is sparkling white. Little clouds of diamonds swirl through the air.

'I've got to get out there – fast!' he whispers.

He dresses, rushes his breakfast and brushes his teeth. Mummy helps him on with his jacket, scarf,

mittens and boots. Out he goes.

First he chugs around the garden, making train tracks and blowing a horn. *Whooo-whooo!*

Then he makes a snowball and throws it at the kitchen window. Mummy jumps and then laughs as she washes the dishes.

'I really LOVE the snow!' he yells to her. 'It's so COLD!' he hoots as he rolls over and over in the fluffy stuff. 'It's so SOFT!'

The friends come over to play. They sweep the snow off the picnic table and jump off it into a deep drift. Mummy comes to the back door. They can see steam rising from big mugs of hot chocolate.

'There's nothing better than a warm drink after a day of snow play', she smiles, handing out the hot drinks.

Hoopla sips his cocoa. 'This was the best day EVER!' Hoopla replies, and the friends agree!

Happy News

27 NOVEMBER

The village hall is buzzing with talk. Mr. Horse has put a sign on the news board. It says he wants to make an important speech today!

Everybody is there. Mr. Horse gets up on his soapbox, smiling broadly.

'My dear fellow villagers', Mr. Horse starts, and the crowd hushes. 'I have important, happy news for you. I have asked Miss Pinto Pony to marry me, and she has said yes!'

Mr. Horse beams at Miss Pinto Pony and asks her to stand on the soapbox with him.

'Hooray!' 'Wonderful!' cry the villagers. 'When is the wedding?' someone asks.

'On 7 December – and you're all invited to the feast!' crows Mr. Horse.

'Excellent!' 'What fun!' exclaim the villagers.

The youngsters are cheering too. They like Miss Pinto Pony, and they love feasts!

'Just twelve days to go', counts Slye Snake. 'I really can't wait!'

A Wedding Album

28 NOVEMBER

'I'm so happy that Mr. Horse is getting married!' Grandmother Brachio tells Grandad at breakfast the next day. 'What should we give them as a wedding present?'

Grandad thinks for a while. 'Baby Cozy really likes that album we gave her when she was born. Do you think Mr. Horse and Miss Pinto Pony would like one too, to collect all the pictures and cards from their wedding?'

Grandmother smiles. 'That's a wonderful thought, dear. I'll get one next week. We can decorate it and make it special for them'.

Just then Bouncer walks in. 'Hello Bouncer! How about some hot chocolate?' asks Grandmother. She tells Bouncer about their idea.

'I could help you with the wedding album', Bouncer offers.

'I took a picture of Mr. Horse and Miss Pinto Pony when they were in the hot-air balloon. They waved at me when they flew over our house'.

'That was when Mr. Horse asked Miss Pinto Pony to marry him', smiles Grandmother.

'Then we can make that the very first picture in their album', Grandad says.

'What a good idea!' Grandmother chuckles.

They all laugh. It will be a fun project and a lovely gift as well!

Snow, Snow, Snow

29 NOVEMBER

It has been snowing for days now. Nobody can use a bicycle or a car. Some villagers are even using skis to get around!

'Nolo, could you get me some groceries from Mr. Ptera's general store?' his mummy asks.

'Yes! Can I use my sledge?' he asks.

'That's a good idea', Mummy smiles.

Nolo drags his sledge to the shop. Mr. Ptera helps him load things onto the sledge. Nolo sets off.

'Hello Nolo!' calls Slye Snake as he goes past her house. 'Do you want to play?'

'Yes! I'll be right back', he calls.

He drags the sledge and its load to his front door, then dashes off to play with Slye.

Hours later, Nolo comes home. His sledge and the groceries are exactly where he left them.

'Hello Mummy, here is your shopping', he calls. His mummy starts to unpack the bags.

'Oh, Nolo!' she cries. 'Everything is frozen – the eggs, apples, potatoes…' she frowns.

'I'm sorry, Mummy! At least the ice cream is perfect', jokes Nolo, and his mother has to smile.

Hats

30 NOVEMBER

The friends are at the Hideout. It's cosy in there because the daddies have put a heater in the corner.

They are doing puzzles and colouring.

'It's lovely in here', sighs Zig Zebra.

'Yes, it is, but I'm getting too warm', answers Baabra Sheep. 'I can take off my jacket and hat, but my woolly fleece doesn't unzip!' she laughs.

Hoopla Hippo has been busy over by their jackets. He turns and says, 'Let's make a snowman outside'.

'Yes!' they yell, and they start dressing.

'Oh!' 'Goodness!' 'Ouch!' cry the friends as they put on their hats.

'They're full of snow!' yells Zig. Snow covers her head and drips down her neck.

'Who did this?' yells Zag. The friends look at each other. Then Zag says, 'Hoopla, you're the only one who doesn't have a hat full of snow. You did it!'

And they gather up the snow from their hats and throw snowballs at Hoopla until he's driven out of the Hideout, laughing all the way!

233

December

Repairing Ivan's Boat

1 DECEMBER

Mr. Horse sees Ivan Monkey trying to repair the hole in his boat. It has half sunk in the water again.

'How are you getting on Ivan?' asks Mr. Horse. 'Will you be able to repair that leak? I really want to go fishing with you next spring!'

'I hope so', answers Ivan, a little embarrassed. 'I'm trying lots of things to plug the hole. Jelly beans, bottle caps, a sock…' he gulps. 'Something should work'.

'Ahem. I'm sure something will', smiles Mr. Horse. 'What about my wooden patch idea? Let's give that a try'.

They find a piece of wood on the beach.

'That looks perfect. Here's the glue', says Ivan.

Mr. Horse spreads glue around the hole and sticks the piece of wood over it.

'Just hold that for a minute, while the glue dries', he says. Ivan presses the patch hard.

'That should do it', says Mr. Horse a little later. Ivan tries to take his hand away.

'Oh, no!' he cries. 'I'm stuck to the boat!'

Mr. Horse stares. Then he starts laughing.

'Poor Ivan, something is always going wrong for you! I'll get some glue remover. We'll get you unstuck quickly'. He runs off, chuckling.

Ivan stands patiently, glued to his boat, as villagers come and go, smiling at him.

Mr. Horse comes back and melts the glue.

'Good news! I'm free, and patch stayed in place!' Ivan cries. Mr. Horse just smiles.

Snow Sculptures

2 DECEMBER

The village is deeply covered in snow now.

The friends are in the Hideout.

'What can we do today?' Slye Snake asks.

'Let's make a snowman in the sculpture garden, next to our wooden statues', suggests Baabra Sheep.

'Snowmen are boring. What if each of us makes a snow creature like ourselves?' asks Slye. 'Right next to our wooden ones?'

'Yes! Last one to the sculpture garden is a rotten egg!' cries Baabra, and they race off.

When they get there, puffing clouds of steam, they stare. The brightly painted wooden sculptures of the friends stand out against the deep drifts of white snow.

'Right. Let's get started', Baabra says. They start shaping their snow creatures, laughing and throwing snowballs as they work.

'Look at me!' laughs Hoopla Hippo after a while. He's made a perfect little snow hippo.

He puts his blue scarf around its neck.

Suddenly the snow hippo's head falls off.

'Oh, no! I've lost my head!' cries Hoopla. He starts laughing. The friends rush over to help him rebuild the snow hippo.

Before long the sculpture garden is crowded with creatures. Some are wooden, some are snow, and some are real.

There are three hippos, three giraffes, three snakes, three sheep, three brachiosauruses and SIX zebras! Each snow sculpture wears its owner's scarf.

Mr. Ptera runs out of his general store with a camera. 'I've got to catch this!' he laughs, and he takes a wonderful picture to preserve the day.

Ivan's Mind Reading Hat

3 DECEMBER

Ivan is excited! He's just finished making a mind reading hat.

'All I needs to do is test it out', he thinks. 'I wonder who could help me'.

Just then, Hoopla Hippo pops in to say hello.

'What are you working on, Ivan?' he asks.

'A mind reading hat!' exclaims Ivan. 'I need to test it on someone. So please sit here', he says.

Hoopla settles into a chair. Ivan puts a metal strainer on Hoopla's head. Wires connect the strainer to a headset that Ivan puts on.

'Think of a number', he tells Hoopla.

Hoopla pauses. He thinks of the number one.

'Three!' cries Ivan. Hoopla shakes his head.

'Think of a different number', Ivan says.

Hoopla thinks of a three.

'One!' cries Ivan. Hoopla shakes his head.

'Try again, and think really hard', Ivan urges.

Hoopla thinks of a two.

'Four?' asks Ivan. Hoopla shakes his head.

Hoopla's eyes wander around the laboratory. He feels sorry for Ivan. His eyes land on a plate of biscuits on the table.

Ivan looks hard at Hoopla, then follows his gaze to the plate of biscuits.

'Would you like a biscuit?' he asks politely.

'Oh yes please! You read my mind!' cries Hoopla, and he laughs his hippo laugh,

'HOOO, HO-HO-HO-HO!'

December

A New Waterfall

4 DECEMBER

The weather has been very cold. It gives Mr. Horse a chance to surprise Miss Pinto Pony.

'Let's go for a walk', he says to her. 'I want to show you something special'.

Quickly, she gets her warm jacket, scarf and mittens. Off they trot through the woods.

Soon Miss Pinto Pony looks at Mr. Horse.

'Are we going to the waterfall?' she guesses.

'Yes. I know how much you like it', smiles Mr. Horse. He can't wait to see her happiness.

'I suppose it's really pretty in the winter', she says. They come out of the woods by the waterfall.

'Oh, my goodness!' cries Miss Pinto Pony. 'It's standing still!'

And it's true. The waterfall has frozen solid. It looks almost like a photograph of the waterfall, with the water motionless. But the water has frozen into ice, so it is pure white.

Mr. Horse turns to Miss Pinto Pony. 'Would you like to slide down the waterfall?' he asks.

Miss Pinto Pony's eyes open wide. She nods.

Mr. Horse carefully goes to the edge of the waterfall. He sits down, and pushes off the edge. He zooms down the slide of ice, laughing as he goes.

'Your turn!' he cries, and Miss Pinto Pony slides down, stopping beside him.

'Fantastic!' cries Miss Pinto Pony. 'I never knew that a waterfall could be a slide!'

Bouncer's Job Visit

5 DECEMBER

'Good morning Bouncer', calls Dr. Henny. It's Bouncer Brachio's job visit day to see how a doctor works.

'Hello, Dr. Henny!' replies Bouncer. 'What will you be doing today?'

'I have appointments with villagers who are unwell this morning. Probably sore throats and coughs – it's that time of year', Dr. Henny answers. 'But first I need to put away some supplies. Would you like to help?' she asks.

Bouncer nods. Dr. Henny goes to a large box tied up with plastic straps. She tries to cut one strap with a small knife. It's not easy.

Suddenly her knife slips and cuts her finger.

'Ouch!' she cries, dropping the knife and holding her finger. A little blood drips out.

'Bouncer, I need a little help, quickly', she says. 'Please get some bandages and tape from the top drawer over there. Don't worry though, I will be fine'.

Bouncer quickly brings them to Dr. Henny.

'Right. Put some of the antiseptic on a cotton bud, and then dab it on my cut', she says. 'Ouch, that stings!' she adds.

'I know what you mean', replies Bouncer, dabbing away and feeling important.

'Now please wrap my finger with a bandage. Good. And now tape it all together. Excellent!' she smiles for the first time since her cut.

'You did a good job. You'll be a fine doctor if you want to be one!'

6 DECEMBER — Getting Ready for the Wedding

'Oh, my', sighs Miss Pinto Pony. 'There's so much to do when you plan a wedding. I'll be glad when it actually happens tomorrow'. Mr. Horse gives her a little kiss and a pat.

'Don't worry, everything will be fine', he says. 'What's left on our list of things to do?'

'Let's see… We've ordered the cake. We've planned the wedding party and our clothes are ready', she says, checking her list.

Mr. Horse isn't listening. He's thinking how happy their wedding day will be.

Miss Pinto Pony smiles. She can just picture Mr. Horse, looking really handsome in his new wedding suit.

'May I have a look at your suit?' she asks.

'My… my… suit?' stammers Mr. Horse. 'Oh, no! I forgot to order it! And now it's too late to get one! What can I wear?' he cries.

'Let's think quickly', says Miss Pinto Pony. She's trying to keep calm. Then she brightens up.

'Let's see if the mummies of the village can help me make you a suit tonight. I have some cloth that will be perfect for it!' she says.

They run from house to house, asking for help. The mummies rush to Mr. Horse's house and start cutting and sewing as quickly as they can.

The hours fly by. But they laugh and talk as they work, so it's fun for everybody.

It is after midnight when they finally finish making the suit.

Mr. Horse tries it on. It fits perfectly.

'Oh, thank you, dear ladies', he cries, bowing to them and blowing them kisses.

Miss Pinto Pony smiles. He looks just as handsome as she pictured him.

And tomorrow they will be married!

237

December

Wedding Day

7 DECEMBER

Mr. Horse is wearing his new wedding suit. 'Don't I look handsome?' he asks his mirror.

He trots to the village hall. The villagers all cheer when he arrives.

Miss Pinto Pony walks towards him. Her long, white wedding dress trails behind her.

'She looks wonderful. More beautiful than ever', Mr. Horse thinks. 'I love her so much!'

Miss Pinto Pony beams. 'I love him so much!' she thinks.

Mr. Ptera performs the wedding ceremony, because he is the oldest villager. He asks, 'Do you promise to love and care for each other all your lives?'

They both answer 'Yes!' and smile happily.

Then Mr. Ptera turns to the crowd and says, 'Dear friends, allow me to present Mr. and Mrs. Horse!'

The villagers clap and cheer and throw clouds of tiny pieces of coloured paper into the air.

'Come to our wedding party tomorrow', says Mr. Horse. 'Wear warm clothes!'

The villagers all wonder. What will happen?

The Best Wedding Party Ever

8 DECEMBER

Everyone is at the village hall for Mr. and Mrs. Horse's wedding party. They're all warmly dressed and very, very curious.

'Listen!' cries Nolo Giraffe. A tinkling sound is getting louder and louder. 'Sleigh bells!'

Suddenly a parade of ponies pulling sleighs loaded with hay comes out of the woods.

Mr. and Mrs. Horse wave from the first sleigh.

Mr. Horse cries, 'My friends, hop on!'

In no time the sleighs are full up. Grown-ups snuggle down in the hay to keep warm.

'Whoooppeee!' cries Nolo, starting a hay fight. He stuffs some hay down Hoopla Hippo's jacket. Hoopla squirms and tries to get the tickly hay out. He throws hay at Nolo.

'Yum! Hippo food!' crows Hoopla, eating a bit of hay and grinning at his own joke.

The sleighs stop at the picnic shelter. It has been beautifully decorated with flowers, candles and ribbons. A band is playing dance music.

Everyone has a drink and pieces of an enormous wedding cake. Then they dance all night. The friends can stay up as late as they want.

It really is the best wedding party ever!

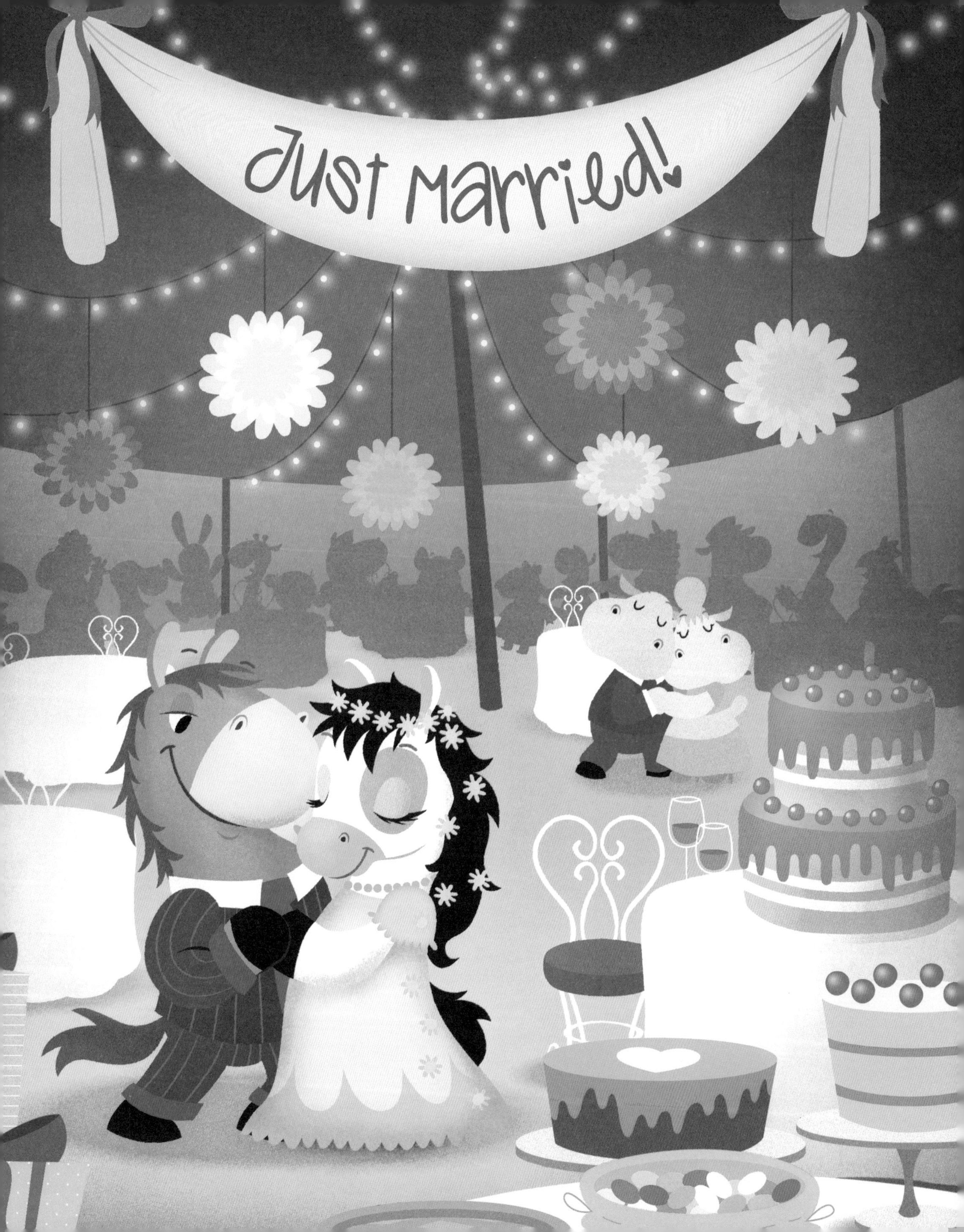
Just Married!

December

Paper Aeroplanes

9 DECEMBER

The friends are at the Hideout, busy with a secret plan. They've been working hard.

'That's my last one', says Bouncer Brachio, adding a paper plane to a huge pile of them.

'Phew! We did it!' crows Hoopla Hippo.

Everyone leans back to admire the pile.

'It's time to take them to the tower', says Slye Snake.

They carefully put the paper planes into bags, and set off for the village hall.

Quietly they climb the stairs to the top of the tower, whispering and giggling with excitement.

'Look. The grown-ups are coming out of their monthly meeting!' whispers Slye.

'Now!' hisses Slye. 'Keep low and quiet!'

The youngsters start sailing their paper planes out of the tower. Soon the air is filled with them.

'What's going on?' 'Look at all these planes!' cry the grown-ups, amazed at all the tiny aeroplanes zooming and diving around them.

'Who's doing this?' someone asks, looking up.

The youngsters peep from the tower, thrilled at their success.

'They look so tiny! And they have no idea it's us up here!' laughs Slye in a low voice. After the last plane lands, the grown-ups go home, chatting about the mystery.

'I can't wait to hear what they say', declares Slye. 'Let's get home fast!'

Ivan's Joke – or Slye's?

10 DECEMBER

'I bet Ivan had something to do with it', Slye Snake's mummy tells Slye at breakfast. 'It is just his kind of joke. But I simply don't understand how he could make it rain paper planes like that. He was with us the whole time!'

Slye pretends to cough to keep from bursting out laughing. The whole thing had been her idea.

'When you think about it, this is the first thing Ivan has planned that worked properly', smiles Mummy Snake, puzzled.

Slye grins. 'Yes, I suppose you're right', she says, biting her tongue to stop herself laughing.

Mummy stands up. 'Hurry up and finish breakfast

240

darling. We need to go shopping'.

Soon they are at Mr. Ptera's general store. It's filled with customers. Mummy Snake spots Ivan Monkey, pushing a shopping trolley.

'Hello Ivan!' she calls. 'Congratulations on your paper plane trick yesterday. I can't work out how you did it, though. You were with us in the town meeting the whole time!'

Ivan looks surprised and gulps. 'I… I…' he fumbles and looks away.

'Now, don't be shy. It was a lot of fun!' Mummy Snake nods, patting his arm. Slye is about to explode with giggles. Nobody knows that it was Slye's idea! 'I wish I could have seen it', Slye tells Ivan. 'It sounds as though it was a brilliant idea!'

Grandmother's Snow Day

11 DECEMBER

'We should do something outside today', Grandmother Sheep announces to Baabra. 'My ankle is fine now and I want to thank you all for your kindness. How about a snow day?' she asks.

'What is a snow day?' Baabra asks.

'It's a day when you do lots of fun things in the snow. Like sledging, or skiing, or…'

'Oh, now I see. Yesss! Let's!' cries Baabra. She runs to get the friends.

Soon they are gathered with their sledges at the top

of the hill above Firefly Meadow.

'Everybody, line up here', cries Grandmother. The friends line their sledges up and hop on.

'Start when I say GO!' she says. 'The first one over the line I drew at the bottom of the hill is the speed champion. The one who goes furthest is the distance champion. Now, 1, 2, 3, GO!'

The friends zoom down, whooping and yelling. Zig and Zag Zebra fall over straight away. They've never been sledging before.

'I'm the fastest! I'm winning!' yells Bouncer Brachio. He crosses the finishing line first and waves his arms like a champion.

Hoopla Hippo is going slower, but he keeps on going, going and going, way past Bouncer.

'I'm the long-distance champion!' he crows.

Grandmother laughs and claps. 'Who wants to do it again?' she calls. They all cheer, pick up their sledges and race to the hilltop to start again!

December

A Very Dark Night

The Zebra family is eating dinner. Suddenly all the lights in the house go out.

'Oh no. It's a power cut', says Daddy.

Zig and Zag are a little scared. It's really, really dark. They can hardly see each other.

'Look Daddy, the lights are off next door as well', says Zag, pointing at the dark house.

'That means that the whole island is dark tonight', Daddy answers. 'Don't be afraid. I have an idea. Let's go outside. Get your coats!'

The zebras step out into the cold, snowy night. They all look up at the sky.

'Oooh! So many stars! Far more than we see on most nights', exclaims Zig.

'That's because we don't have any house or street lights on now. They hide the smaller stars', explains Mummy.

The family stays watching the stars until they get cold.

'Let's go back inside and get warm. I'll light some candles', Daddy says.

'And I'll make some hot chocolate', Mummy adds, putting an arm around each twin.

They sit in the kitchen, filled with warm, soft candle light, sipping hot chocolate.

'Let's sing something', suggests Zag. Mummy starts a song and they all join in.

'I wish we could have more nights like this', says Zig, yawning.

'Me too', answers Zag, catching Zig's yawn.

'Time for bed', smiles Mummy.

'By candlelight?' asks Zig.

'Of course', laughs Mummy.

The twins head for the bathroom to get ready for bed by the flickering candle light.

Northern Lights

The youngsters are chattering about the exciting dark night they had yesterday.

'And do you know what?' exclaims Baabra Sheep.

'We saw the Northern Lights!'

'What are they?' asks Slye Snake, curious.

'They looked like a curtain of coloured lights. Blue, green, red and yellow, rippling in the sky. Mummy says we were lucky to see them'.

'I wish we'd seen them', says Slye sadly.

At dinner Slye asks Mummy and Daddy if she can look for the Northern Lights before she goes to bed.

'Certainly! In fact, we can go to Firefly Meadow to look for them. And you can stay up a bit late if they are out. They are very special and they don't happen very often', says Daddy.

After dinner they walk to Firefly Meadow. With no street lights, it's really dark there.

'Now face the north – that way – and see if you can spot them', Daddy says, pointing.

Slye is silent, staring at the sky.

'Is that them?' she cries suddenly.

'Yes! We're lucky tonight!' smiles Mummy.

The Snake family stares up in wonder at the shimmering, shifting colours in the night sky.

'They really are fantastic! I don't want to go to bed at all tonight', says Slye.

But it's really cold and before long they head back towards their home.

'Thank you, Mummy and Daddy', says Slye sleepily as they tuck her into bed.

Falling from the Pocket

14 DECEMBER

'I just love my new grown-up bed!' thinks Baabra. Lammie is too big for his crib now, so he has her old bed.

'And I really love sleeping in the pocket', she says, as she falls asleep tonight.

Baabra sleeps on the side of the bed, where her blanket is tucked in under the mattress. She calls it her bed's pocket. It's really cosy sleeping there.

Soon Baabra is fast asleep, but in the middle of the night, her blanket becomes untucked.

Baabra falls out onto the floor with a thump! She rolls under her bed without waking up.

'What was that?' thinks Mummy. She runs to Baabra's bedroom in the darkness.

'Baabra, are you alright?' she whispers.

There is no answer, and no Baabra in the bed. Mummy is a little worried.

'Baabra, where are you?' she whispers a little more loudly. Still no answer.

Then Mummy hears a sound, like a tiny snore from under the bed! She tiptoes closer.

Mummy bends down and peers under the bed. There is Baabra, snoring quietly.

'That's amazing. She never woke up, even when she fell out', chuckles Mummy.

She gently puts Baabra back into her bed.

'Baabra's pocket really makes her sleep deeply', she thinks. 'Perhaps I should try it!'

December

Grandmother Brachio's Password

15 DECEMBER

Grandmother Brachio is so upset!
'I just can't remember it!' she says, typing away at her computer keyboard.
'What *was* the secret password that I chose?'
Grandmother wants to show Bouncer the photos that she took at the wedding sleigh ride last week.
'What could it be?' she wonders.
'Sleigh?' She types it in. 'No, not sleigh. Wedding? No. Snow? No, not that either'.
'I should have written my password down', she says, shaking her head. 'There are really good pictures of you, Bouncer!'
Bouncer nods. He pats Grandmother. 'Don't worry. You'll remember it. Was it hot chocolate? That was yummy'.
'Hmmm. No', she says, after trying that.
'Sorry, Bouncer', Grandmother says. 'Maybe I'll think of it later today', she shrugs.
Bouncer feels sorry for his grandmother.
He thinks.
'What about me?' he asks.
'Hmmm. Me', Grandmother types it in.
'Sorry, Bouncer, that didn't work', she says.
'No, I mean my name – Bouncer!' he laughs.
'Now that makes sense', smiles Grandmother. She types in Bouncer's name. Hey presto! The photos appear. 'Silly me', she laughs.
And Grandmother was right. They *are* good photos!

Bird Feeder Sneeze

16 DECEMBER

Baabra Sheep and her little brother, Lammie, are in their garden shed.
They are doing an important winter job.
It's Lammie's first time helping to feed the birds.
'Birdies! Food!' chants Lammie.
Baabra scoops some bird seed out of a huge sack.
Then they walk to the bird feeder in the garden.
Lammie watches as Baabra pours seeds into the bird feeder. 'Yummy! Food!' he laughs.
The feeder looks just like the village hall on Firefly Island. It even has a tiny clock in its tower! Baabra opens the roof for the seeds.
All of a sudden Lammie sneezes.
Aaah-chooo! Aaah-chooo! he explodes.

244

Baabra jumps in surprise. She spills some of the bird seed on the ground.

'Uh-oh!' cries Lammie. He feels awful. He starts picking up the seeds, one at a time.

'It's fine Lammie', Baabra tells him, smiling. 'The birds will find their food anyway, even if it's not in the feeder'.

'Fine? Fine?' asks Lammie doubtfully.

'Yes, it really is fine', comforts Baabra.

Lammie looks at Baabra carefully, thinking. Then he reaches up and takes the bird seed scoop from Baabra. He throws all the rest of the seed up high into the air!

'Fine! Birdie! Food! Fine!' he yells.

Icicles

17 DECEMBER

All the houses in the village have really long icicles hanging from their roofs now. The sunlight twinkles on the shiny ice.

'I think they are sooo pretty', sighs Zig Zebra, looking out of the window at them.

'Me too', answers Zag, her twin. 'I wish I could touch them'. They have never seen these beautiful things where they lived before.

But they can't reach their icicles.

'Wait a minute!' cries Zig suddenly. 'The roof of our garden shed is really close to the ground! Maybe we can reach those icicles!'

The twins put on their boots, jackets and mittens and run to the garden shed.

Yes! They can reach the icicles there.

'Oooh, they're cold!' cries Zag, breaking one off. She starts licking it like a lollipop.

'They are!' laughs Zig, breaking another one off for herself. She gets an idea.

'Let's send one to Scruffy Hyena', she suggests.

'What a lovely idea!' answers Zag.

They break off a big one and run inside.

'It will be a Christmas present', says Zig.

Soon the icicle is all wrapped up.

'Mummy, can you please write Scruffy's address on this box for us? We're going to send it to him. It's a present', explains Zag.

'Of course', Mummy says. 'But it looks as though your present has got wet somehow'.

'Oh no!' say the twins together. They unwrap the box and look inside.

'Just a puddle of water!' moans Zig.

'We forgot that icicles melt!' giggles Zag.

Bouncy Castle

18 DECEMBER

The friends and their parents have gone to a really enormous Christmas market on Big Island.

A blue and white striped circus tent is filled with homemade gifts to buy. But it also has wonderful things for youngsters to do.

First they try knocking some teddy bears off a shelf with snowballs. Hoopla wins one of the teddies when he makes three of them fall.

'I'm a snowball professional!' he laughs, waving the bear around.

Then they go to the bouncy castle.

'It's like a giant bed filled with air. You can bounce as much as you want', explains Nolo Giraffe to Zig and Zag Zebra, who haven't seen one before.

'You have to take your shoes off so you don't make a hole in the bed', he adds with a smile.

Soon they're all bouncing, rolling, falling and diving around on the rubbery floor. Everyone is having a great time. But suddenly…

POP! HISSS! The floor slowly sags and goes flat.

'What happened?' everybody cries.

'Something made a hole in the bed and all the air rushed out', answers the owner.

'I… I… think it was me', says Nolo quietly. 'My feet are pointy, even without shoes'. He looks down at them, feeling awful.

The owner comes over to Nolo. 'No, it wasn't you', he says, putting an arm around Nolo.

'It was this!' He shows everyone a small, sharp stone. 'Don't worry, I'll have this hole repaired in a minute', he says, getting to work.

Soon they are all bouncing again, and loving it!

Roota's Present

19 DECEMBER

Roota Rooster is looking at his collection of treasure.

In the pile in front of him are all kinds of shiny finds. Keys, pieces of coloured glass, bottle tops and mysterious things.

'I have no idea what this is', he says, peering at something with his little eyes. 'But – look, there's another one, almost the same!'

He puts the two pieces of yellow china together.

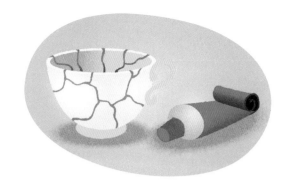

'Look!' he exclaims. 'They fit like a puzzle!'

He picks out every yellow china piece that he can find.

'I think all these pieces were once a cup or something', he murmurs, admiring them.

Suddenly he dashes to his kitchen, grabs a bottle of glue and gets to work.

Many hours later, he has finished. 'There!' he says proudly. It is a yellow teacup, though quite lumpy and is still missing a few pieces.

'I'll surprise Henny with this. She'll love it!'

When Dr. Henny comes home from the clinic that night, Roota hands her his gift.

'I made something for you', he says proudly.

'Oh, how sweet of you!' Dr. Henny exclaims. She unwraps the cup and stares at it.

'Oh', she says, not quite knowing what to say.

'Thank you, dear. You've worked really hard. But don't you recognise this cup?' she asks.

Roota shakes his head, confused.

'It's the one you broke two weeks ago. I had to throw it away. But it certainly is pretty!'

Pasta Treasures

20 DECEMBER

Baabra Sheep, Zig and Zag Zebra, and Slye Snake are at Baabra's kitchen table. They are making beautiful jewellery for their mummies for Christmas.

'Let's see', says Mummy Sheep. 'We have raw pasta, wool, glue and glitter. All ready!'

'What do we do?' asks Slye.

'First put some glue on the pieces of pasta, then sprinkle them with glitter. When the glue is dry, cut a long piece of wool and thread it through your pasta pieces. Then tie a knot and you have a lovely necklace', says Mummy.

The friends get busy. It's quiet for a while.

'We've done the glue and glitter part. Let's go and play in the snow while the glue dries', announces Baabra.

After a fun snowball fight, they're back. Mummy Sheep gives them each a mug of hot chocolate.

'Now we can thread our glittery pasta on the wool', Baabra says. They work quickly.

'These look really beautiful!' says Slye.

'Let's ask your mummy to take a photograph of us. Look at these four film stars!' Zig calls. The friends line up and smile. Click!

'You all look wonderful!' laughs Mummy.

'I'll make prints of this picture so you can give them with your necklaces to your mummies at Christmas', she adds.

'It's not a surprise for you', says Baabra, hugging her mummy.

'That's fine. I love being part of the secret', laughs Mummy Sheep!

247

December

A BIG Surprise

All the parents have brought the friends to see the *Tinker Bell* arrive this morning.

'We have a big surprise for you all', says Daddy Zebra to everyone.

Captain Cow blows her horn and docks the ferry. Two daddies carry off a big square wooden box tied with a red ribbon off the boat. The friends gather around excitedly. What can it be?

Daddy Zebra unties the ribbon and knocks on the box. There's a knock back, from inside.

The box opens, and out climbs Scruffy Hyena!

'Merry Christmas!' he cries. It takes a second for the friends to believe their eyes, but then they start cheering and clapping.

'I was missing you all so much that my mummy and daddy said I could visit you again for Christmas and New Year', he explains, bursting with happiness.

'Oh, Scruffy, you're the best present we have ever had!' cries Zig Zebra. 'We've missed you too!'

'Please all come to our house for some Christmas treats', says Daddy Zebra. So the whole crowd goes to the Zebra house, chattering and laughing along the way.

Scruffy looks around and sighs, 'I love my family and my homeland, but this is my second home. It's lovely to be back', he says in a trembling voice.

'We are really glad you're back', answers Nolo Giraffe. 'You'll love Christmas on Firefly Island!'

22
DECEMBER

Wish Chain

The Zebra family has just brought a beautiful pine tree into their home.

'Time for our wish chain', calls Mummy Zebra. Daddy, the twins and Scruffy Hyena hurry to the kitchen table.

'We make a wish chain every year', Daddy explains to Scruffy. 'I'll write our wishes on strips of coloured paper. Then we'll make a paper chain from them to decorate the Christmas tree'.

'I wish everyone could be as happy as I am', laughs Scruffy, beaming at the Zebras.

'I wish Scruffy could spend every Christmas with us!' cries Zig. Daddy is writing fast.

'I wish I had hot chocolate', giggles Zag.

Mummy laughs and starts making some.

It's Daddy's turn. 'I wish everyone has lots of love', he says, hugging Mummy.

'I wish I could see the golden fish', declares Zag wistfully. Everyone nods.

'I wish I looked like my beautiful twin sister, Zag', exclaims Zig. Zag is speechless.

'I wish I could think of another wish!' says Zag at last. Everybody laughs and claps.

They go on making wishes and writing them down until they have a long paper chain.

'Let's put our chain on the tree now', says Mummy. They loop it over the branches.

'It's lovely! And I have one last wish', says Mummy.

'I wish for all our wishes to come true!'

Golden Fish

Scruffy Hyena is at Mr. Ptera's general store. He likes Mr. Ptera a lot, ever since his job visit to the shop during the summer.

'Scruffy, did I ever tell you about our golden fish?' Mr. Ptera asks mysteriously.

'No', replies Scruffy, 'but please do!'

'There are supposed to be many giant golden fish, but only a few villagers have ever seen even just one', explains Mr. Ptera.

Scruffy feels goose bumps rising on his arms.

'So we've been really lucky that one wanted to visit us this year', adds Mr. Ptera.

'I wish I could have seen him', says Scruffy.

'Well, you may have one chance', says Mr. Ptera slowly. 'Sometimes we see one on New Year's Eve, so let's hope that happens this year. I know you have to go back home soon'.

'Hmmmm', says Scruffy. 'I have to go now, but I'll come back tomorrow, if I may!' he says, running out of the store.

'Of course you can', Mr. Ptera calls after him.

Scruffy hurries to the beach. He shuts his eyes and whispers, 'I promise to behave better if I get the chance to see a golden fish'.

Then he opens his eyes and stares out over the water. Nothing, just waves and sparkles.

Then suddenly a huge golden fish leaps out of the water and splashes back in.

Scruffy can't believe his eyes! 'I saw one! I saw one!' he yells.

The fish leaps again and again.

Scruffy is breathless with excitement. He even pinches himself to make sure he is not dreaming.

After a while the fish stops leaping.

Scruffy thinks to himself, 'Now I REALLY do have to behave!'

December

24 DECEMBER — The Village Tree

It is Christmas Eve and the sun is setting.

Villagers have brought their wish chains to the park. Mr. Horse, the mayor, stands on his soapbox by the tall pine tree.

'My fellow villagers', Mr. Horse booms into his megaphone. 'It's Christmas Eve and time to decorate our village tree. Let's get started!'

Each family brings their wish chain to the tree and joins it to the other families' chains. 'I see hundreds of wishes!' says Mr. Horse. They loop the chain around the tree.

'Pretty! Pretty!' cheeps Cozy the chick.

Next the daddies put lots of coloured lights on the tree. By now the sun has set and it's dark.

'The oldest villager always lights the tree', booms Mr. Horse. 'Mr. Ptera, that's you!'

Mr. Ptera turns on a switch. The tree bursts into a rainbow of colours.

'Ahhh!' breathes the crowd.

Suddenly the tree lights flicker and it goes dark.

'Oh, no!' cries the crowd.

'Wait, let me fix this!' cries Ivan Monkey. He twiddles the plug. The lights spring back to dazzling life.

'Hooray for Ivan!' cries the crowd. He's finally repaired something, and this time it works!

25 DECEMBER — Christmas Magic

Christmas morning is still and sunny. Snow sparkles and the icicles, hanging from the roofs of the houses, look like long, glittering diamonds.

Hotta Toucan and Chilly Penguin have invited Mr. Ptera to share the day with them at their house. He and baby Cozy have a special friendship. After all, he was the one who taught her to whistle. He has a gift for her.

Hotta has decorated their table with pine branches, flowers and candles.

'We have the youngest and the oldest villagers at our table', smiles Hotta. 'What did you wish for in your wish chain, Mr. Ptera?'

'I wished that Scruffy Hyena could see a golden fish', answers Mr. Ptera. 'And he did!'

'I wished for Cozy's good health', says Chilly.

'And I wished for Chilly's!' laughs Hotta.

'And you, Cozy?' asks Mr. Ptera gently.

Cozy sits up tall and fluffs her little feathers. She bursts out, 'Berry Kickmast!'

Then she whistles the most beautiful song anyone has ever heard!

Mr. Ptera has tears in his eyes. He gives Cozy a cute little doll and says softly, 'It is a Merry Christmas, Cozy! Your wish also came true!'

December

Super Sour

Bouncer Brachio is thirsty. He has been playing all morning, and now he really wants a drink of water. Mummy is busy upstairs.

'I'll just get some for myself', he thinks as he goes to the kitchen.

Bouncer looks in the refrigerator for a bottle of water, but there isn't any, so he goes to a cupboard to get a new one. There are lots of tall bottles inside.

'Hmmm', he thinks, 'here's a new kind!' He picks a bottle with a pretty label.

'This one has a different sort of cap on it', he says to himself. But he can open it by himself without a problem.

Bouncer gets a glass from another cupboard and carefully fills it. He is so thirsty!

He takes a big sip.

'Eeeuw! Ugh! Blaaah!' he cries, spitting it out on the floor.

'Sour! Eeeuw! Ugh! Blaaah!' Bouncer goes on spitting.

Mummy comes running down the stairs to see what is going on.

'Bouncer! What in the world?' she exclaims.

Bouncer is red in the face and can't talk. He points to his glass and the bottle on the table.

'Oh, Bouncer, you didn't!' Mummy cries, but at the same time she's laughing. 'You didn't try to drink white vinegar, did you?'

Pavement Sliding

It is strange outside.

There is a really thick layer of ice over everything.

'Look! I can walk right across the top of the snow!' yells Hoopla Hippo to the friends at the Hideout. He goes stamping around, but the ice holds him up. Until he slips and falls on his bottom!

It's true – the ice on top of the snow has made a hard, really slippery surface.

'Let's go pavement sliding!' cries Slye Snake.

'What's that?' asks Scruffy.

'You just run as fast as you can and then slide, as if you're snowboarding or skating', explains Slye with a smile.

The friends slip and slide their way to the village. The pavements are as smooth as glass.

'Watch this!' cries Slye, taking a run and then slowly turning around so that she's sliding backwards down the pavement.

'Here I come!' yells Scruffy, and he runs fast, then slides along, waving his Firefly Island cap as he zooms past Mr. Ptera's store.

'Look out, everybody, here I come! I'm a penguin!' yells Hoopla.

He runs and then dives on his tummy on the pavement.

As he slides along he laughs his hippo laugh.

'HOOO, HO-HO-HO-HO!'

'HOOO, HO-HO-HO-HO!'

Mr. Ptera comes out of his store to watch.

'You youngsters are so funny!' he laughs. 'Come on in and pick out a sweet, you slippery sliders. The treat's on me!'

Wrong Door

28 DECEMBER

Mrs. Trico, the postmistress, spots Roota Rooster flapping and stumbling his way towards the post office on this sunny morning.

'I do hope he's not expecting any post', she worries. I've already sorted all of today's letters, and there were none for him'.

Roota crashes into the post office door.

'Ouch!' he cries.

Mrs. Trico hears him fumbling around with the door handle. 'What *is* going on?' she wonders.

In a second or two, the door swings open and Roota stumbles in.

'Be careful, Roota!' Mrs. Trico cries.

Roota catches himself from falling.

He peers around, blinking his little eyes.

'Doctor Henny! Doctor Henny! I need help!'

Mrs. Trico stares at Roota in surprise.

'Henny, where are you?' cries Roota, looking all around and rubbing his eyes.

'Roota, what's wrong?' asks Mrs. Trico. She's really quite worried. Has he gone mad?

'I really think I need glasses! I can't see properly any more!' Roota exclaims, rubbing his eyes.

'I'm certain that you do need glasses Roota', laughs Mrs. Trico. 'This is the post office!'

December

29 DECEMBER

Giraffe-eety

Mr. Horse is standing with the youngsters in the sculpture park next to the village hall.

'The grown-ups want me to ask you to decorate this wall', he explains, pointing.

The friends stare at Mr. Horse in wonder.

Mr. Horse hands out cans of spray paint.

'So paint us a nice picture', he says, smiling.

'You mean we can make giraffe-eety?' Slye Snake asks. Nolo Giraffe giggles.

'Yes. Actually, the word is graffiti – that's spray painting on public places! You'll get into trouble if you do it without permission. But we WANT you to do it here!' Mr. Horse explains.

'Wonderful! What should we paint?' Slye Snake asks the friends. They think for a while.

'How about a summer's day, with all of us playing here in the park?' asks Nolo at last.

'Yesss!' the friends cheer, and they get busy.

Bouncer Brachio has green paint, so he starts painting grass and bushes. Hoopla Hippo has yellow. He makes a lovely smiling sun.

The others fill the wall with pictures of themselves, playing games, having picnics and reading books on the park benches.

'This is so much fun!' laughs Nolo. 'I suppose this makes me a giraffe-eety expert!'

Mr. Horse chuckles, steps back, and looks at the wall. 'It looks perfect! Thank you very much!'

30 DECEMBER

Mrs. Horse Starts Writing

Mrs. Horse is really very happy living on Firefly Island. She and Mr. Horse are very much in love.

'It's such a lovely place, full of friendly villagers. And I love the rest of the island too', she tells Mr. Horse as they eat breakfast.

'The waterfall is my favourite place, but I also love the woods, and the fire tower, and the ferry boat, and...'

'I know what you mean', smiles Mr. Horse.

'Why don't you write a story book for children, about our island?' he asks.

'Hmmm. That might be fun', Mrs. Horse answers. She's quiet for a while, thinking.

'There are so many stories to tell', she adds.

'Perhaps I could write one story for every day of the year'.

'What a good idea. Why not try it?' says Mr. Horse, putting his jacket on. He gives her a kiss and leaves for work.

Mrs. Horse gets out some writing paper and a pen and starts thinking. She pours a cup of tea and looks out the window.

'Let's see. Where should I start?' she thinks.

'Perhaps I could begin by writing about the bonfire that happens on the first day of every new year'.

She starts writing...

1 JAN. BONFIRE DAY
Bouncer Brachio is
excited! For the first
time, Mommy and Daddy
are letting him help
build their village's New
Year's bonfire. This is the
way we start our
Boun...

31
DECEMBER

Wishes Come True

Mr. Ptera is locking up his general store. 'The end of the day and the end of the year', he smiles. 'Nearly time for our New Year's Eve party!'

All the villagers are gathered by the dock, chatting and laughing. They can't wait for sunset.

As Mr. Ptera joins them, Ivan Monkey cries, 'What was that?' pointing out over the water. The villagers go quiet and stare.

Far out in the water, right in front of the setting sun, there is a huge splash.

'It's our golden fish!' cries Bouncer Brachio.

Then there's another splash, closer to the dock. And another, even closer.

'There are THREE golden fish!' yells Hoopla Hippo. 'I can't believe my eyes!'

All of a sudden, right beside the dock, *another* huge golden fish leaps out of the water, wriggles in the air, and splashes down. Soon the harbour is full of enormous golden fish, each leaping and splashing in the water.

'There are dozens of them!' cries Mr. Horse.

The villagers clap and cheer, hoping the golden fish can feel how happy they are.

The sun sets and the fish stop leaping.

'That was unbelievable', says Scruffy Hyena to Mr. Ptera. 'I was happy that I saw just one, but I never thought I'd see more!'

Mr. Ptera smiles. 'All our wishes came true!'

Booom! Bang! Booom! fills the air as fireworks go off over the water. The villagers cry 'Oooh' and 'Aaah' after each one.

A band starts playing. Everybody dances and dances, until the clock in the village tower shows it is almost midnight.

'Ten! Nine! Eight! Seven! Six! Five! Four! Three! Two! ONE!' chant the villagers.

'Happy New Year!' they all cry, throwing confetti and balloons up in the air and hugging each other. Another year has started on Firefly Island.